A Cultivated Reason

The Pennsylvania State University Press
University Park, Pennsylvania

A Cultivated Reason

An Essay on Hume and Humeanism

Christopher Williams

Library of Congress Cataloging-in-Publication Data

Williams, Christopher, 1960–
 A cultivated reason : an essay on Hume and humeanism / by Christopher Williams.
    p.   cm.
 Includes bibliographical references and index.
 ISBN 0-271-01820-8 (alk. paper)
 ISBN 0-271-01821-6 (pbk. : alk. paper)
 1. Hume, David, 1711–1776. 2. Rationalism—Controversial literature. I. Title.
 B1499.R4W55   1999
 149'.7—dc21   98-16935
                                                              CIP

Copyright © 1999 The Pennsylvania State University
All rights reserved
Printed in the United States of America
Published by The Pennsylvania State University Press,
University Park, PA 16802-1003

It is the policy of The Pennsylvania State University Press to use acid-free paper for the first printing of all clothbound books. Publications on uncoated stock satisfy the minimum requirements of American National Standard for Information Sciences—Permanence of Paper for Printed Library Materials, ANSI Z39.48-1992.

Contents

	Preface and Acknowledgments	vii
	List of Abbreviations	ix
1	Rationalism	1
2	Bodies and Disembodiment	21
3	The Sceptic's Version	61
4	Irrationalism	93
5	Persons and Artworks	129
	Retrospect	175
	Index	181

For Jack Kelly

Preface and Acknowledgments

As history instructs us, philosophy can be done in a remarkably wide array of genres—from the mathematical proof to the aphorism—and I suppose that if I had to identify the genre to which this book belongs, I should have to confess that it is the essay, in a familiar sense of the word, even though the fit is a loose one. A book that develops a single point of view, argumentatively (at times), over consecutive chapters cannot literally cultivate the casual, unsystematic air that is the cachet of the great essayists' "attempts"; one might wonder, too, whether an academic work should even aspire to possess that air. Yet I hope that the claim my work has to being an essay is neither entirely inapposite nor ultimately unmotivated. Genre always matters to philosophy: this is an important fact about the subject, and it was an imperishable insight of Plato, the logical positivists, and others to have recognized just this fact. How it matters is another question. If I am a fortunate author, perhaps it will be enough if the thoughts that I offer here, derived from Hume, on the nature of true reasonableness seem appropriate to their vehicle.

This book began its life as a dissertation, and I wish to thank my dissertation adviser, Annette Baier, who performed a very valuable office for me. If we are in a skeptical mood about the powers of philosophy, which is not an uncommon mood in our century, the real discovery—if I may irreverently co-opt a famous remark by Wittgenstein—can be the one that lets us continue to do philosophy when we want to. Annette showed me how to continue, and why philosophers should not pander to gloom while they are in the cool hour of reflection. Her nimbleness in noticing, and in making others notice, the ordinary but oddly significant aspect of a problem has been an inspiration also.

Another member of my dissertation committee, Jennifer Whiting, deserves a special mention for her unfailing beneficence, confidence, and encouragement over the years—many of them unproductive ones for me. Had some of her good deeds been left undone I rather doubt whether I should have had a history that includes the writing of this preface today.

I am indebted to a former teacher, James Edwards, and particularly for his course in the philosophy of religion, which helped to shape certain of the ethical intuitions that inform this book. I shall be pleased if he discerns an image or two of his own thoughts, glimmering obscurely, in the mirror here.

Thanks are owed to Emily Hauptmann and Róbert Haraldsson for reading earlier versions of the manuscript, to Sanford Thatcher of Penn State Press for his support and good humor, and to Kathy O'Keefe for invaluable assistance in preparing the final manuscript.

Finally, for his unwavering faith in me and my work, I shall always be grateful to Jack Kelly. In a noble poem that celebrated the idea that human worth is not a respecter of persons, Robert Burns wrote:

> The rank is but the guinea's stamp,
> The man's the gowd for a' that.

Jack exemplifies, to my mind, the reason why the poetry of Burns will remain noble. This book is dedicated to him.

Reno, Nevada
February 1998

List of Abbreviations

Throughout this work I use the following abbreviations, in the body of the text, accompanied by page number, for Hume's writings:

D   *Dialogues Concerning Natural Religion*, ed. Richard Popkin (Indianapolis: Hackett, 1980)
E   *Enquiries Concerning Human Understanding and the Principles of Morals*, 3d ed., ed. L. A. Selby-Bigge and P. H. Nidditch (Oxford: Clarendon Press, 1975)
MPL *Essays Moral, Political, and Literary*, ed. Eugene F. Miller (Indianapolis: Liberty Classics, 1985)
NHR *Natural History of Religion*, in *Hume's Philosophical Works*, ed. T. H. Green and T. H. Grose (London: Longman, Greens, 1882)
T   *Treatise of Human Nature*, 2d ed., ed. L. A. Selby-Bigge and P. H. Nidditch (Oxford: Clarendon Press, 1978)

Virtue, which is nothing but a more enlarged and more cultivated reason, never flourishes to any degree, nor is founded on steady principles of honour, except where a good education becomes general.
—Hume, *History of England*

Because if intellect does not deserve the crown of crowns, only intellect is able to award it. And if intellect only ranks second in the hierarchy of virtues, intellect alone is able to proclaim that the first place must be given to instinct.
—Proust, *Contre Sainte-Beuve*

1

✼ ✼ ✼

Rationalism

Hume's account of the relationship between reason and passion in "Of the Influencing Motives of the Will" often elicits a less-than-warmhearted response among philosophical readers. We regularly discern, both in conversation and in print, a certain impatience with Hume, a certain querulousness in our reactions to him, when he casually claims that "reason is, and ought only to be the slave of the passions" (T 415) or that "'tis not contrary to reason to prefer the destruction of the whole world to the scratching of my finger" (T 416). I select these passages as emblems. Virtually any Humean text on the place of reason—or on philosophy—can be substituted to equivalent effect, as, for example, "'Tis not solely in poetry and music, we must follow our taste and sentiment, but likewise in philosophy" (T 103). Asserting such a connection between music and philosophy (not to mention poetry and philosophy, whose quarrel is ancient, according to one ancient authority) grates upon our ears in the same way that the reason-slave identification does.

Let us look more closely at that identification. By itself the reaction of annoyance to Hume's pairing is perhaps not of great moment: one of the few constants of philosophical life is that philosophers are impatient with each other. And it is likely, too, that some of the reaction depends on a particular interpretation of the slave metaphor: we may find it tempting to regard Hume as offering us a picture of the mind as a battleground between two warring subsystems, reason and passion, which are then naturally conceived as protopersons vying for hegemony within the larger person. Given this interpretation, it can seem perverse or paradoxical on Hume's part to throw reflective support to the side of passion. For we apparently rely on reason (in some suitably commonsensical understanding of that word) in order to arrive at the judgment that reflective support for passion is warranted.

Once we accept the warring-subsystems picture of the mind, the philosophical question concerning which combatant to endorse is, interestingly, already over. The normative victor has to be reason. But the warring-subsystems picture is not one that we must accept. It is one thing to say that feeling and intellect give a single person differing perspectives on life, and quite another to personify the differences between those perspectives. The personification has to be seriously meant if the mind is going to war with itself, but there is no reason to treat the personification as anything more than a misleading flourish—even though it is a flourish we can easily and unconsciously fail to recognize for what it is.

Because slaves are persons, however slighted their claims to personhood may be, Hume's slave metaphor resonates unfortunately. Furthermore, to the extent that our annoyance requires the optional, problematic picture, we can account for the reaction in a straightforward manner: we are justifiably dissatisfied with Hume's endorsed combatant. However, the slave metaphor itself need not be read as sustaining the conception that psychological faculties are protopersons, and (what is more important) Hume need not be read as a defender of that conception. In another passage, which is less remarked upon, Hume writes, "Where reason is lively, and mixes itself with some propensity, it ought to be assented to. Where it does not, it never can have any title to operate on us" (T 270). Although we need to get clearer about what "mixing" comes to, Hume is presenting, in a less misleading form, an idea that is much the same as that which animates the notorious remark—the idea that pure intellect is unreliable and that feeling has to inform, or give shape to, our sense of what is reasonable.[1] We might say that

---

1. T 270 speaks of "propensity" rather than feeling, and propensities extend beyond feelings (to include habits, for example). But since propensities always pair off with feelings, the talk of feeling here seems unobjectionable.

Hume's view of the reason-passion relation is, properly speaking, reconciliationist in tenor. It is this tenor that the slave metaphor obscures.

Hume's conception of reason, as I am reidentifying it, can still make some of us uneasy, for it seems to involve a downward revision in our understanding of reasonableness, a relaxing of our standards of rational assessment. If the "mixing" of reason and propensity is something other than a mechanical combination of psychical elements—and we should hope that it is other than that, since a mechanical combination would help to reinforce the warring-subsystems picture—we apparently have to think of reason, from the inside, in a new way. This can still be a frightening thought, if we are in an elevated mood.

I want to exorcise the frighteningness from that thought. The observation I begin with is that any fright here has a peculiarly philosophical flavor. There is little reason to believe that Hume's conception of reason would scandalize anyone *except* philosophers; most persons who are not committed to the explicit cultivation of reason are not at all disturbed if the power or scope of reason is cried down. Divergences between specialists and nonspecialists are not unusual in our experience—physicians and their patients often have sharply contrasting views about the etiology of a disease, for example—but what is unusual in this instance of divergence is that the object of disagreement is hardly arcane. Reason and passion lie very close to the surface of our experience, and the Humean claim about their relationship does not, and should not, take us outside our phenomenology for its assessment. Why then the divergence of opinion? I am prepared to hazard the hypothesis that Hume's stance toward reason can be irritating to philosophers in an almost ideological way. That is, philosophers tend to react adversely to Hume's account because in it they do not hear a "good Hume" speaking, a constructive philosopher who (say) shows us how to answer the fools who deny morality in their hearts. Instead, they hear a "bad Hume" whose motivation is literary fame, or a Hume who irresponsibly leaves the skeptic ("just when the discussion is getting serious") to dine and play. It is felt that by arguing for the primacy of passion as he does, in his famous "careless manner," Hume deserts the colors of careful philosophy instead of serving under them.

The bad-Hume reading encourages us to scrutinize the prima facie contrast between reflective responsibility and unreflective irresponsibility. To bring out this contrast, we might consider, for a few moments, our response to a supremely eccentric philosophical system, Berkeley's. (By "eccentric" I merely wish to register, in a single word, the gap between Berkeley's views and those of nonphilosophers.) If we think Berkeley wrong about the existence of enduring objects outside the mind, as most of us do, how do we make a reply to him?

Hume thought that Berkeley's arguments were unanswerable (in this he agreed with Samuel Johnson, a nonphilosopher who had a knack for bumping philosophically into things), but since they produced no conviction, they were frivolously skeptical in nature and hence ignorable (E 155). Here we have a kind of crucial experiment for our inclinations. To some tempers, usually the more philosophical among us, the thought that Berkeley is wrong implies that Berkeley has a faulty assumption or has made an inferential misstep *somewhere* in his system and that it behooves us to find the error, the finding of it counting, then, as the answer to Berkeley. Hume, however, leaves open the possibility that no error might be directly exhibited, or rather that the error is of a special sort, not fundamentally intellectual in nature and not answerable in purely intellectual terms (as Johnson's gruff kick or Moore's more mannerly inspection of his hands inadvertently point up).[2] It is possible that the difficulty lies with the reasoner's self-understanding, and that a proper self-understanding will change the identification of the kind of error involved.

For Hume there is, no doubt, a problem that Berkeley presents to us: we might call it the problem *of* Berkeley rather than the problem *in* Berkeley. His system shows us what can happen if the impulse to intellectual clarity and maximal logical consistency is given free rein, unconstrained by the less lucid, less articulate beliefs and sentiments we rely on when we cease to think explicitly. To deal seriously with Berkeley, in Humean terms, is to show that Berkeley's conclusions are a reductio ad absurdum not so much of common sense as of the uncritical reliance on pure intellect; and once we see where the longing for total clarity leads us, we have some reason—not perfectly conclusive, of course—to think Berkeley answered. The matter-denying bishop may not especially feel as if he has been answered, but then the sort of intellectually clear answer he seeks is precisely the sort of answer that Hume, allying himself with the "many honest gentlemen" who never ensconce themselves in the philosophical closet (T 272), denies, in effect, that he can give. When we have someone who denies the experientially obvious but intellectually dark fact of matter,[3] and who denies the fact solely because

---

2. The peculiar character of the error is worth emphasizing: it can only be revealed indirectly, and the machinery by whose means we reveal it will not be a standard sort of argument. I shall say more about this machinery in Chapter 2.

3. We can deny matter in more than one sense. If "matter" refers to a featureless substratum

of that darkness, there is little we can do about it by way of explicit reflection if we suppose that cognitive transparency has a limit. With the denier of material objects we must proceed as we do with the denier of equally obvious but dark moral distinctions: "The only way, therefore, of converting an antagonist of this kind, is to leave him to himself" (E 170). Boredom, fatigue, or self-deprecating laughter may convert where no argument can.

This scenario, brief and imperfect though it is, shows us why the issue of responsibility or seriousness might be no laughing matter. The Humean response looks frivolous to those who think that philosophers' reflections are the palladium of reason, whereas the Humean is apt to locate frivolity just where the non-Humean locates seriousness, in those byzantine arguments about the obvious that are, for the Humean, a sterile labyrinth. (We might reap a comic pleasure, after all, and perhaps an additional consideration in favor of Humean carelessness, from this philosophical case of complementarily mistaken identities.) The pathos of the non-Humean position is not itself eccentric, however. I believe that something in Berkeley's conceptual extravaganza strikes a very deep and sympathetic root in the philosophical imagination, and that to deny Berkeley in the Humean fashion naturally leads us to think we are denying philosophy as such. (So purely does Berkeley incarnate the impulse to clarity that I fancy had he never existed it would have been necessary for Borges to invent him.) But my own view, all things considered, is that the Humean position is in fact the truly serious, and the philosophically most respectable, position to have.

I think, in other words, that we have neither a Jekyll nor a Hyde to sort out in Hume's writings, and that the lack of seriousness some readers see is only apparent because Hume, among other things, invites us to reconsider the very idea of philosophical seriousness itself, of what counts as a serious answer to a philosophical perplexity. Mounting a full-scale defense for this conviction would be a large undertaking—and even too large, since full-scale projects

---

for perceivable properties to inhere in, then Berkeley is indeed not departing markedly from the commonsense understanding of the world by denying its existence. If "matter" refers to objects solely insofar as they are ensembles of primary qualities—the world according to scientific realism, as we may say—then again there is no marked departure in denying it. But if "matter" refers to continuously existing bodies, which may possess determinate features, then we do have a major departure. Throughout my discussion of Berkeley I am construing the denial in this third sense. (Although his commonsense critics often proceed with the third sense as well, Berkeley himself had the first two senses very much in mind: the multiplicity of possible targets makes responding to Berkeley a complicated affair, but I wish to focus only on the most counterintuitive aspect of his position here.)

arguably excite more incredulity than respect in our quizzical, unsystematic age. Yet a number of local considerations might be adduced to show that it is reasonable not to expect too much from reason, and the ensemble of our reflections may provide an informal systematicity, an approximation of an argument, for the Humean point of view. This I seek to provide.

At this point, however, a reader might slyly wonder what the purpose of the arguments will be, given my professed Humean aspirations (which must include an aspiration to be true to Hume's sensibility). Am I not declining to "leave the antagonist to himself"? In a sense, yes. What I should like to do, in the first place, is to banish the bugbear that a Humean view of reason has irrationalist implications. That Hume is a nonrationalist is clear: he denies the primacy of reason in assorted ways. But there is a tendency to regard nonrationalism as tantamount to the view that the guidance of reason should be rejected, and the rejectionist stance is the signature of the irrationalist. It is desirable to show that nonrationalism need not lead to irrationalism, that clasping Hume to our bosom is not a preliminary surrender to the dark gods in the blood.

In the second place, I should like to show how very modern, or even postmodern, Hume's reconception of philosophical seriousness is. The issues concerning responsibility that Hume broaches have deep similarities to issues that arise when we read Nietzsche or Richard Rorty or Jacques Derrida. All of these authors try to activate our disposition to laughter, or to smiles, in the course of their thrusts and parries, and this type of writing increasingly disorients the mind as the mind itself becomes increasingly accustomed to the intellectual brand of sobriety. Accordingly, these irreverent (or, rather, casually reverent) writers are not uncommonly regarded as being unserious qua philosophers, and it would be useful to offer some principled resistance to such a perception. Hume, however, has advantages these writers do not possess. There are fewer distracting alarums and excursions in Hume, and so we can see, in a vehicle of classical simplicity, the concepts that await us. Moreover, Hume in some respects has a more advanced conception of things than his successors do, and I suspect that much of the opprobrium that attaches, for this or that reason, rightly or wrongly, to what these other writers say results from important elements that they retain of the older views they reject. Our beginning is sometimes our end, and Hume's version of nonrationalism will perhaps be the music of the future.

Nonrationalism, without some further argumentative support, easily suggests irrationalism, as the following observations make plain. If we share Hume's convictions about reason, and if we come to those convictions without a great deal of thought, then it is perhaps safe to say that we will readily accept the proposal that Hume's offhand statements are motivatedly offhand because the position Hume offers us is not meant to "draw too much" (E 8) from the perspective of unreflective common life. Now let us suppose that in a euphoric access of extreme Humean identification with our common life, we construct an efficient and relatively unreflective defense of the Humean position along these lines: The warmth of the anti-Humean responses to Hume's views tends to confirm those views because the warmth is strangely disproportionate to the texts that produce the response, texts that are themselves notably cool, unvexed, and ironic in their tone. Of course, the coolness of a particular stance may justifiably call out for warm indignation in a response (irony about a serial killing would, and should, revolt us), but in this case, where reasonableness and relative emotional detachment are explicitly at issue, we might think that the anti-Humean's tone assorts ill with the content of the anti-Humean's message. Accordingly, the passionate dismissals of Hume easily make us wonder whether the anti-Humean doth protest too much. And if the anti-Humean indeed protests too much, then we could scarcely have better evidence for the nonprimacy of reason, since the polemical passions of the anti-Humean are so thinly concealed by the arguments themselves. The anti-Humean's heart, not his head, leads the charge.

The import of this argument (if I may use, in a resolutely prereflective sense, a word dear to our philosophical hearts) would thus resemble my earlier embryonically dialectical aside about the comic possibilities lurking in the standoff between the defender of Hume and the defender of Berkeley. This kind of argument could be quite persuasive, I think, on its own terms. But such is the misfortune of our arguments that, insofar as they are addressed to no one in particular, the most elegant and persuasive of them are usually those which fail to carry an air of plausibility, let alone conviction, with a preferred target audience. In this case, the target is the class of non- or anti-Humean philosophers whom we might call, for the sake of a handy label (and without overzealous concern for historical accuracy), *rationalists*. The problem is that we have not thrown any sop to them, and thus we do not have a conversation. If the Humean cannot hope to convince the rationalist that the Humean is right, she or he must at least hope to convince the rationalist that the Humean is, by rationalist lights, a good egg; and the distance to this second goal is traversable by the arguments I shall give. In any genuine conversation there must be not only give and take, but a willingness to assume imaginatively the evaluative stance of our interlocutor in the candid hope that he or she will so assume ours, and such conversational seriousness should, on nonrationalist grounds, be the ultimate mark of seriousness *tout court*.

Since we now have a rough-and-ready contrast between the nonrationalist Humean, who is supposed to be insufficiently serious, and the rationalist, who is a representative of seriousness, at least on one understanding of it, I should now like to develop our portrait of these two figures; and to do this I need to justify my choice of nomenclature. Obviously, reason is the central notion for the drawing of the contrast between the figures, so let us proceed by considering their possible relationships to reason.

It would be useful to emphasize at the outset that Hume, or the Humean, is not averse to reason, but to a certain theory of reason that ascribes extensive normative powers to it. In other words, Hume is opposed to rationalism, not reason. This pithy statement calls attention to a distinction to be drawn, and maintained, between nonrationalism and irrationalism, inasmuch as the irrationalist wishes (in probably a confused way) to abjure appeals to reason altogether. Unfortunately, our work of differentiation cannot stop with a mere insistence on the distinction between reason and one sort of metareason, because a rationalist theory encourages us to regard a rejection of that theory as ultimately involving a rejection of reason. This is indeed a peculiarity in our reflection about reason. We seemingly have a *bonum* that self-reflexively implies that it is *summum*. And this peculiarity, together with the occlusions that attend self-reference, makes argumentation against rationalist claims a hard matter. If reason does not have the normative power with which a rationalist theory invests it, such a shortcoming offers an indirect argument concerning the limits of self-reflexive thought. The nature of normative power is not a neutral token in this rencontre between Humean and rationalist, however, and this adds to our already egregious difficulties in differentiating nonrationalism from irrationalism. These difficulties will not be adequately removed until Chapter 4. Be that as it may, we should be able to make a start on this project by identifying rationalist commitments, using reason, but seemingly without having to accept rationalism itself. To do so, let us show a little more care for historical fidelity than we did initially.

Rationalism has a rich and colorful history, and although we find positions that are called rationalist both in Plato and in the twentieth century, we typically associate the name with the Continental philosophy of the seventeenth century—with Descartes and his successors, who include Spinoza and Leibniz. The seventeenth-century tradition is the purebred specimen of the breed, and I should like to state a view of rationalism that plausibly captures the distinctive flavor of this central case but is flexible enough to make the more peripheral cases comprehensible. Let us say that rationalism is aboriginally the thesis that mental contents derive, in some fashion, from the mind itself and that these contents have, in virtue of their origin, systematic logical interrelations. This is the fundamental rationalist commitment in its undiluted form, as I think a few considerations will convincingly reveal.

Leibnizian monads are self-contained, self-regulated systems that are set up in such a way as to make possible, in principle, inferences from one of the monad's thought contents to another. Alexander the Great has a makeup that would permit an ideal observer to trace the whole of Alexander's life from any part. Leibniz perhaps affords us the most vivid illustration of the rationalist commitment, but we easily encounter it elsewhere. Descartes supposes that we can, with sufficient care, safely advance from the *cogito* to the belief that a veracious God exists who guarantees the existence of a material world from which we are metaphysically distinct (but to a part of which we are intimately connected). I rehearse this familiar synopsis of the Cartesian system only to point out how the seemingly slender stream of the meditator's first truth is supposed to flow into what is a rather grand estuary of belief, and the connection between stream and estuary makes sense only on the assumption of the rationalist commitment. And Spinoza, also, conforms to the model: his *deus sive natura* contains all possibilities within him or it as essential exfoliations.

Since I hope we shall be impressed, and stably impressed, by other seemingly slender streams to come, I should say a few words about these fertile fragments and their wholes. In the rationalist systems, we or God can make mental transitions over these connections without any *external assistance*. (Externality is to be cashed here as externality to an individual intellect.) God descries the carpet of Alexander's life in the figure of his program, and he does so in virtue of his extraordinary intellectual abilities. So too for the Spinozist God and (on a more modest level) the Cartesian meditator. These vessels of intellect are strongly self-correcting, self-sustaining, or self-expressive. If we compare other things in the world to these vessels, we can see that there is a great deal of distinctive power in them, and their actualization will inevitably have the appearance of a heroic progress or (if temporal categories are infelicitous) a heroic event. We will not come across these varieties of self-sufficiency outside rationalism.

There is a question, of course, about the extent to which the mind is the source of its contents in these systems. To the question "How much?" the answer may be "All" (as in Leibniz) or "Only the basic explanatory principles" (as in Descartes, arguably, despite occasional pronouncements that are more confident). Answering this question is an in-house debate within classical rationalism, and pursuing that debate is not to our present purpose. It is the framing of the problem space itself that is of interest, and that indicates a rationalist agenda.

My formulation of the rationalist commitment also ties together various strands in the classical package that are perhaps more familiar indications of rationalism: the deductivism, the countenancing of innate ideas, the distrust of sensory inputs (which for the rationalist are similar, I think, to the static on a radio or television set, sensory experience being at best problematically classifiable as having mental content, just as the static is problematically "what we hear"). This tie between ostensibly disparate components is pleasing on rationalist grounds, and naturally inclines us to think (though not unerringly!) that the proposed identification of the rationalist commitment is correct.

We can explain the non-seventeenth-century cases too. Plato's view that all learning is recollection and that our sublunary existence involves a falling away from a less distorted cognitive situation is conformable to the model. Similarly with Hegel, who thought that *Geist* posited its own embodiment and so contained its history within itself implicitly. (To be sure, *Geist* posits a contradiction-engendering embodiment for itself; and in that light Hegel is in fact leaving the rationalist commitment behind, while professing to be a rationalist and retaining the aprioristic language. This language is awkwardly maintained in the face of all the talk of experiential contradiction. Yet it is, once again, the language, or rather the conception that originally informed the language, that I wish to call attention to.)

If we have a fair representation of rationalism, we have the makings of a discernible target. At this point, however, we might think that the target is little better than Don Quixote's windmill. We can elaborate an objection on these lines: "Who accepts *this* rationalist commitment now? To the extent that Hume was at all concerned to lay to rest the purebred specimen, it is all well and good; but there is then no need for us to revisit the scene of a contest long settled in the nonrationalist's favor. Nothing is easier to resist than this theory, and so we certainly do not need to suppose that reason encourages us to embrace it. If there is a living worry regarding rationalism, as well as living rationalists, the commitment has to be something different from the more or less historically accurate version given here."

The objection is just to a point, but only to a point. The body of classical rationalism indeed molders in its grave, and before we examine the limitations of the objection, let us consider the real cause of the death (since it may turn out that the cause is mediately related to some important posthumous effects). The cause I wish to cite may appear unusual at first, but this cause is more fundamental, and so more likely to be hidden, than other candidate causes. The great difficulty with old-fashioned rationalism, the great impediment to our taking its projects as literally feasible, is that it is extraordinarily difficult to tell a *naturalistic* story about the minds, or mindlike entities, whose contents are so putatively rich in implication; and within a naturalistic story I would include all the historical and social factors that shape the always uncertain mental progress of an embodied organism. If we are unable to fit ourselves (as described by rationalism) into our more encompassing conception of things, then we have a more serious problem than those presented by any retail failures in a rationalist project, because the project itself will cease to be an object of potential belief.

It is with misgivings, however, that I use the terminology of naturalism in order to state the chief objection to rationalism. "Naturalism" is an unhappy word, in extensive philosophical use but signifying nothing very definite (and indeed having incompatible significations).[4] To a great extent the problems can be traced to the reactive origin of the concept, which contrasted with a better-defined supernaturalism. When I speak of naturalism in these pages, I intend a view of human beings that takes us to be continuous with, and to bear highly relevant resemblances to, the other mammals we know. Naturalism, so understood, is most Humean. For Hume proposes that the resemblances between us and other animals provide us with an "incontestable argument" for his doctrines and "a kind of touchstone" for philosophical systems generally (T 176). Understanding ourselves as denizens of the earth involves a certain self-reconception, and a consistently naturalized image of human beings will extend the reconception to the norms of ethical and rational assessment that our species engages in.[5]

---

4. This is a large topic, but P. F. Strawson, in *Skepticism and Naturalism: Some Varieties* (New York: Columbia University Press, 1985), identifies what I take to be the central tension between different kinds of naturalism, which Strawson labels "reductive" and "non-reductive." This central tension also surfaces in my remarks about naturalism in the next footnote.

5. Naturalism, for my purposes, is not the view that science offers an exhaustive, or unequivocally privileged, account of the universe, or the view that values are not part of the universe's basic "fabric." Such positions can, and do, go by the name of naturalism as well, but here we come up against the kind of naturalism I wish to defend. The more scientistic perspective is one that refuses to regard science itself as a human practice or that refuses to acknowledge its own rationalistic proclivities. For an exposition of a naturalistic program that

To discern the recalcitrant unnaturalness of the rationalist mind, we need only to consider a few examples of it unsentimentally. Let us begin with Plato. If all learning is finally recollection, and if we cannot make sense of the idea that knowledge comes from without, then it trivially follows that this knowledge is already in us in some form or other. Since our phenomenology does not give much, if any, support for this hypothesis, we then have to conjecture that perturbing factors are causing our phenomenological reports to come out as they do, to have the manifest content they display, and so it is natural, and perhaps inevitable, to conceive of the mind as having fallen away from a more pristine state. We smile when we read Socrates' questioning of Meno, because we are skeptical of pristine states and fallings away; we do not fathom how such a mind as Plato hypothesizes could ever have arrived in a manner consistent with a naturalistic, evolutionary account of our origins. (We also smile because we can easily explain Meno's answers through Socrates' patently leading questions, and this style of explanation is naturalistic in its own right.)

Our incredulity has a parallel when we read *Meditation Three*, which presents us, after all, with a variation on the Meno theme. The meditator thinks that he would not be able to recognize his errors unless he already had within him some idea that would make the recognition possible, and this idea is the idea of a perfect and fully actualized God. It is remarkable, we sense, that the meditator's mind could *already* contain an idea with the semantic repleteness that the idea of God must have if it is to be as clear and distinct as the meditator thinks it is. Too remarkable to be true, because cognitive organisms do not start at the top, however implicitly, and then work down; they go in the other direction, from less to more, with the sometimes serendipitous threat of mistake attending their inquiries.

The noncredibility, for us, of historical rationalism has the consequence of making its spiritual revenant far more credible than it would otherwise have been. This is a curious phenomenon, but our cultural experience amply attests to its genuineness, and the phenomenon is expressible in the following maxim: when the letter dieth, the spirit gaineth life. The high para-Christian moral earnestness we associate with the Victorian period coexisted with the sense, often agonized and poignant, that the divine lawgiver was no longer

---

resembles the Humean in some respects, but whose confidence in science is also strangely unnaturalistic (in my sense), Daniel Dennett's *Darwin's Dangerous Idea* (New York: Simon & Schuster, 1995) is instructive.

with us, and the latter fact helps to explain the former. (The eighteenth century was more cosmopolitan and insouciant in its moral outlook, but also more Christian—or closer to the Christian—in its cosmological.) The Greek myths were much more closely scrutinized for their ethical content, by Socrates and others, in an age that had ceased to believe them. The quest for a comprehensive logic of science became evident at a time, the early twentieth century, when the practice of science had become so diversified and untidy as to resist all attempts at codification. Moralistic politicians of the present day invoke the virtues of a more agrarian culture when that culture has all but vanished (and it was a culture that called less attention to its virtues than do its present-day invokers). These examples are so obvious and so numerous that we scarcely need to dilate upon them further. In all of these instances, we have an object of perceived value that disappears on us, and, the absence of the valued object being keenly felt, we relocate the value in other objects that are more amenable to our manipulation and involvement—namely, our thoughts.

Accordingly, I submit a set of parallel observations regarding rationalism. After ceasing to occupy our imaginations in a descriptive fashion, it returns to us more vigorously in one that is normative—or that is more abstractly normative (for normativity is no longer connected to actual practices). We do not believe that the mind contains its contents implicitly, but it is natural for us to think that, however we come by our contents, we should then make them as intellectually transparent as possible, and that the mind should be guided, and guided solely, by these transparent deliverances. This is not the same as simply making them interrelated (a task we perform, when—to use T. S. Eliot's example—we show how reading Spinoza is related to falling in love). Rather, the interrelations are of a certain sort: they are, or should be, clear and distinct to an individual intellect inspecting them. We do not speak of "clarity and distinctness" nowadays, and so my way of putting the matter could sound unavoidably quaint, but the notion survives, and we might instead speak of intellectual states that have an unrestricted license or imperative to guide our thoughts. This imperative would then be the target I wish to bring into sharper (that is, intellectually clearer) focus.

There is a passage in Descartes that can be usefully reworked into the form of the imperative I am looking for. When the meditator reflects, in *Meditation Four*, on the judgment he has paradigmatically taken to be true, that which concerns his own thinkerly existence, he observes, "I could not but judge that something which I understood so clearly was true; but this was not because I was compelled so to judge by any external force, but because a great light in the intellect was followed by a great inclination in the will."⁶ The meditator is merely reporting a necessary connection between his understanding and his will in optimal conditions of clarity, and it is hardly controversial as such. But if we convert this claim into a purely normative commitment, then we have the rationalist imperative: from a great clearness in my mind alone, there ought to follow a great inclination of my will. In other words, my will approvably disposes to the extent that the intellect explicitly proposes; and hence we have a demand in principle for unlimited explicitness. This formulation is an adequate statement of a view whose interest is not merely antiquarian, since it involves none of the historical rationalist ontology, and, moreover, it is a view that a non-Humean philosopher often has. This last point is perhaps unobvious, but it will become more obvious, I hope, after we forestall a possible misunderstanding of the formulation.

The misunderstanding arises if we suppose that the intellect-following will is to follow in all action contexts whatsoever. Descartes himself held, in *Meditation Six* and in his letters, that the exigencies of living prevented us from following the deliverances of our intellect, and that our will thus had to receive some guidance other than the intellectual. And surely, it will be said, nobody would ever hold that the will should follow the intellect at all times and in all places, and the reason is just that the conduct of life will never permit such a luxury. Consequently, it may be thought that we are once again tilting at windmills.

In answer, I would be happy to add the rider "in theory, not in practice" to the formulation, except that I would prefer to do without the theory-practice distinction, which is as difficult to state precisely as it is intuitively apparent. A distinction between theory and practice makes best sense if the respective objects of theory and practice form disjoint classes, as they ostensibly do for Descartes, for whom theory is concerned with general truth and practice with goodness for mind-body compounds. But these classes are not in fact disjoint. On the one hand, we can have theories expressly about practices (and what is more, all theories presumably have some tacit reference to practice), in which case pragmatic considerations must infiltrate the content of the theories; on the other, our theorizing exemplifies, and is informed by, reflectively endorsed practices, in which case the infiltration goes in the other direction. In the light of these considerations, the theory-practice distinction is probably best regarded as not being theoretical (or intellectual) at all, but

---

6. *Philosophical Writings of Descartes*, trans. John Cottingham, Robert Stoothof, and Dugald Murdoch (Cambridge: Cambridge University Press, 1984), 2:41.

pragmatic. And so, the distinction we seek perhaps reduces to the difference between movements of the will that occur in a deliberatively propitious setting and those that do not. Let us endorse this interpretation, and having done so, let us then elaborate the formulation of the imperative as follows: if and only if there is a great clearness (or transparency) in my intellect alone, and if and only if the time and place are propitious for unhurried movements of the will, then the clarity of the intellect should incline the will.

We need one further clarification before we have the matter for our debate. Clarity or transparency are notoriously unclear and nontransparent notions, and therefore they demand some commentary. The idea that comprehension is fittingly comprehended by images drawn from the family of diaphanous phenomena (mirrors, lifted clouds, withdrawn veils) is so intriguing that it deserves a study of its own, though it is enough for present purposes to note that there is surely a connection between the transparency idiom and the exercise of our power. When a problem is explained to us and we say, "I see!" we are serving notice that we can go right up to the object of our quondam puzzlement and interact with it, as our purposes require, without any further ado: there are none of the erstwhile obstacles between us and it. Because we have already seen that the rationalist mind is able to exercise peculiar powers denied to other worldly things, the clarity imperative is not arbitrary or gratuitous. But it would be desirable to have an unpacking of the clarity idea that is more precise and less metaphorical.

Here is a proposal. Let us call a state of our mind intellectually clear if the content of that state can be grasped, or expressed, as a *followable rule* or if it can be understood as an instance of a followable rule (understood, that is, as a followed rule). I include "followable" because without the qualification we have an ambiguity between rulings and recipes, so to speak. A ruling does not necessarily guide action, and it need not be intellectually clear. Custom or habit is, in Hume's account, a rule in the sense of a ruling: we appeal, for example, to custom for our final verdict about what to believe concerning a continuously existing world, but the "principle of custom" does not guide the mind as the rationalist would want to have it guided. A rule in the sense of recipe guides our mental action because, if we have the rule, we are able to subsume instances under it, thereby allowing us to deal with the instances. This proposal enables us to acknowledge a vestige, and hence the historical descent, of the imperative from classical rationalism. If we have the rule, there is a sense in which we already have the instance; our processing of the instance is just the application of the rule, the finding of relevant rule-conformities.

Hume of course does not deny—nor should we—that we rely on followable rules. The ease with which we deal with novel occurrences of fire and water suggests that we subsume present instances under rules obtained from constantly conjunctive associations (though it is not altogether apparent that such graspable, action-guiding regularities must literally qualify as rules). But Hume does not suppose that we can formulate a rule enjoining us to follow our followable rules. Rule following has its limits, and these are more interesting than they might appear, because our mental stability actually depends on crucial rule-avoidances. These avoidances occur straightforwardly in unreflective life, but they become more problematic when we reflect. Thus Hume, as I read him, takes recalcitrance to formulability in rules—on whose importance Kant had insisted, somewhat peripherally, in his account of our understanding of creative works of genius—and places it squarely in the center of the mental stage.

My elaborated version of neorationalism, or something like it, is what many reflective people either believe or have a responsive disposition to assent to. In my view, only a further or more complete reflection can show its unsoundness. Ultimately the imperative may not even be coherently statable, but it looks coherent on an initial glance, and that impression suffices for now. Hume provides us with two basic arguments, the first concerning our natural belief in the continued existence of objects around us and the second concerning the correction of our sentiments. But before turning to the first argument, I want to announce that I shall be excluding from view two well-known strands in Hume's thinking about the claims of reason—strands that are so well known and so closely associated with the name of Hume that my exclusion of them is apt to seem like an abandonment of what is most distinctive about Hume's discussion of reason. On the contrary, I fancy that I shall be attending to what is truly distinctive (and important) about Hume's discussion. But more on this by and by. The first strand concerns the kind of reason whose normative power we are calling into doubt; the second concerns the kind of argument to be used for that purpose.

The first exclusion. Hume has achieved a notoriety of sorts for holding that the mind is not "determin'd by reason" (T 88) when it makes a causal inference, and for noticing that ought-statements differ from is-statements, that the two are often conflated in moral discourses, and that it "seems altogether inconceivable, how this new relation [of oughtness] could be a deduction from others, which are entirely different from it" (T 469). The reason whose incapacity is flagged in these instances is unreconstructed rationalist reason, or what Hume frequently calls "demonstration" (at, for instance, T 31, 42, 70). Demonstrative reason traces epistemically secure relations of ideas; its powers have been extolled by the original rationalists; and for Hume its proper province is arithmetic, algebra, and (with modest qualifications) geometry. It is one of Hume's achievements to show just how restricted the field of application for demonstrative inference really is. When we detect a causal relation our inference does not rely on a principle of uniformity ("the future either must or probably will resemble the past"), which renders the inference demonstratively circumspect, or at least more circumspect than it would be without the principle. Similarly, when we detect a moral relation, our inference does not draw forth an evaluation of an object from our conception of what that object is (just as we might draw forth a recondite proposition about triangles from a careful consideration of triangularity).[7] In each of these cases, demonstrative reason does not effect the transition of the mind, but rather something else. For causal inference, that something else is habit-assisted imagination; for "moral inference" (as we may, for the sake of symmetry, call the counterpart for ethical deliberation), it is sympathy-assisted imagination.

Given the successful debunking of demonstration in these very important practical domains, we can then naturalize the concept of reason so that it applies to the imagination-dependent operations that Hume documents. And this naturalization project is something that Hume plainly commits himself to unreservedly, as the most casual review of his use of the word "reason" shows. But when he is making his eye-catching claims about the crucially unreasoned bridges in causal and moral inference, he reverts to the old way of speaking about reason, intending thereby, so it seems, to throw into high relief the inappropriateness of the rationalist talk.

These Humean campaigns are justly celebrated. I shall not revisit them, however. For I want to say that Hume has an argument against rationalistic metaclaims that can be made on behalf of his own preferred, naturalized version of reason, metaclaims that in part undo the naturalism of the version. These arguments are less well known but more ambitious. As I have already suggested, it would be a mistake to consider the antidemonstration arguments the heart of Hume's nonrationalism, but it is a mistake that perhaps receives

---

7. When Hume speaks of the impotence of reason in moral reflection, at the beginning of Book Three, he uses the term "deduction," not "demonstration," for the missing reason-guided mental movement. Although deduction is a broader notion than demonstration in eighteenth-century usage (it includes nondemonstrative inference), we are probably safe in assuming that Hume is thinking of a demonstrative inference at T 469.

aid and comfort from Hume's own classification of his causal-inference account in the first *Enquiry* as a "sceptical solution" to "sceptical doubts," the classification not only making it appear as if Hume were primarily concerned with demonstration but also suggesting that he endorses the primacy of demonstration. This is unfortunate, because in the *Treatise* Hume places the causal-inference account in Book One, Part III, carefully segregating it from the skeptical engagements of Part IV. Hume, as many of his readers have noted, does not try to undermine naturalized causal inference. (Even the Part IV engagements do not try to undermine it, on my view, but rather the metaclaims regarding its adequacy for our epistemic purposes.) And so, I respect the treatment of the story we get in the *Treatise* more than the one we get in the *Enquiry*; and if we attend to the earlier treatment, we shall lose much of the feeling that demonstration occupies the center of Hume's attention, or occupies it wholly.

If we wonder why the Hume of the *Enquiry* made the causal-inference account "sceptical," and omitted most of the skeptical Part IV entirely, we have no ready answer, but I do not think that we can blandly acquiesce in the view that the *Enquiry* must be a more mature instrument for Hume's thought than the *Treatise*. The argument I exhume primarily from Part IV is decidedly more abstruse than the antidemonstration argument, and perhaps more purely philosophical in tenor (by virtue of its counterfactual component); and both of these reasons might have induced Hume to leave out a reprise of Part IV. He was, we must remember, greatly afflicted by the misfortune of his dead-born *Treatise* and cited its "manner," rather than its "matter," as the explanation. That being so, he wanted to make the recast as reader-friendly as possible, and it is therefore unsurprising that the reader-unfriendly Part IV was largely deleted.

And now the second exclusion. Hume sometimes writes that our lives are too important and our reason too uncertain for our lives to be guided by reason alone. When he writes in this vein, demonstration is not the kind of reason he has in mind. (Mathematics is useful for life, but mathematical decisions seldom play a very grand role in our actions.) This general line of argument is, like the antidemonstration campaign, commonly associated with Hume. For example: "Nature must have provided some other principle, of more ready, and more general use and application; nor can an operation of such immense consequence in life, as that of inferring effects from causes, be trusted to the uncertain process of reasoning and argumentation" (E 106; cf. T 187). In other words, if animals depended on their reasoning for the bulk of their beliefs, they would depend on a faculty maladapted to the occurrent and unavoidable demands of living. We should notice that it is reason*ing*, and not reason as such, that Hume is downplaying here, inasmuch as a few sentences back Hume observes that animals are not "guided in these inferences by reasoning," and so we have a distinction between a kind of mental operation, the inference, and an extended exercise involving that operation, the reasoning. The problem with reasoning is not completely clear, but it probably has much to do with the fact that reasoning takes place over time that is in relatively scarce supply. This brings us to Descartes's caveat about reason, again. A lack of time alone, however, would not explain the "uncertainty" of reasoning, unless we explain uncertainty as the result of a too cautious weighing of evidence. Hume may have intended to gloss the uncertainty in this manner. For a variation on this real-time worry is also arguably behind Hume's reflections on the rules we use to fix property relations. We fix those relations in ways that are natural for the imagination to grasp but that invite dispute when they are spelled out in particular cases; yet fuzzy rules are better than nothing because less fuzzy rules, we sense, would be too controversial and too time-consuming (because controversial) for us to work out. A similar pattern of thought is to be found in Hume's views on the origins of government.

This type of argument (which has a recognizably conservative flavor, though it is not narrowly political in its purview) is not one I want to consider, because the worry about time, if that is the core worry, merely concerns a deliberatively unpropitious factor. Hume's remarks about the importance of our active lives are unexceptionable so far as they go: we do have to act and cannot forbear acting while we wait for the reports of our reasoning to come in. But they just do not take us very far: combinations of persons, especially transgenerational combinations, are not subject to the exigencies that affect individual persons, and so the worry that we do not have enough time largely disappears if the "we" is a true first-person plural. I am not suggesting that Hume himself would disagree with any of this, and these remarks are not intended as criticisms of the content of the argument, but only of an extension of its scope that some might want to make.

That an extended scope is not envisaged by Hume becomes rather evident in the concluding paragraph of the essay "The Sceptic." There Hume somewhat elegiacally observes, "While we are reasoning concerning life, life is gone," but then he wryly goes on to end the essay by saying, of reasoning, that "this occupation is one of the most amusing, in which life could possibly be employed" (MPL 180). If reasoning were *truly* prodigal, then the amusement of the occupation would be vicious, and similar to playing the violin while your city burns. But of course Hume never makes the remotest suggestion of this kind. Hence, although reasoning may be problematically time-intensive for individuals, a culture advanced enough to contain not only sublime philosophers but their whimsical shadows, the skeptics, is a culture that can afford to have persons who squander their individual apportionments of time in refined reasonings. In fine, then, I think we can relegate the conservative argument to the background, and despite its occasional prominence in Hume's texts it is a device whose import for our evaluation of rationalism is negligible.

Even if we lay aside the time argument, we should notice that scaled-back conceptions of reason frequently accompany conservative cultural stances. Since conservatism, by its complacency, can easily become excessive, it seems that we have another problem to worry about besides irrationalism. I do not think that Hume's argument, despite the (partial) conservatism of Hume the man, has untoward or excessive conservative implications.[8] But I will have to return to this topic when I return to irrationalism.

Now that we have removed the obvious candidates from play, it is time to take up the argument that has antirationalistic import. And it may emerge that this argument will have a somewhat larger and more positive import as well.

---

8. As the response of James Beattie and Thomas Reid made evident, however, the worry about Humeanism in Hume's own time was quite the opposite—that it was too destructively revolutionary. (For a discussion of this reception, see David Fate Norton's *David Hume: Common-Sense Moralist, Sceptical Metaphysician* [Princeton: Princeton University Press, 1982], 192–208.) We have a great temptation, when we do philosophy, to think that what we do either razes our concepts to their foundations or else leaves everything as it was. These outcomes rarely obtain, and a naturalized philosophy should admit as much to itself.

2

✻ ✻ ✻

Bodies and Disembodiment

In this chapter I present the first of two critiques of rationalism, and here the critique is aimed at rationalism concerning belief. The source of this critique is the section in Book One, Part IV, of Hume's *Treatise* called "Of scepticism with regard to the senses." This section of Hume's work offers a sustained series of reflections that I would label an argument, inasmuch as Hume conducts the reader to a particular conclusion about the human mind that the reader is invited to deem acceptable on the basis of the mental movements that terminate in that conclusion. But it is not an ordinary deduction that leaves the mind's self-understanding where it was. The ultimate conclusion of this unusual—and, in the broadest sense, therapeutic—argument can be put in this form: If it were possible for us to follow our reason unreflectively, the objects of our belief would cease to resemble their prereasoned counterparts and, by ceasing in the particular manner that they do, would also cease to be objects of belief. We, as ex-believers in bodies, would then be in a condition that could be aptly described as "disembodied." Before entering into this argument, I want to explain some of the component parts of this formulation of the conclusion.

Not without a little reluctance, I include the phrase "follow our reason unreflectively" in the statement above. My justification for including it is to remind us that reason is not the source of mischief, but rather that a conception of the power or scope of reason is. Concisely specifying that conception, however, is not an easy task. We could speak of a "faith in reason," but that formulation has religious overtones that may not be altogether helpful (although rationalism does indeed foster a spirit of gravity about reason), since the faith in question is not really a faith but only something akin to one, namely, an uncritical trust. "Uncorrected reason" is better, but this may suggest to some ears (my own included) that there is a higher-order faculty that does the correcting, a truer Reason that surveys the soul-making vicissitudes of its experientially more naive partner. Not all of this picture is unwelcome to me: I do think that there is a distinctive point of view, or perspective, that we must occupy if we are to regard reason as corrected. But talk of correction, unless corrected itself, is apt to encourage the thought that the correcting point of view is successful because of something that is intellectually clearer to it than to the point of view it corrects. Wishing to eschew intellectualist connotations, I have therefore decided to eschew the correction talk.[1] "Unreflective reason" is freer of undesirable connotations and has pleasantly Humean associations to boot, but it also has, besides a portentous ring, an air of stasis or passivity. And so, I choose "unreflectively followed" in order to capture the element of mental activity that accounts for the untoward effects. This choice makes for a slight sacrifice of elegance in the statement, but I hope that the resulting perspicuousness justifies that sacrifice.

A few comments about "skepticism" and "skeptics" are in order as well. Sometimes these notions will be pejorative, sometimes laudatory. The explanation is that skepticism comes in two varieties. The first can be called *malign* skepticism, and it results from rationalistic arguments for which we cannot furnish rationalist-acceptable answers. The second can, by parity of terminology, be called *benign* skepticism, and it results from the abandonment of the rationalistic stance through the Humean procedures.[2] Hume thus deploys a malignly skeptical argument in the hope of realizing a benignly skeptical perspective. This opposition of skepticisms sounds more confusing in theory than it is in practice, and the context usually makes clear which skepticism

---

1. Hume himself speaks of the "correction of sentiments," and so I am departing from his usage. I do think, though, that my eschewing of correction talk is more in keeping with Hume's antirationalistic intentions than his embracing of that talk is.
2. This terminology was suggested to me by Annette Baier.

I am talking about. Where it is not, I include the adjectives "malign" and "benign."

And, as a final preliminary, I should say something about the relationship between Parts III and IV of the *Treatise*, a subject that will take us right to the doorstep of the argument. This is a subject that all readers of Hume must come to terms with and have a view about. For there is, on the face of it, a strange bifurcation in Hume's consciousness between these Parts. In III we encounter a worldly Hume, a cautious naturalist who observes how the human species acquires beliefs about the inventory of the world (and, in particular, beliefs about those inventory items that lie outside the immediate experience of the persons involved); in IV we have an unworldly Hume, a suspicious denizen of the Cartesian study who shows us how we might shed most of those same beliefs (but who does so without Cartesian optimism about their ultimate reacquisition). In other words, a forceful contrast in sensibility awaits the reader of Book One, and the difference in textual atmosphere is replayed, in curious and instructive ways, by a certain difference in Henry James's novels between the earlier and later periods. In the earlier works we have a clearly discernible public world with all the familiar signposts of shared experience. But in some of the later works we have, as Edmund Wilson observed, a world whose experiential structure combines "the lifeless trickery of logic and the ambiguous subjectivity of a nightmare."[3] I introduce this otherwise irrelevant remark because it is such a stunningly accurate description of the phenomenology of Hume's Part IV. Here we enter a dreamy, private space of endless self-analysis. Here we have arguments galore, many of them byzantine and relentless, and Hume a number of times remarks upon the difficulty and abstruseness of the views he presents— uncharacteristic admissions because he elsewhere generally plumes himself on the obviousness and nonabstruseness of his claims. This atmosphere is utterly unlike that of Part III or, for that matter, the rest of Hume's writings. How do we account for this?

Now it may be the case that we are witnessing one of those "delicate revolutions" Hume later discusses, changes in sentiment that make people "different not only from each other, but also from themselves in different times" (T 438), and although the suggestion is not entirely without value, it is unsatisfying unless we can provide a motivation for supposing that a change of sentiment here is anything other than a whim. A more promising suggestion would be that Hume wants to reduce Part IV to absurdity. This,

---

3. *The Triple Thinkers* (New York: Harcourt, Brace, 1938), 152.

too, has value, because Part IV houses the malignly skeptical arguments, but is not entirely satisfying either, because we do not yet have an internal relation between Parts III and IV: reducing rationalist reason to absurdity is compatible with the naturalist account of reason, but as we well know, *mere* logical compatibility is not an especially interesting property for sets of sentences to possess. And if IV is a reductio, it is a very long and strangely clamorous reductio—much as if Plato's use of poetic imagery were to be explained solely as the result of a desire to give the reader self-verifying illustrations of Plato's claims about the cognitive poverty of poetically expressed thoughts. My view is that Part IV ultimately continues the work of Part III, by showing what happens if we unreflectively put unrestricted confidence in the reason that is so proudly expounded in Part III, causal inference. If Hume's preferred version of reason runs into self-reflexive embarrassments itself, we have reason then to think that the faculty on which we rely has been truly naturalized. For we, as careful (and carefully reflective) students of human nature, need to know that we have "no choice but betwixt a false reason and none at all" (T 268), a choice that will in no wise count as an objection to our continued reliance on the "false" faculty.[4]

The portion of Part IV that chiefly interests me is, as I said at the outset, Section 2. This is a very difficult section of the *Treatise*, and some prominent commentators—Barry Stroud, Robert Fogelin, and David Pears—are on the whole dissatisfied with it.[5] But it seems to me that the real subject of Hume's discussion is perplexity of a kind that our rationalist proclivities make it hard for us to acknowledge, and so our dissatisfaction, if we have it, may in fact disclose the inescapability of reflective bafflement as well.

It might be helpful to start with a brief (though selective) review of Hume's theses in this section, which I shall identify with letters, and then consider their upshot, as Hume apparently sees it. Hume is concerned with our belief

---

4. More generally on the view I am offering, our inability to avoid contradiction while using reason on reason does not impugn the credentials of our intellectual faculty. By contrast, Annette Baier has recently argued that successful self-reflexivity is ultimately the work of Humean endorsability; see *A Progress of Sentiments* (Cambridge: Harvard University Press, 1991), especially chap. 12. Although I think that the Humean expects the mind "to bear its own survey" (T 620), I do not see that looking into the mirror, as it were, is an *explanatory* device on Hume's part. Moreover, the mind that bears its own survey is the *whole* mind, not a particular faculty seeking accreditation.

5. Stroud, *Hume* (London: Routledge & Kegan Paul, 1977), chap. 5; Fogelin, *Hume's Skepticism* (London: Routledge & Kegan Paul, 1985), chap. 6; Pears, *Hume's System* (Oxford: Oxford University Press, 1990), chaps. 10 and 11.

in the external world (to use old-fashioned language), and he distinguishes between the *continued* and *distinct* existence of objects. The table has a continued existence (we think) when we turn our head and are no longer looking at it; the table has a distinct existence (we think) if we subtract ourselves from the world. Although continuation and distinctness are distinguishable, Hume holds (a) that they are "intimately connected together" (T 188). He generally writes in such a way as to suggest that one of these modes of existence obtains if and only if the other does.

(b) Despite the intimate connection between continuation and distinctness, our belief in continued existence (but not necessarily distinct existence) results from the tendency of the imagination to stay in easy motion by gliding across perceptions that resemble each other. Where belief in distinct existence comes from is less evident, but our commitment to it is most clearly in focus once we distinguish perceptions from objects.

(c) Now there are "experiments" (T 210) that, while sharpening our sense of the perception-object distinction, undermine our confidence that anything actually has a distinct existence. In Section 2 the experiments are easily performed (eye pressings, moving around objects at different distances); but Hume envisages, in principle at least, the more sophisticated experiments of science, which really accomplish the confidence-undermining work. Section 4 ("Of the modern philosophy") significantly extends the suggestions about "experiments" in Section 2, and Hume's conclusions in Section 4 can be regarded as a more detailed expression of the suggestions in Section 2.

(d) A philosophical response to the foregoing experiments that attempts to preserve our commitment to an external world is the doctrine of "double existence of perceptions and objects" (T 215), according to which the world exists twice over, once as perception and once as object. Hume thinks that this doctrine is not one that we can believe (for reasons that I shall return to). Our minds are left in a condition of aporia, which can only be remedied by our not attending to the considerations that forced the aporia upon us.

Thus the upshot is not to think. Such a remedy may be psychologically very satisfying to a thinker, but it does leave us hanging in the air regarding the content of the worldview that Hume wishes to leave us with. Where exactly, for example, does Hume want us to stand with respect to the conclusions of the "modern philosophy"? The unbelievability of the double-existence doctrine is at odds with Hume's modernist-inspired conclusions about distinct existence. In the face of this conundrum, it may be that Hume would simply want us to answer, "We don't know where to stand, and we don't know what we should do in order to find out." But this sort of answer is not satisfying: we will retain some view of the world, even if we do so willy-nilly, after we finish with Hume's arguments; and we would at least want to understand, and reflectively approve, the route we take to our view, even if we do hold it willy-nilly.

I think that we can fill in, on Hume's behalf, the details of a worldview, though, in order to do the work, we have to make some modifications in (a)–(d) above, in ways affecting either the content of the theses or the import that the theses are supposed to have. I confess, however, that such a project is not what I wish to pursue here, save incidentally. What interests me more are the implications of either attributing to Hume or withholding from him a definite view regarding the bodies around us. If we attribute to him the view that I think we should—broadly, the metaphysics of the "vulgar" (if I may speak as only the "learned" nowadays do)—we shall have to admit that the only world in which we can believe is a world that resembles our perceptions of it, and the explanation of this result will involve an endorsement of the imaginative tendency mentioned in (b). If we withhold that view, then we shall make the same admission, and offer the same explanation and endorsement. Hence, whichever position we adopt, I believe that the conclusion will be uncongenial to the rationalist.

These general points are worth making because the strand of Hume's thinking that I am concerned with is open to objections that do not detract from the nonrationalist moral I hope to draw. That strand is a progression of thought that has structural affinities with both the Hegelian progression that terminates in the Unhappy Consciousness and the Nietzschean progression that shows "how the 'true world' finally became a fable."[6] Like Hegel's and Nietzsche's progressions, Hume's charts a progress of alienation and its removal: it belongs to the *Bildungsroman* line of reflection, as we may call it, in which changes in the sensibility of thought are meant to be enacted (or reenacted). Because the movement of mind is intricate, let us begin with a précis of the different moments, along with some minimal textual indications:

1. When we believe, before philosophical reflection ("vulgarly," in other words), in the continued existence of body, we do not mark a distinction between perception and object. (T 193)

---

6. Hegel's discussion of the Unhappy Consciousness (and its preludes, Skepticism and Stoicism) is found in *Phenomenology of Mind*, secs. 197–230. Nietzsche's fable is the fourth section of *Twilight of the Idols*.

2. Causal inference rests on belief in (this version of) the continued existence of body. (T 195–96)
3. Belief in continued existence rests on a resemblance-based inference. (T 197–98; explained at T 199–210)
4. Our perception is itself susceptible to causal explanation. (T 210–11)
5. Causal explanation of perception requires us to distinguish between (interrupted) perceptions and (continuing) objects, and so the uncorrected intellect generates the "philosophical" doctrine of the double existence of perceptions and objects. (T 211–15)
6. The double-existence thesis destabilizes the resemblance-based inference. (T 226–27)
7. If perception and object are separated from each other, there is no resemblance-based inference to support belief in the distinct, continued object. (T 228–31)
8. Lacking a resemblance-based inference to support belief in the distinct, continued object, the mind cannot occupy the philosophical conception of double existence and so falls back into the vulgar version of the belief in continued existence. (T 216)
9. Lacking confidence in resemblance-based inference, the mind occupies the vulgar conception without endorsing it. (T 217–18)
10. Therefore, reason creates a problem for the mind that only something apparently extrarational ("nature") can resolve. (T 218)

This précis looks at the various moments from an above-the-battle point of view, but the making of some of the transitions depends on unreflective exercises of reason, the kind that Hume will chasten by means of the progression. Thus, the benign skeptical strategy must embed the malign if it is to remove the alienation that the malign unwittingly exemplifies.

For greater ease of exposition, we might think of this progression as an argument, provided that we do not interpret it as a standard deductive set of inferences. If the argument is successful, it will show that the price for the mind of having an overly intellectualized self-understanding is a self-reflexive imaginative impasse, since the mind, no longer finding itself at home in its prereflective doxastic environment, cannot find itself at home in the reflection-derived environment either. (Because being at home is tantamount to being embodied, in one sense at least, we could give the steps leading up to, and including, the impasse the sobriquet the "Disembodiment Argument"). Let us now turn to explicating each of the steps.

Step 1. We believe in the continuous existence of the world around us, and we do so without any prompting from philosophy. This much is uncontroversial. But now let us begin to characterize the content of this prereflective belief: what exactly are we committed to, without benefit of philosophical intervention, when we acknowledge this belief? Here we enter more problematic waters. According to Hume, at this stage of our mental life we "confound perceptions and objects, and attribute a distinct continu'd existence to the very things [we] feel or see" (T 193). Alternatively, we think that perceptions and objects are the "same." What this means is that we do not explicitly draw a general distinction between the way we perceive things and the way the things are, between the way they are for us and the way they are in themselves, or (more portentously yet) between appearance and reality. I do not think Hume is claiming, as Pears thinks he is, that our vulgar attention is fixed on items that are categorially *neutral* between perceptions and objects.[7] Neutrality implies an isolation of elements common to two different frameworks, and the awareness of categorial neutrality is always a sophisticated affair, and it is even doubtful whether a putative awareness of this sort commonly occurs independently of philosophical analysis. (Descartes looked for true beliefs whose causal provenance was neutral between waking and dreaming, and found them in mathematics, but this view of the status of mathematical—as well as metaphysical and theological—beliefs hardly suggests itself to us when we do our sums in ordinary contexts.) Our vulgar attention is fixed rather on items that are categorially *mixed* or *indeterminate*. Hume does not use this language, to be sure, but since it is clear that the vulgar conception involves, for him, a nonmarking or nonnoticing of the perception-object distinction, to speak of a (tacit) mixture or indeterminacy would seem to be licit.[8]

This point about categorial mixture, while seeming to be pedantic or carping, is actually of some importance, for it allows us largely to disarm a generic criticism that can be advanced against the attribution of beliefs to the vulgar. Sophisticates are in no position to say what the man or woman in the street believes—so the criticism goes—because the commonsense framework is a tangled skein of views and half-views, and it is accordingly possible to extract from this original framework any number of successors that more or

---

7. Pears, *Hume's System*, 153.

8. My way of putting things in this paragraph may suggest that a perception-object distinction can be successfully drawn. Intuitively, that seems right; but the impression could be mistaken. For one reaction to the Humean argument is to deny that we can neatly separate perceptions from objects.

less qualify as refinements (or articulations) of the original and that are incompatible with each other. (The history of British empiricism is particularly illuminating in this regard. Locke, Berkeley, and Hume are alike eager to claim a "natural" or commonsense basis for their very different systems, each exploiting different strands.) Therefore, we might be inclined to be dismissive of all attributions of recognizably philosophical belief to the vulgar, for the reason that the prereflective view does not even admit of being stated. But at this inauspicious pass the virtue of the Humean attribution becomes apparent. For Hume is not attributing to us a positive or a negative thesis, but one that is murky, inexplicit, unexamined, and underexplored. To the extent that the worry about sophisticated attributions is well motivated (and I think it is), the blurry Humean-type attributions acquire greater plausibility. And thus we have reason to regard the Humean conception of our prereflective view as being less a revisionary than a rival conception.

If we can disarm the generic criticism, we may still wonder whether Hume's ostensibly confident, unqualified assertion that we "confound" the categories is warranted. For if we run through the familiar gamut of illusions with which we regale first-time visitors to the epistemologists' closet—wet patches on summertime roads, bent sticks in water, and so on—the very readiness with which the visitors understand and appreciate the force of the examples suggests that qualification is necessary. I do not think, however, that this phenomenon should afford Hume much vexation, if any, and for two reasons. First, aware though we generally are of optical illusions, we do not regard their occurrence as especially common or numerous, and these illusions certainly do not have for us the fascination of a potentially unrestricted generality as they do for the epistemologist. We note the occurrence of a few illusions here and there, are mildly amused by them, and delight in showing them to children and naïfs (which is one of the few options we have for preserving our original, prone-to-fade amusement in them). We correctly treat illusions as the exception, not the rule. (We require a special light for seeing if we are to countenance the serious possibility of a radical, wholesale illusion that pervasively infects our experience.) And so, Hume's claim stands unimpeached for what has to be the vast majority of our beliefs.

But second, even within the comparatively tiny subset of our beliefs for which the awareness of an illusional component is unreflectively unavoidable, we are surely stacking the deck against common life if we think that this prosaic awareness involves, in turn, the awareness of a wholesale appearance-reality gap (and this additional awareness must be present if the Humean claim is to be in trouble ultimately). When we see the bent stick in water, we do not suppose that the real stick is different from the way it appears, but that our first view merely needs to be corrected or supplemented. We are at one of those places where it is difficult to say what we want to say without being cajoled into saying it, and so I will refrain from bold pronouncements, but I would assimilate illusions to the following sort of case (and then leave undecided the categorization that applies to both). Suppose that you arrive home to discover that your stereo system is missing and that your window (closed when you last saw it) is open. You naturally infer a burglar. On the next day, however, when you return home again, you discover a new, upgraded system and a well-wishing note from your spouse and family. Revising the burglar inference, you then say: I have been the sport of my lovely, wicked near and dear. In other words, more evidence comes to the fore, a fuller view supplants a narrower, and the addition translates as a difference in judgment. Beyond this minimal characterization, I believe there is little we can confidently aver regarding the change in your belief, but to say that the first judgment concerns a mere appearance is obviously a tendentious graft onto the common rootstock.

Optical illusions behave no differently, and further consideration makes the tendentiousness of the graft more visible. We may think that the stick is bent at first, but as we learn more about sticks and water, our relationship to the original perceptual pool changes; later and richer viewings effortlessly replace the earlier and poorer. Our first experiential contact is with the tip of any particular perceptual iceberg (and we may, for our ease, think about icebergs themselves), but additional contact reveals more than the tip, and moreover shows us what the world must be like if it is to have such things as genuine tips in it. We never see the whole of the iceberg, even after we know what icebergs are, and yet the merely visible tip does not pose any difficulties that lead us to think, "How odd. Icebergs are more than their tips, but tips are all we see." Embodied persons do not see, and ordinarily do not expect to see, all that there it is to look at, and in this setting the very idea of an appearance-reality *gap* contains a hidden demand *to see everything at once*.

The presence of this demand is seldom sufficiently acknowledged. When Descartes disparages the senses, his complaint arises because we cannot rely on any single batch of sense perceptions when we make perceptual judgments. On one view, the demand looks simply petulant ("Can't you just walk up to, and around, the towers for half an hour or so, and gather a fuller set of perceptual readings?"); but on another, it is not, since the intellect creates expectations that the object before it be wholly before it and that our mental access to the object not be essentially mediated by anything so pedestrian as *walking.* (It is his faithfulness to this intellectual presumption that makes Descartes such a deep and intriguing thinker—and so, at times, like a pitiless machine too.) This divergence in assessments of the demand adumbrates a divergence between the Humean and the rationalist, and we will give the elements of this kind of case the widest of berths. At present, it is enough if we see that a wholesale appearance-reality distinction requires for its drawing here a special trip we do not ordinarily make (or if we think that we do make it, the drawing occurs so far behind our backs that we are then forced into a self-ascription of a luxuriant Meno-like psychology).

Step 2. When Hume begins his explanation of how perceptual coherence gives rise to the belief in continued existence, he observes that there is an important difference between external objects and our passions, despite notable similarities between them in our perception. Both passions and external objects exhibit a certain order to us, and they both become present to our minds via impressions, but we do not suppose that our passions continue to exist when we are not perceiving them, whereas we do make that supposition with external objects. If I believe that the table exists, I believe that the table has a causal structure we rely upon in our dealings with it, and so the existence of the table is at least perceiver-indifferent if not perceiver-independent. (This is a general claim about existence, and our passions do not invalidate the claim. It is natural to say that I am angry, but not that my anger exists, for the second locution, but not the first, suggests that the anger is ongoing and thinglike.) This basic model is complicated, but only complicated, when we incorporate causal incursions into that portion of the world that our senses and memory present to us. If I believe that the porter has just brought a letter to my table, then I do not believe that the porter materialized out of thin air (he had to climb the stairs to reach my room), and I do not believe that the letter materialized in the porter's hand (it had to cross the ocean on a ferry from a distant friend). Although Hume typically insists that cause-effect relations connect us to perceptually absent realities, his theory of belief has another aspect that is just as important, and that the story of the porter and the letter brings out, namely, that cause-effect relations stabilize perceptually *present* realities by making changes that occur before us intelligible and nonmiraculous. (Consequently, Hume's earlier exposition, at T 107–8, of the "two systems" of belief, one drawn from the memory and senses, the other from causal inference, needs a little articulation. The first system it is not as self-contained as Hume's exposition suggested.) And so, not only a particular kind of belief, that of existence, but a particular mental operation, causal inference, presupposes belief in continued existence.

We should have nothing to cavil at in step 2; let us turn then to step 3. Hume tells us that if we "consider these phaenomena of the porter and letter in a certain light," we will find that they are "contradictions" and "may be regarded as objections to those maxims, which we form concerning the connexions of causes and effects" (T 196). As Hume goes on to explain, the belief in continued existence is a belief that arises through a psychological mechanism that is strikingly different from the mechanism in which he has reposed the utmost confidence thus far, that of causal association. Forming a belief regarding continued existence is unlike forming a belief regarding causes and effects, because the first belief, and not the second, involves "a habit acquir'd by what was never present to the mind" (T 197). When we trace causal relations, the mind needs to be accustomed to constant conjunctions before we are able to infer the causal connection between the relata. But when we believe that something continues to exist, the mind makes a move that is not underwritten by accustomed conjunctions. That the mind does not have the reservoir of custom to draw from is more easily visible if we consider what our mental lives would look like if the habit were "acquir'd" in the normal way.

It seems to me that our lives would have to be utterly unlike what they are now. Our minds would in effect have to be free, to some extent, of our present bodily constitutions: we would need an experiential awareness of absent objects that would somehow, at the same time, not make them present objects, and this unusual juxtaposition is necessary if we are to have something "present to the mind" on which the habit can grow. In other words, it would have to be possible for us to be somewhere when we were not, strictly speaking, there. Doubtless, this conception is exceedingly difficult to make intelligible, but the traditional theological attribute of omnipresence (which may not be intelligible either) gives us at least an intimation of the direction in which our psychology would be turning. And perhaps we can put the point this way: that only an omnipresent (or multiply present) being could believe in the continued existence of things on the basis of a habit that conforms to the regular pattern of habit acquisition. Only a being that could be everywhere (or "manywhere") and simultaneously nowhere would have the requisite psychological endowment, if what is needed can even be characterized as psychological. Of course, with such a redoubtable being we may become unentitled to speak of habits altogether, or else lose our grip on what a habit is, since certifiably habitual behavior may in the end depend on embodiment. But the issue is nugatory, for it is entirely safe to say that we do not exemplify even weak multipresence. It is true that our minds are not confined "like those of beasts, in that narrow circle of objects, which are the subject of daily conversation and action" (T 273), but we are elsewhere only in our imaginations. To suppose otherwise is to succumb to a high-grade (optical?) illusion.

Causal inference, the habit-presupposing procurer of our beliefs, requires for its success a belief that cannot itself be procured through the same habits. This is the "contradiction." Before we take up the question of the alternative mechanism, it would be useful to consider the status of this contradiction. Admittedly, it is informal, but I also believe that when Hume acknowledges the contradiction, he is at most shedding crocodile tears. Our belief in continued existence "arises," he says, "from the understanding, and from custom in an indirect and oblique manner" (T 197), and we only have a true informal contradiction, a tension worth worrying about, if we think that we need to have a unified (that is, direct and nonoblique) explanatory model for belief acquisition. I see no evidence at all for believing that Hume was disturbed by the discovery occasioned by the porter and letter. That the all-important belief in continued existence has a peculiar causal history is just another lacuna of the sort that fascinated Hume and that he never tried to explain away. Throughout Hume's writings we witness a near obsession with causal gaps, false starts, dead ends, exceptions, irregularities, and the wherewithal we have for filling, removing, or concealing them. The keynote discussion of the missing shade of blue furnishes a kind of leitmotiv for the whole philosophy. Thus, for example, when Hume is unable to explain to his satisfaction why causes are always necessary, he enjoins himself and us to be like those who "beat about all the neighbouring fields, without any certain view or design, in hopes their good fortune will at last guide them to what they search for" (T 78). We then get our answer, but only after a lengthy indirection. Similarly, the impression that provides us with our idea of necessary connection is invisible to direct inspection, and the invisibility is maddening if we demand a straight mental trajectory for an idea of such great moment as this. But the mind, on Hume's analysis, does not move on a linear track. Although this nonlinearity may seem to be an accidental feature of Hume's mode of presentation, it may emerge as a defining property of the embodied mind.

We could cull many other examples of Hume's lively awareness of lacunae, but we would do well, perhaps, to forgo them. But one exception to this general rule is worth a digression. There it is a very revealing throwaway remark Hume makes in "The Sceptic," and it can be usefully retrieved to show the depth of his gap-mindedness. After reviewing various kinds of lives, the Sceptic informs us, "And in general, business and action fill up all the great vacancies of life" (MPL 167). A remarkable statement, and not merely because of the rather imperious "all." It is remarkable for the Pascalian association between a certain emptiness and what undoubtedly constitutes the greatest part of our waking adult life, the getting of our livelihood: empty times, we are tempted to say, occur after our work is done (and the filling of which calls for the usual sorts of divertissements), but here work itself is the filler, and the remark leads us to suspect that the Sceptic discerns more gap than nongap in our mental life. On this view, work loses the transparent intentionality we thought it had, becoming, as it were, an unconscious screening device that hides the expressionless Great Vacancies from sight. Too large a world can sometimes be seen in a grain of sand, and I would not want to erect a theory of Hume's philosophical sensibility on the basis of the Sceptic's one remark, nor would I want to burden the Sceptic, who is a fairly cheery fellow, with a black load of angst. And, on the suggestion I am making, there is arguably a new worry about positing a Meno psychology (though dispellable, I think, because the vacancy avoider hardly needs to be a sophisticated intellect—a careening id will do). Nevertheless, I present the remark as providing us with a modest index of Hume's standing expectation that the timber of the human tree will be crooked; and unlike Kant, he did not think that the crookedness of our timber was necessarily a cause for alarm or self-congratulatory regret.

Doubtless, we need a wide context in which to situate Hume's response to the "phaenomena of the porter and letter," a context wider than I can give now, but I trust that we have enough reason to believe that Hume's talk of contradiction is plausibly seasoned with irony. It is important that we detect this irony, because the course of the skeptical argument is apt to seem increasingly bizarre if we regard Hume as committed to the unassisted supremacy of causal inference. For it will look as though Hume is autistically tearing down the very house he is attempting to build up. And having thus dealt with the status of the contradiction, we can return to the thread we left hanging, the special mechanism for the belief in continued existence.

Hume says that the imagination, "like a galley put in motion by the oars, carries on its course without any new impulse" (T 198). This galleylike mental motion is the source of our belief in continued existence. The imagination responds to patterns of perceptual coherence and constancy and extrapolates those patterns beyond our occurrent perceptual ken. If we unpack the simile, the implied original impulse for the oars is furnished by the senses, but when the sensory input fails, as it must (because we are not multipresent), the imagination is able to continue the path the sensory input has opened, without renewing itself at another sensory fount. How the imagination is able to perform this feat may seem dark, but the feat is really no different from ordinary instances of legerdemain, where we always get effects that astonish us because the apparent effects seem unsuited, if our experience is standard, to the causes that we see. The imagination is the original magician, beguiling us with illusionistic improvisations on the props with which the senses equip it. Hume devotes quite a few pages (T 199–210) to showing how easy it is for the imagination to execute the continued-existence trick, and I want to take what he says in these pages for granted, since I doubt whether we need an argument in order to be convinced that the imagination has a smooth passage here. Instead, I want to replace my ungainly "galleylike mental motion" with a seemingly more august term for the activity in which the mind is engaged.

To begin with, Hume twice refers to this motion (at T 197 and 199) as an *inference*. Continued existence is not something we "just believe"; we require an action of the mind, however slight or self-effacing, if we are to make continued existence an object of belief. This observation is not so startling. But calling this mental transition an inference may yet raise hackles, because we think that inferences are amenable to formal codification and it is hardly credible to suppose that we have promising material for such a codification here. ("Rules by which to judge of conclusions based on galleylike mental transitions" is an unwritten—and presumably unwritable—section of the *Treatise*.) Hume's terminological liberalism thus goes beyond what many of us would be prepared to accept. We may interpret this liberalism as a further indication of Hume's naturalistic program, however, and I am content to acquiesce in Hume's usage. And following Hume's lead in gentrifying the galleylike motion with the name of inference, I am willing to extend the gentrification by calling it the resemblance-based inference, or the *resemblance inference* for short.[9] Since neither Hume nor (to my knowledge) his commentators use this expression, it is incumbent on me to justify this term of art.

The imagination reacts, as we know, to patterns of perceptual coherence and constancy, but of the two patterns constancy seems to be the more

---

9. The resemblance inference is the same as what H. H. Price more prosaically called "inertia" in *Hume's Theory of the External World* (Oxford: Clarendon, 1940). I am not opposed to a label that is more standard, but for my purposes I want to emphasize the role played by resemblance in the inertial mental movement, and so I will stay with my label.

important. Hume mentions constancy first, and we encounter it in our perceptions when objects recur unaltered to our view. "My bed and table, my books and papers, present themselves in the same uniform manner, and change not upon account of any interruption in my seeing or perceiving them" (T 194–95). Coherence, which we encounter, for example, when we return to a burning fire after an hour's absence and see the changes in the logs, appears to be a degenerate form of constancy, since Hume introduces coherence by saying that constancy is "not so perfect as not to admit of very considerable exceptions" (T 195). The presentation of constancy and coherence mirrors Hume's earlier presentation of causation and probability, in Part III, where the reader learns that probabilistic inference is imperfect causal inference, not that causal inference is a perfecting of the probabilistic. It is somewhat difficult to grasp how coherence could merely be imperfect constancy, since judgments of coherence would seem to presuppose causal inferences in a way that judgments of constancy do not: I would not regard the charred embers in my hearth as "cohering" with the blazing flames I saw earlier unless I knew that fires tended to burn themselves out. But perhaps the very presence of causal, appearance-altering factors is what enables us to understand the imperfection. When we have constancy, we have a recurring scene that recurs because there are no causal irruptions that prevent the recurrence; when we have coherence we do witness these irruptions. Accordingly, we can make a good deal of sense of the way Hume makes his pairing. He reinforces this pairing, a few pages later, just after he unveils the galley image. He tells us that coherence is "too weak to support so vast an edifice, as it is that of the continu'd existence of all external bodies," and that we must have constancy in place if the edifice it is to be supported (T 198–99). Constancy, not coherence, is the wind that really blows our galley, and this conclusion is borne out by Hume's subsequent explication, which is concerned exclusively with constancy.

    The reason I am at pains to stress the greater importance of constancy is that our judgments of constancy are made possible on the basis of observable resemblances between batches of perceptions. My bed and table *look the same* to me as they did a moment ago, before I turned my head away. With coherence, this resemblance fails, more or less, wholly or in part. The embers have a partial visual affiliation with the blaze, and the resemblance is breached to the extent that causal factors have been active. (If I had returned to the fire earlier, I would have had a perception more nearly resembling my first perception, but then the causal series would have unfurled itself less completely as well.) And so, we have a resemblance-based inference for continued existence that complements the cause-based inference we have for cementing the various parts of our universe together. By setting up parallel streams for these two Humean associative principles, I am of course implicitly making a more ambitious claim for the resemblance-based inference than Hume officially does, and so I now need to show that the resemblance inference has quietly acknowledged citizens' rights in Hume's system. Establishing these rights requires a brief detour into Parts I and III, but this excursion will handily tighten the tie between Parts III and IV, thereby yielding us no small occasion for gladness.

On Hume's basic model of the mind there are two kinds of mental entities, impressions and ideas. Impressions are the cause of ideas, but ideas are also said to resemble the impressions that cause them. In the primal scene of the mind, we can observe, then, two of the three relations that ground the association of ideas. By itself this observation is not very important, but we are able to see that resemblance figures along with causation in Hume's most elementary mental occurrence, the manufacturing of an idea, and this may prompt us to accord more respect to resemblance-based associations than we otherwise would as we move forward in the *Treatise*.

But the real evidence that favors the importance of the resemblance inference comes in Part III, Section 9, "Of the effects of other relations and other habits." In this section Hume considers the way the three associative relations affect our propensities to belief. Cause and effect, understandably, is given pride of place. Hume then dispatches contiguity in a single paragraph. But then he devotes four extremely interesting pages (T 111–15) to resemblance, and the *kinds* of beliefs whose ideas are approvingly assisted by resemblance relations have a striking similarity to the belief in continued existence.

Hume's idea-examples are these: the ocean, miracles, and the afterlife. A person standing on a promontory receives a more lively idea of the ocean than in his study because the view from the promontory, which reveals a vast body of water to him, has a stronger resemblance to the ocean than his unassisted imaginative perception has. Another person is more likely to believe that a reported miracle is true merely because it is reported, a hypothetical resemblance between the reporter's ideas and the supposed event obtaining. Another person is not concerned about the future state of his soul, because there is not enough of a resemblance between his present state and the future one.

These pages are interesting in part because Hume the practical moralist clearly strides across the pages of the *Treatise* for the first time. The second case is plainly condemned. The first is either neutral or meets with mild approval. The third seems to meet with a definite approval, and this impression is reinforced when Hume notes that the Roman Catholics condemn the St. Bartholomew's Day massacre, which was committed "against those very people, whom without any scruple they condemn to eternal and infinite punishments" (T 115). We have the feeling here that the absence of resemblance relations causes the mind to go astray, to lose its humanity, to silence those sentiments of horror that naturally present themselves when we behold flesh-and-blood sufferers who resemble us.

There are many niceties in this discussion that could keep us busy for quite a while, and that would deflect us from the immediate task at hand. I take it for granted that Hume is right to condemn the second case, and I retire it from further consideration. I assume also that there it is mild approval in the first case. We then have the ocean and the afterlife to consider, and both of these items are things that we, as embodied perceivers, have trouble perceiving, on account of our embodiment. We cannot grasp the ocean very well in our imagination, and so we need a revivifying perception from our senses that suitably intimates the largeness of the thing. The same would be true for the afterlife. We would need a revivifying perception of times to come in order to keep those times before our minds. We can then explain why we care about the kind of world our children will live in after we are dead, because we can vividly discern the relevant resemblance relations.

On the basis of Part III, Section 9, I wish to advance this thesis: whenever an object is such that the conditions of our embodiment make it intrinsically difficult to keep up either a stable belief in, or a stable concern for, that object through the usual avenues for belief or concern, the resemblance inference has to do nontrivial work that cannot be done by any other action of the mind. Hume, of course, does not say this, but I think the thesis captures the logic of his thought, and the argumentative machinations of Part IV, Section 2, provide it with a kind of defense. We are shortly going to try to do without the resemblance inference, but at this point, suffice it to say that continued existence is the sort of item that qualifies for coverage under this thesis. We ordinarily believe something either because it is present to our memory and senses or because it is connected to what is present via cause and effect relations. We are not multipresent, and so continuously existing objects cannot ever be present to our memory and senses. Nor can we make out causal relations to such objects.

If, on a Humean view, causal inference it is not enough for the securing of all beliefs, then Parts III and IV, which have different presumptions regarding causal inference, do bear an internal relation to each other. In Part III there is no implicit claim that causal inference is enough; in Part IV there is. We can return now to the main thread of the argument, and with a newfound confidence.

Step 4. At T 210 the malignly skeptical becomes noticeable. Hume notes that "a very little reflection and philosophy" will convince us that our "sensible objects or perceptions" cannot have a continued existence. He thereupon furnishes us with the little philosophy that we need in order to acquire the conviction, and that philosophy consists of the perceptual-variation arguments that show that our perceptions are dependent on our constitutions: pressing our eyes with our fingers and seeing double, changing our position and thus changing the apparent size of objects, the alterations in what we see on account of physiological illness—and there are "an infinite number of other experiments of the same kind" to make the case (T 211). In other words, the little philosophy is the standard gambit of what Hume two sections later calls the "modern philosophy," which cuts us off (in his view) from any stable conception of the world.[10] Since I believe that Hume either wants or should want to distance himself from the "modern philosophy," I think that his (ostensibly uncritical) use of the opening arguments of that philosophy has to be understood in a way that carries no endorsement of the later moves. I propose, then, that we interpret Hume as doing a bit, just a little bit, of what he told us, at the beginning of the *Treatise*, he would not be doing, namely, a causal explanation of our perceptions, a subject that "belongs more to anatomists and natural philosophers than to moral" (T 8). All that Hume's breezily mentioned "experiments" really show is just that there is a causal story to be told about perception, that perception is not external to the causal order, and Hume's lack of interest in pursuing that story is perfectly consonant with his professed intentions. He only needs the fact, as we might call it, of causal explanation of perception to keep the remainder of the argument moving.

We should notice, though, that the kind of causal inquiry Hume adverts to here is different from the kind to which we have been treated thus far in Book

---

10. As Annette Baier has suggested to me, it is possible to read Hume as committed to the view that the modern philosophy is just a mistake, and that the little philosophy we need is simply an awareness that not all of our prereflective beliefs can be held true. This reading would then save Hume, or prepare to save him, from the modern philosophy, but it seems to me that we are forcing the text on this point.

One. Until now Hume has been tracking horizontal causal relations between perceptual contents, between, for example, fire causes and heat effects. Here he is shifting our view to vertical trackings, from perceptions *as such* to something that causes them (and that includes our bodily constitution). Because of this shift, it is perhaps tempting to regard the skeptical argument as being tantamount to a reductio ad absurdum of vertical causal explanation. This interpretation is not entirely inapposite. Vertical explanation does seem to be (in Hume's language) more "irregular" than horizontal in the sense that we do not attain results in the two directions with comparable success rates. We continually add to the general fund of our knowledge horizontal causal claims that are both detailed and defensible. But with the vertical our claims are much less secure, and (in some respects) we have scarcely advanced since Hume's day. Nevertheless, I do not think that Hume wants to rule vertical explanation out of bounds, nor should we want to. The vertical suffers from complications of which the horizontal is free (the perceiver himself is not up for study in the case of the horizontal), and so we can count on greater hurdles. And relatedly, it seems pretty clear that vertical trackings are almost completely undoable by single minds: we can gather data and test hypotheses on each other in a way that we cannot replicate with ourselves, because finding the data and funding the hypotheses require studiable interruptions in the consciousness of those who are the subjects of the hypotheses, and we cannot interrupt our own consciousness, in the multifarious ways that are necessary, to see what happens. The eye pressing that Hume mentions is about the most we can do on our own.

It is possible that first-person-singular vertical causal trackings are reduced to absurdity in Hume's text. Even so, there is more going on than that. For in responding to the fact of explanatory susceptibility, the intellect-enamored philosopher will espy an opportunity that allows him or her to disown the resemblance inference. Hume considers this philosophical response to the scientific discovery about perception a disaster, and it seems that this response would never have been dreamt of unless we had had the itch to accommodate the scientific discovery in a globally coherent (in the logical sense, not Hume's) and regular (in Hume's sense) conception of things. Let us advance to that response.

Step 5. We (who begin our philosophical careers as Lockeans) reflectively respond to the fact of perception-directed causal explanation by a "new system" (T 211) that distinguishes between (interrupted) perceptions and (continuing) objects. This is the doctrine of "the double existence of perceptions and objects" (T 215), and besides being a decisive revision of the vulgar conception, it ontologizes a wholesale appearance-reality distinction. We had, before, an indifferent perception-or-object. From this turbid solution, as it were, we now precipitate out two items, an object that is mind-independent and a perception that is conceptually world-independent. (Part of the picture here is that causal relations obtain between sets of the two items, although Hume does not explicitly say this.) Accordingly, then, a thing exists twice: first as an independent object, and again, in the manner of a doppelgänger, as a dependent perception. We arrive at this revised conception because (i) the perceptual-variation arguments apparently reveal that some aspect of our perception has no existence outside the mind, in virtue of its causal dependence on the mind, and (ii) we have a powerful conviction that our minds do not simply produce and consume their objects, that something remains after we subtract the mind from the perceptual transaction.

The doctrine of double existence is essentially the Lockean view of the relationship of mind to world, and so insinuating is the view that it crops up time and again (as in the drawing of the Kantian distinction between noumena and phenomena). Hume considers the doctrine a "monstrous offspring of two principles, which are contrary to each other, which are both at once embrac'd by the mind, and which are unable mutually to destroy each other" (T 215). The first "principle" is our causal inference, in which we repose so much confidence; the second is our resemblance-based inference, which we are disinclined even to acknowledge, but whose presence is crucial because we would not have the powerful conviction that perceptions do not consume their objects unless our imaginations were set in motion by the various sensory constancies. Striking as Hume's image of this battle royal is, his discussion of it actually makes it seem less striking than it is. For the *disavowal* of the resemblance inference will be necessary for the production of the "monstrous offspring," as we shall presently see.

Step 6. The resemblance-based inference is not exactly respectable; it is déclassé. We can easily understand why. The thinness of the inference becomes manifest simply by our becoming aware of its occurrence. We vulgarians rely on it for our belief in continued existence, but plainly the way in which the imagination is "seduc'd" into extrapolations of constancies does not stand up to scrutiny. Hume calls the belief in continued existence a "fiction," and I do not take him to be saying that this belief is unverifiable, but rather that the belief has a discernible causal origin that does not stir our confidence, which embarrasses us. This belief is "really false" (T 209), and although Hume does not have a theory of truth, he does not need one to make this claim. All that he needs is an exhibition of the relative frivolousness of the imaginative operation that leads us to the belief, and this he supplies. In the same way we can explain the "fictions" that those "liars by profession," the poets, make: we have no confidence in their deliverances, because of the circumstances of their production. Our minds are uneasy if we acquire our beliefs from romances, just as our minds are uneasy when we discover our embarrassingly unartful seduction to the continued existence of bodies.

To strengthen this claim about the weak credentials of the resemblance inference, and incidentally to strengthen the claim about the nature of Humean fictions, we should briefly consult Hume's discussion of personal identity, which conducts us to a similar conceptual tableau. The inference that gives us continued existence also gives us personal identity: the mind has a smooth ride from perception to perception, and the ride is so smooth that we take succession for sameness. "This resemblance is the cause of the confusion and mistake, and makes us substitute the notion of identity, instead of that of related objects." That the mind is embarrassed by this slide is apparent in the readiness with which we feign "the notion of a *soul*, and *self*, and *substance*, to disguise the variation" (T 254). What is easy for the unreflective imagination to swallow sticks in the craw of the reflective, and so the mind attempts to disown the shaky inference by pretending to perceive a psychological state of affairs, a substantial self that is strictly identical over time, that in effect transforms the inference into a thoroughly solid interior-observation report. The notion of the substantial self it is a fiction-concealing *fiction*, however, because it arises to satisfy a higher-order version of the same need that provoked the first fiction—a desire for comfortable mental transitions—and in a higher-order fashion. (As a fiction concealer, the new fiction may do a splendid job until its own standing is unmasked, and then its downfall is much harder than that of the initiating fiction, false consciousness having been necessary for its production.) The substantial self has double existence for its opposite number in Section 2. Here too we have a proposal that seems to disembowel the shaky inference via redescription of our mental topography: no inertia-loving galley would ever wander into double existence, and so we find solace in the thought that the continuing object is secured through respectable, albeit labored, inference. And to realize the same end, we might even redescribe the galleylike activity of the mind in a non-inference-involving way (perhaps by viewing the apparent motion as a static series of images that the mind scans quickly, though a process similar to that which gives us cartoons).

Hume plainly thinks the metafictions are ultimately less creditable than their fostering fictions, and much of the explanation surely has to derive from the greater naturalness of the originals. We have a situation that involves two operations of the imagination, where one is "permanent, irresistable, and universal" and the other "changeable, weak, and irregular" (T 225), and the saner preference is for the former. But I think that there is another reason for the disapprobation of the metafictions. The resemblance inference is shaky on its own terms—and shaky enough, in view of its strategic importance. But the metafiction makes the inference appear shakier than it in fact is. This superadded shakiness, ideologically imposed, attaches to the inference if we examine some further implications of the double-existence doctrine. We do not get these in Section 2, but we do in Section 4, and at this point, therefore, we have to breach Hume's narrative order slightly. The breach is well motivated, though, because we shall only be enlarging upon, and adding details to, our picture of the "monstrous offspring" whose visage we are surveying at T 211–15.

In Section 4 Hume gives us a slightly more extended presentation of the perceptual-variation argument (though its scope is more limited), and he also draws a conclusion from it: "'Tis certain, that when different impressions of the same sense arise from any object, every one of these impressions has not a resembling quality existent in the object" (T 227). If we observe how things look different to us under various perceptual conditions, and if we hold that the independent object cannot vary *pari passu* with the conditions, we begin to question whether the variable qualities, which are found in our perception, resemble the object that causes them to occur in us. If we accept the double-existence thesis, we lose confidence that the resembling perceptions over which our mind effortlessly glides, and by gliding continues, are perceptions of items that have an existence beyond our minds. Consequently, the double-existence thesis weakens the imaginative credentials of the already weak resemblance inference further: why should we rely on resemblance in our extrapolations from what is present to what is absent when we have such a strong reason for supposing that the world that continues in our absence has at best problematic resemblances to our perceptions of it in our presence? The philosophical turn that results in our acceptance of the thesis, as we can see, does not leave the evidence against the resemblance inference unaffected. By attenuating the resemblance relation between the two separated halves of the vulgar perception, we think even less well of our mental operations, and of the beliefs we form by means of those operations.[11]

At this point I want to register a divergence from Hume's official view (and my most substantive one in the course of this argument). I have claimed that the severing of the resemblance relation follows upon the double-existence thesis in conjunction with the perceptual-variation argument. Hume, however, does not wed the denial of resemblance to double existence. Instead, he treats the denial as following simply from the perceptual-variation argument.[12] This divergence is important because Hume nowhere treats the denial of resemblance as the product of a *questionable* inference. He says that the resemblance-denying conclusion is "as satisfactory as can possibly be imagin'd" (T 227), and this judgment is never retracted, never recalled with irony. Hume, in this particular, *accepts* the modern philosophy—specifically, the doctrine of secondary qualities, taking over without critical reservation the lesson Locke purported to draw from his perplexed musings on the color of porphyry in a darkened room. It is highly revealing that when Hume came to write "The Sceptic," an essay that seemingly delights in putting all nonobvious philosophical ideas up for a laugh, he let the Sceptic have one footnote where, somewhat apologetically ("Were I not afraid of appearing too philosophical, I should remind my reader . . ."), he embraces the nonobvious philosophical view about secondary qualities as part of an effort to *shore up* the more obvious (though not utterly obvious) and less philosophical view that values are projected and not found (MPL 166). Surely the strategy of this footnote is fairly strong evidence that Hume is an unreconstructed modernist regarding secondary qualities.[13] I, on the other hand, am more inclined to consider this view a new-generation monstrosity, sired by double existence

---

11. I do not mean to suggest that the materials upon which the resemblance inference operates—the phenomenal constancies and coherences—are themselves necessarily vitiated by the acceptance of the double-existence thesis. We still have them, and largely (but not perfectly) intact. The principle of belief formation, if we wished to represent the galleylike motion as a principle, is the increasingly undermined party.

12. It should be emphasized that Hume's discussion of perceptual variation in Section 2 does not betray a commitment on his part to the modern doctrine of secondary qualities. His discussion in Section 4, however, does treat the secondary-qualities doctrine as a philosophical response to the fact of perceptual variation, and it is this discussion that I am concerned with.

13. Simon Blackburn has proposed that "while Hume is prepared to tolerate the [sc. modernist] inference, he does not present it with any great enthusiasm," and that "the tone is one of distaste for the issue" of secondary qualities ("Hume on the Mezzanine Level," *Hume Studies* 19 [1993]: 274). If Blackburn it is right, then in my view Hume should have the courage of his distaste.

and physiognomically displaying its paternity. I believe that Hume's skeptical argument would have been both simpler and stronger had he seen things this way. Part of my conviction concerning Hume's argument is founded on the pleasing shape I think my overall reconstruction has, but part of it has independent (or semi-independent) sources, which I will briefly indicate. (In what follows, I let colors represent all the secondary qualities.)

First, I tend to think that we cannot coherently state the denial of resemblance without covert reference to the double-existence thesis. All that the example of porphyry in the dark might show is that colors are not, in Locke's terminology, simple ideas: we cannot simply tell, just by looking at a sample of porphyry at a given instant, what its color is. Locke's thought experiment with the porphyry, by itself, would then be little different from Wilfrid Sellars's thought experiment with John in the tie shop, who misidentifies the colors of the ties because of the effects, unfamiliar to him, of electric lighting.[14] Alternatively, if we wanted to insist on the simplicity of color, we could say that the variations in lighting are actually variations in the thing lighted, and so porphyry in the dark and porphyry in the light are two similar, but not identical, objects, that the lighting and our eyes make a subtle but important difference. Alternatively again, and with some auxiliary corpuscularian premises, we could conclude that color is only in the superficies of the porphyry, not down in the constituent particles. None of these conclusions requires us to make additional philosophical commitments about the perception-object relation, and these are accordingly the more natural conclusions to offer after flicking the light on and off our porphyry. To get the porphyry example to yield Locke's desired conclusion, we seemingly have to have an antecedent attachment to two orders of things: *if* there were a double order, then these variations in our porphyry perceptions would be just what we should expect to observe on the perception side of the divide, and so we would have an encouragement to believe that the two orders do not resemble each other. If we pull the double order out of play, though, it becomes difficult even to see what the connection is between perceptual variation and the nonobtaining of resemblance. Therefore, we have reason to separate Hume from the modern view on secondary qualities, inasmuch as Hume wants to separate himself from the double order.

14. The example is found in "Empiricism and the Philosophy of Mind," recently reprinted in a volume of the same name (Cambridge: Harvard University Press, 1997), 37–45. The upshot of the thought experiment, according to Sellars, is that the concept "looks X" (where X it is a color term) presupposes the concept "being X."

Second, rejecting the modern view is arguably more consistent with Hume's naturalism. Our first impression may be that naturalism *requires* the modern view, but this impression is mistaken. If we move colors from the perceiver-and-world to the perceiver alone, we automatically raise a question about "where the colors are," a question that is certainly extraordinarily difficult to answer in naturalistic terms. If we suppose that we shall not be finding little red triangles and little pink cubes when the surgeons peer into our skulls with the more refined instruments of the future, then I surmise that we will say either that the problem is scientifically insoluble or that the lost qualia reside in a medium that is recalcitrant to scientific investigation. Neither conclusion is ultimately consonant with naturalism; neither engenders confidence in our truth-collecting abilities; both give indirect aid and comfort to a Cartesian-type dualism. Such cloying puzzles as this do not arise if we put colors back where we find them, out in public space, and if we give up, as Hume did in his science of man, the prejudice that regards quantifiable and microscopic entities as the objects that are preeminently tractable to scientific investigation. (There is indeed a sense in which natural science is itself not naturalized so long as we are of the view that some things are more naturally amenable to it, on purely intellectual grounds, than others.)

Third, rejecting the modern view accords better with Hume's generally reconciliationist psychology.[15] Hume believes that we do not have to make a choice between freedom and determinism, reason and passion, self-interest and morality. He wishes to deconstruct, if you will, these enshrined oppositions and take us beyond them (as Nietzsche wished to take us "beyond" good and evil). An implication of such a project is that we need to reject the view, criticized earlier, that the soul is a site of interminable conflict, where protopersons pursue intrinsically incompatible agendas. By accepting the modern view, Hume has in effect saddled his psychological model with a gratuitous conflict, one that becomes manifest in the Conclusion of Book One. He tells us there that the principle of the imagination that allows us to trace causes and effects is the same principle that persuades us of continued existence, and "tho' these two operations be equally natural and necessary, yet in some circumstances they are directly contrary" (T 266). He then refers us to the section on the modern philosophy for confirmation. But what sort

---

15. One indirect illustration of the reconciliationist tendency is found at T 215, where Hume says that because we are "unable to reconcile" reason and nature, we opt for double existence, which is an awkward reconciliation attempt. But then we are not reconciled to double existence itself, and so the mind seeks to move beyond it.

of confirmation do we get? Just whatever the Lockean-type arguments provide.

On my view, we rely on the imagination for these two mental operations, but the "principles" are not quite the same—one is resemblance-based, and one is cause-based. More important, these principles do not conflict; they supplement each other. Moreover, I am at a loss to see how they could conflict, *except* on the hypothesis of double existence: if causal analysis of our perceptions were to show us that our perceptions do not resemble their causes, then we would have evidence that the imagination is self-subverting, inasmuch as the imagination would lead us to posit causes that we could not make imaginatively intelligible. But if, as I suggest, causal analysis shows us no such thing, then that evidence dries up. Hence, I think that Hume should have been content, in the Conclusion, to have founded his (initial) melancholy solely on the "seeming triviality" of the principles that keep our mental life going, and that he should have therefore abjured the (fortunately) brief passage concerning incompatible operations before it went to press and became sedimented as T 266. His marshaling of the incompatible-operations idea also muddies the interpretive waters considerably, and perhaps unavoidably: we are invited to accept the modern argument about secondary qualities at the same time that we are invited to reject the accompanying conclusion for double existence, and it is never clear why, on the basis of Section 4, we can be so selective in our endorsement—or at least not clear without becoming unwilling Berkeleyans into the bargain. Yet we both bypass this difficulty and neatly avoid an ineluctable intrapsychological conflict if we clarify Hume's position vis-à-vis the modern philosophy.

I do not pretend to have given a satisfactory account of the secondary-qualities problem, nor do I want to give the impression that naive realism about colors is free of serious difficulties. I have hoped, much more modestly, only to motivate a Humean rejection of what I take to be Hume's official acceptance of the modern solution. And so, let us now return to the Disembodiment Argument proper.

Step 7. By this stage we have separated perceptions and objects, on the one hand, and have cut their tether of resemblance, on the other. Since the object does not enter our perception except in the most theory-laden way possible, as the hidden explanatory cause of what we do perceive, we find that we cannot make sense of the object. Once stripped of the perceptual qualities by which we prereflectively identify it, the object becomes a mere cipher. This it is the conclusion Hume draws in the second half of Section 4. After we draw the distinction between primary and secondary qualities, and position them respectively in objects and perceptions, we can explain the primary only by means of the secondary. Hume's paradigmatic primary quality is solidity, and his discussion suggests that we prephilosophically understand it on the basis of tactile sensations, which clearly have to be in the perceiver (if we are making all-or-nothing assignments of qualities to perceivers or objects). If we subtract solidity, as we prephilosophically understand it, from the catalogue of independent existents, and thus if solidity proves to be disconcertingly unsolid, then it would appear that we have no other qualities left on which to pin the independent existence of the object: "When we exclude these sensible qualities, there remains nothing in the universe, which has such an existence" (T 231).[16]

Hume is making a pair of moves here that we associate with Berkeley. The first move is that there is no intelligible cut between the primary and secondary qualities, and so whatever we say about the status of one set of qualities we should say about the status of the other. Berkeley of course wants to assimilate the primaries to the secondaries, and so the stage is then set for the second move, which is to hold that anything that remains of a material object after we relocate all of its experienced qualities within the perceiver is an unintelligible abstraction. It is possible—and I think an argument could be made to show that it is desirable—to execute this entire maneuver in reverse, beginning with abstraction (and its discontents) and proceeding to an assimilation of the secondaries to the primaries. Still, at this point in the dialectic we are operating on the assumption that perceiver-contained qualities can be certified as such, owing to the double-existence commitment, and so we seem to be poised for the orthodox Berkeleyan execution, which leaves us with immaterialism.

Hume, however, does not think that we are wired, as it were, for immaterialism: we do believe that something remains after we "exclude these sensible qualities." We should try to explain what interferes with the working of our wiring, for the interference is curious (and indeed too curious if we go with the Berkeleyan). The explanation, at this stage, seems obvious enough: since the imagination can only grasp a mind-independent object *falsely*, through mind-dependent qualities, the truth-seeking imagination finds noth-

---

16. When Hume says that "tho' bodies are felt by means of their solidity, yet the feeling is a quite different thing from the solidity; and that they have not the least resemblance to each other" (T 230), I take him to be speaking of the Lockean reinterpretation of solidity, that is, impenetrability, which is not tactilely understood. His point, as I follow it, is that our tactile sensations do not underwrite Lockean impenetrability, but I do not see that he is endorsing the reinterpretation.

ing to grasp. That is, the "true object" is one that bears no resemblance to those the imagination can successfully grasp. In other words, the belief in the mind-independent object must be supported by something other than the resemblance inference because, in this setting, that inference is unavailable.

Step 8. Without this inference, we are unable to sustain belief in the mind-independent object. Philosophers "immediately upon leaving their closets, mingle with the rest of mankind in those exploded opinions, that our perceptions are our only objects" (T 216). Hume sarcastically remarks that philosophers are able so to mingle because of the "similarity" their system of double existence bears to the vulgar; both systems are able to "humour our reason for a moment," and both are easy to ignore. There is a definite irony in this remark too. If the philosophical system were very similar to that of the vulgar, then the two systems would sit with equal ease in our minds, and there would thus be no out-of-closet backsliding on the philosophers' part. The real reason that the philosophers mingle is that their system does not sustain belief, and therefore the philosophical system fails to have an extremely important similarity to that of the vulgar; if the systems were interestingly similar, the philosophers' objects would resemble their perceptions, and the awareness of that resemblance would be possible only through the resemblance inference. Again, the Sceptic comes to our aid when he succinctly observes, apropos of natural religion, that "an abstract, invisible object . . . cannot long actuate the mind, or be of any moment in life," and that "we must find some method of affecting the senses and imagination" if the mind is to be actuated (MPL 167). Exactly parallel observations are appropriate for natural metaphysics. The mind-independent object is as abstract, as invisible, as unaffecting as ever the god of the reasoners was. Heart, fantasy, and sensibility should not be sent away empty-handed, and if we do send them away, they in turn will leave us empty-minded, unable to keep up our beliefs.

One feature of the philosophers' return I particularly want to stress. When they return to the "exploded opinions," they do so uncomfortably, with a bad conscience. They do not *want* to mingle with the vulgar. The reason is that double existence carries their endorsement, and they find themselves in a position where they can easily attribute their want of belief to perturbations arising from their human frailty. (These perturbations can be thought as being analogous to the static on the radio, as before.) We can imagine the philosopher uttering the following soliloquy, sotto voce: "Would that I could maintain my belief in the abstract, invisible cause of my perceptions, but though my spirit is willing, my flesh is weak—I believe; help thou mine unbelief." My choice of "backsliding" to describe the psychological posture of the closet-leaving philosopher is quite deliberate, for I want to emphasize the hectoring, ever-vigilant censor whose residence in our minds we shall perforce imagine when we endorse a position that we cannot occupy. Such a censor "tells" us that want of belief reflects badly on us, not on the content of the belief—and it is the felt opposition here between our normative notions and our life that produces the illusion of the censor.

Even so, inability to occupy a position may be the best reason possible for withholding endorsement.[17] This is one formulation of Hume's own view of reflective equilibrium, but the charm of our mental life is such that we can accredit so obvious a view only by a very unobvious chain of reasoning. It is a more natural option for the inward-turning mind to think that a gap will open between endorsement and occupation, and hence that a disparity between conception and performance is its natural condition. In a sense, this condition is natural because the self-representation that has this condition as part of its content is reflectively natural. In another sense, however, this condition is not natural, because an awareness of the instability of the self-representation leads us to repudiate it and this awareness can be purchased only at the price of taking the reflectively natural wrong turn. We must follow the "highway of despair" (in Hegel's haunting phrase) in order to see that we have been on despair's highway, and as soon as we are able to conceptualize our itinerary thus, we at once exchange our melancholy mental path for a sunnier.

And so we continue in our miscellaneous way of reasoning toward the better destination that we hope for. Before proceeding to the next step, which will complete the stage-setting for the malign skeptical impasse, I think we already have enough light to be somewhat suspicious of the self-recriminating philosophical stance. (Light not only dawns but also sets slowly over the whole, and we are entering a twilight moment for the stance in question.) For the unoccupiable belief has a definite irregularity about it that ought to excite our misgivings. If we peruse the works of historians, or of scientists, we almost never find an author tacitly chiding either himself or herself or us for not being able to maintain a belief. We do not read historians who put forward a hypothesis (for example, that some villain plundered the treasury of Rome

---

17. The idea that *inability* to do something intrinsically supplies a normative reason against doing it is controversial. For one presentation of a view that dissents from mine, see Galen Strawson's *Freedom and Belief* (Oxford: Clarendon, 1986), chap. 5. Strawson's topic is the "nonrational commitment" we have to personal-reactive attitudes such as resentment, which is similar enough to my present topic to make the criticisms of that commitment germane.

and thus helped to weaken the republic at an especially inopportune time) but who have to *work themselves up* into believing it: either the belief comes effortlessly, without encouragements, after the appropriate spadework (which is usually far from effortless itself) has been done, or the belief does not come at all. Scientific theories may be extremely non- and counterintuitive, and yet we detect the same pattern. On the other hand, in the arts belief can sometimes arrive precipitately—we read a deeply moving novel and may be prepared to accept all of the author's implied ethical propositions without further delay—and so we have to pour cold water on our native epistemic ardor. But, again, we do not have this straining after a belief that we think we ought to have but cannot. It is only in religion and philosophy that we behold the spirit toiling on this rack, and this prospect must give us pause, and should incline us to seek out less stressful religions and philosophies.

Step 9. Not only does the philosopher have trouble occupying the endorsed position, but he also cannot endorse the position he does occupy. He has worked himself into a belief, all right, but that belief is the rejection of the resemblance inference. That inference becomes disownable to the extent that the philosopher makes it explicit. Consequently, besides pining for his unoccupiable beliefs, the philosopher avails himself of the vantage point that those beliefs afford actively to condemn his occupiable beliefs. He uses the one as a yardstick for making invidious assessments of the other. Let us attend to Hume's language, which is telling: "I begun this subject with premising, that we ought to have an *implicit faith* in our senses, and that this wou'd be the conclusion, I shou'd draw from the whole of my reasoning" (T 217, my emphasis). This "implicit faith in our senses" is what Hume ultimately leaves us with, in a sense, but for the moment I just want to call attention to Hume's next sentence, in which he stands down from an intimation of his final point of view and imaginatively identifies with the incomplete point of view of the rattled philosopher: "But to be ingenuous, I feel myself *at present* of a quite contrary sentiment, and am more inclin'd to repose no faith at all in my senses, or rather imagination, than to place in it such an implicit confidence" (Hume's emphasis). An explicit vote of no confidence rather than an implicit affirmative: this is the position we have attained through copious deliberations, and the outcome of the vote is traceable to the "trivial qualities" and the "false suppositions" of the vulgar (and not merely vulgar) imagination.

We have completed the skeptical circle and can tighten the knot. The mind, able neither to advance to its desired position nor to retreat from its undesired, is stranded in an uncomfortably suspenseful condition. This is a remarkable corner for the mind to be in, and we may liken it to a stalemate in chess. To see why the analogy has some merit, we could delineate the moves that are available to the mind at this juncture, and we can derive them conveniently from some options Hume considers in the Conclusion of Book One. (By a "move" I intend a followable rule that the mind can extract from a calm and judicious survey of its skeptical plight.) Three basic moves are available.

(i) *We should follow the imagination wherever it leads*. This could be the first candidate to present itself to the philosopher, who might very well infer, after considering how our reflective attempt to shore up our naturally occurring mental weaknesses only compounds or magnifies them, that the vulgar are not in such bad shape, and that we should therefore follow the untutored promptings of our imagination. This option cannot win assent, however, because the promptings of the imagination are a mixed bag, and if we give license to them all, we shall rue the inference. The "errors, absurdities, and obscurities" the imagination proposes would make us "asham'd of our credulity" (T 267). The vulgar may be comparatively better off than the learned in the sense that their absurdities are both less baroque and less pretentious than those of the more refined, but that is about the only advantage. The very baroque flavor of learned absurdity usually suffices, when left to itself, to preclude it from having wide-ranging, harmful public effects, and so what is comically a disadvantage in one context becomes a weighty advantage in another. Imagination-fueled madness does not have its root in reflection; the root is already there in common life, and the root can send forth hideous shoots, as Hume was well aware. Ethnic, social, and religious hatreds all take their cue from promptings to which highly imaginative people are prone, and these people, because of their dash and swashbuckling, are able to communicate their visions to others (cf. T 122–23, 600–601). "Men of bright fancies may . . . be compar'd to those angels, whom the scripture represents as covering their eyes with their wings" (T 267), and those who are blind, as another scripture informs us, will fall into a ditch along with those whom they lead. And thus, the laissez-faire approach to mental management will not submit to formulation in a general rule.

(ii) *We should follow the promptings of the more orderly division of the imagination, our reason*. Patient examination of (i) might lead the philosopher to retrench. Let us bite the bullet, he says, and escalate our commitment to reflective management. This is not a workable option, either. Since we were already in a muddle because of our attempt to give our minds more order than they apparently had, this proposal is a summons to make the muddle more profound. We have every expectation that the exceptional wakefulness of reason will, like its sleep, breed monsters. And of course, if we are too shrill about the importance of reason, there will be an intensification of the pragmatic difficulty concerning the believability of such sublime exoticisms as our exuberant philosophers tend to retail. And thus, the full-dress command-economy approach fails as well.

(iii) *We should follow the promptings of reason when its findings are not too revisionary of our beliefs.* Examination of (i) and (ii) together might point us toward this sensible-looking option, which certainly has a Humean ring to it. Interestingly (but consistently), Hume does not think that we should have a general rule here. "Consider well the consequences of such a principle. By its means you cut off entirely all science and philosophy" (T 268). Many good results flow from highly refined reasonings, and the general rule would discourage the occurrence of those refinements which terminate in the good along with those which terminate in the bad. Science furnishes abundant instances of refined reflections that withstand unforeseen experimental tests, and we do not know in advance which ones will survive. Much the same is true in philosophy; we need to sow a great deal of silliness in order to reap an occasional insight. These are also Hume's views, I believe. Despite the notoriety of the book-burning finale of the first *Enquiry*, Hume's keen observation of the ways adjacent cultural communities reveal the flaws in each other's intellectual productions and strive to emulate and surpass each other's achievements—as displayed in the essay "Of the Rise and Progress of the Arts and Sciences"—serves to show that the detection of nonsense is a far-from-simple matter, and may suggest, further, that the preservation (and even mildly self-aware promotion) of nonsense has its purpose. The book-burning is a half-joking flourish—or quarter-joking (since Hume is not sounding the tocsin to light the pyres)—and was rather too solemnly received in some quarters. Hume is not a positivist.

The core problem with (iii), as I see it, is that we do not know how much refinement is too much, and what kind is too much, and so the rule instantly falls into inapplicability as soon as we try to apply it in a concrete situation. And thus, our third option leaves our inspection with fewer teeth than it promised at the start, and we are then back with the other two.

Step 10. With our deliberative options effectively cashiered, we at last reach the resolution of the impasse, and the conclusion of the argument. Malign skeptical doubt is the condition of our philosopher, and it is "a malady, which can never be radically cur'd," because no measures can be taken against it. "Carelessness and in-attention alone can afford us any remedy" (T 218), and this resolution is significant because carelessness and faulty attention are not objects of an agent's choice. These are states of soul that steal upon us; they *happen*. Of course, we might elect to be careless, but our election transforms the scenario, and we can then ask what is the reason for our action, putting ourselves back into the difficulties we have just canvased. The authentic Humean resolution does not have an elective element in it, and we can therefore say that the way out of the skeptical impasse is deliberatively opaque to the person whose impasse it is. In the operations of the mind itself, we can discern an analogue of what Bernard Williams has called intrinsic luck,[18] though it would be preferable not to call it luck at all but rather intrinsic externality. And with this, we have a vindication of the nonrationalist, for we have shown that reason creates problems that are only solvable in a different court.

It could be argued that there is no vindication in this outcome, because carelessness and inattention are merely causal influences, not rational ones, and so their appearance on the scene is not interestingly different from that of any brute natural force. And if a rupture of a blood vessel in the brain hardly carries any vindicative weight with us, it could be said that Humean fatigue should not be accorded a different status. But I think that such a response misconceives the Humean impasse breaker, and consideration of a parallel phenomenon can bring out the misconception. Random selection often contrasts with reasoned choice, but there are certainly instances where randomness is the rational policy: Buridan's ass (to take a celebrated instance) would have done well to pick one of two equally attractive bales of hay randomly. In our skeptical scenario, we have a situation in which there is no prospect of an internal resolution of the impasse, and so an ostensibly external factor can legitimately claim to be a rational influence. (For this reason also, the cure that Hume proposes is radical enough.)

The resolution of the impasse is not one that the nonrationalist can congratulate himself over, however, because the egress from the impasse does not involve the privileging or glorification of any element of our psychology, except those elements that are the least exciting or prepossessing. The mind that is inattentive operates in a manner similar to that of the mind when it makes the galleylike motion I have perhaps too mightily called the resemblance inference. We enter with facility into associative tracks that extend resemblance relations; we enter with difficulty into those which do not, and

---

18. In "Moral Luck," in the volume of the same name (Cambridge: Cambridge University Press, 1981), 25. I have adapted Williams's wording.

so our attention falters. In fact, we should say that the resemblance inference is not an inference for the mind to make so much as an inference that happens to the mind when it is off guard. The acceptableness of this type of operation is what chiefly makes the nonrationalist a benign skeptic. The nonrationalist is a skeptic because he contends that there is no internal radical cure, but is benign because he recognizes that the only nonradical cure is so unheroic. Unsurprisingly, we later find Hume saying of the benign form of skepticism, "By flattering no irregular passion, it gains few partizans: By opposing so many vices and follies, it raises to itself abundance of enemies, who stigmatize it as libertine, profane, and irreligious" (E 41). The transition to the unheroic viewpoint is itself unheroic. We sense merely that (in a phrase of Schopenhauer's) our will has turned, but this turning is no mystical event, as it was for Schopenhauer and the early Wittgenstein, for the turn is too banal for mysticism. We fill the vacancy of doubt by going about our daily business, as we are wont to do.[19]

I should like to throw the structure of the argument, and the shape of its critique of rationalism, into sharper relief by turning once more to the Conclusion, which epitomizes Hume's Book One strategy in addition to being a splendid send-up of the heroic viewpoint. As Edgar Wind has shown, Hume was a party to a controversy that was not transacted entirely on a philosophical plane, for the portrait painters of Hume's day were parties also.[20] The Humean undercutting of heroism is complemented by the aesthetic stance of his contemporary, Thomas Gainsborough, who sought to represent his subjects in natural but affecting poses. The Hume-Gainsborough approach contrasts with that of James Beattie and, on the side of aesthetics, Joshua Reynolds, who wanted to give *their* subjects a larger-than-life grandeur. And so, just as we can profitably oppose the attitude toward portraiture in Reynolds's *Mrs. Siddons as the Tragic Muse* to that in Gainsborough's *Mrs. Siddons*, with its mere (mere!) eponymous title, so too, in the framework of Hume's Conclusion, we can contrast the exaggerated posturings of the rationalist with the more discreet decorum of the nonrationalist.

---

19. In this connection, it is strange that Pears titles his last chapter "Hume's Heroic Solution." Only a philosopher would ever be inclined to call Hume's inattention "heroic," I think.

20. *Hume and the Heroic Portrait* (Oxford: Clarendon, 1986), 1–52. Wind has a particularly fine discussion of Allan Ramsay's portrait of Hume, in which (Wind says) the "immense mass of fat" in Hume's face becomes expressive of the indolence that "prevents fanatics from carrying out their world-shattering plans and strengthens sceptical philosophers in their aspiration to moderation and gentleness" (30).

In the first half of the Conclusion we can discern a movement of thought describing a beautiful arc that begins with our frail prereflective condition, serenely passes through the febrile skeptical thickets, and returns to our frail postreflective condition (which more or less mirrors the starting point but whose subtle difference eludes the direct survey). After Hume's initial histrionic ventilation of a faintly dandified paranoia (which reads like a parody of the persona yet to come in Rousseau's *Reveries*), he cools down a bit to lay out, in more detailed fashion, the cause of his spleen. It derives from a survey of the crucial, pervasive offices that habit performs in our psychology, and thus ultimately derives from a survey of our psychological anatomy. The vivacity enhancement that habit makes possible for some of our ideas is a quality "which seemingly is so trivial, and so little founded on reason," that we behold ourselves amazed (T 265). The contrast between the richness and order of our extraphilosophical system of beliefs, as inventoried in Part III, and the slenderness of the system's underpinning is stunning: the documentation of this slenderness would doubtless earn the "dis-approbation" of heroically minded rationalists, as well as produce the melancholy of the documenter who, in Part IV, tries to replace the slender underpinning with one more substantial. This takes us to the second station of the arc.

We try to disown the "seemingly trivial" resemblance inference in Part IV, and the hope is to make ourselves over in accordance with an image of the self whose causal history we would prefer to have. We make a mess of everything we touch, and find that our prereflective world disowns us: we desert the resemblance inference at the price of having resemblance between our reflective and unreflective lives fade. This loss of a recognizable *Lebenswelt*, and hence a recognizable self to inhabit it, discloses my ultimate reason for referring to this critique of rationalism as the Disembodiment Argument. For while we are in the grip of the self-authorship project, we put imaginative space between us and our embodiment. This pass is where rationalism leaves us unless something else comes to break the spell. And that something else is habit once more, though in a slightly unexpected guise, which takes us to the third station.

The impasse breaker is "that singular and seemingly trivial property of the fancy, by which we enter with difficulty into remote views of things" (T 268). The recurrence of the "seeming triviality" formula is deliberate on Hume's part, I believe, and underscores the similarity between pre- and postreflective states. It is as though Hume were offering us an instance, after a fashion, of a Newtonian principle: the trivial actions of the mind, which account for the production of our nebulous conundrums, ultimately elicit equally trivial and opposite reactions as corrections. From this new-old standpoint Hume finally announces his nonprovisional conception of the place of reason, which is both naturalistic and skeptical, honoring the partial perspectives displayed in both Parts III and IV while not yielding wholly to either: "Where reason is lively, and mixes itself with some propensity, it ought to be assented to. Where it does not, it never can have any title to operate upon us" (T 270). We assent to reason from our enlarged perspective, and the enlargement of our perspective is naturalistic because it is the result of a genuinely causal progression that carried us from the point of view we occupied when we relied, uncritically, on causal inference in Part III to that which we presently occupy. Our perspective is (truly) skeptical because reason has a circumscribed authority, but the circumscribing power is not a higher form of reason. We thus avoid the near paradox that Hume propounded at the end of Section 1, "Of scepticism with regard to reason" (T 186–87): if the authority of reason is undermined by argument, then the underminer partially accredits reason insofar as the argument is successful, and so the success of the underminer, too, is partial. This internal circumscription of reason does not restrict the authority of reason so much as it appears, and not so much as the external one that we get in the Conclusion. Hence the true skepticism.

Hume's conclusion about reason does not give us a rule, except in a relaxed sense. The "propensity" that is to mix itself with reason is neither supplied nor wholly accredited by reason. It merely arrives to be aligned with reason in an intrapersonal cooperative venture. We are immediately shown an example of this intellectually unpredicted but friendly alliance between reason and nature in Hume's return to philosophy in the remaining paragraphs. The hysterical preoccupation with philosophy at the start of the Conclusion was "unnatural" in the sense that it was too overwrought to last (just as fits of rage typically burn themselves out and leave us in a cooler and less volatile state). The malign skeptical impasse was the instrument for the extinguishing of this self-lacerating hysteria, and the hopelessness of the skeptical malady, which becomes manifest at the impasse, gives us a case study for appreciating Hume's later dictum that "the moment we perceive the falshood of any supposition, or the insufficiency of any means[,] our passions yield to our reason without any opposition" (T 416). The reason to which the hysteria yields is the properly appreciated reason of T 270, reason-as-supplemented, a perspective that has an entitlement to be called "reason" if we are careful not to convert it into a faculty of the soul. (The highest normative court of appeal, whatever it is, invariably attracts, and should attract, the reassuring name of reason.) This perspective we occupy is simply the good sense that acknowledges the frailty of all things human, itself included, and we then go off, relieved, to play our backgammon.

But the backgammon cure, like the talking cure, is no panacea (though it may be a placebo). For in time I will find that "I am tir'd with amusement and company" (T 270), and this reaction is to be expected. "Human life is so tiresome a scene," as Hume remarks in an aside on what is his principal discussion of amusement, "and men generally are of such indolent dispositions, that whatever amuses them, tho' by a passion mixt with pain, does in the main give them a sensible pleasure" (T 452). And so we are led to games where the agreeably painful "sudden reversals of fortune" put boredom at bay. But as this description suggests, our minds will have trouble keeping up the purring the more we grow accustomed to the game, for satiety will begin to set in. We then *return* to our solitude, through another unheroic reclamation, out of boredom and not because our arguments have boxed us into a retired (and retiring) methodological solipsism. After giving himself over to solitary dreaming and rambling, Hume introspectively observes, "I feel my mind all collected within itself, and am naturally *inclin'd* to carry my view into all the controverted subjects of interest to human beings (T 270, Hume's emphasis). We reenter philosophy just as we reentered common life, and in each case we return through the intellectually cloudy mechanism of natural inclination.

Hume stresses—rightfully, on my interpretation—the causal role that natural inclination plays in the return. He emphasizes that the possibility of greatness, of making a mighty name for himself, is the lure for his philosophical curiosity, and this admission is certainly remarkable in the light of that powerful deflation of heroic pretension we have so recently witnessed. Yet Hume says that "these [fame-seeking] sentiments spring up naturally in my present disposition; and shou'd I endeavour to banish them . . . I *feel* I shou'd be a loser in point of pleasure; and *this is the origin of my philosophy*" (T 271, first emphasis Hume's, second mine). Hume does not explain why "these sentiments" spring up so naturally, but with a little reflection I think we can uncover some explanations, and these will only confirm the benignly skeptical point of view.

First, even if Hume has truly laid bare the seemingly trivial principles that animate our minds, the laying bare itself, the accurate anatomical discovery, is anything but trivial. (This is the point about the unobvious modes of the obvious once more.) Accordingly, he who claims the accurate anatomy as his achievement is apt to think that he has a few more surprising discoveries up his sleeve, and hence the desire to begin getting them out of the sleeve is thoroughly appropriate.

Second (and less frivolously), the Humean discovery is of the sort that is likely to make us seek out first-person embodiments of it, provided we are convinced that the discovery is veridical. Nothing interests us so much as ourselves, and a discovery that affects our self-conception—and affects it by introducing an element that is prima facie ludicrous—draws us like an unseen sun toward itself, and we become its walking illustrations. Unconsciously, we try to steal a march on the unflattering conception, and by enacting it through a tacit choice, we partly attenuate the assault on our dignity. It always makes us feel better to jump rather than to be pushed. Possibly, the power of Descartes's evil-genius thought experiment derives from a concurrently active desire of this kind, since it is hard to grasp how an extravagant, merely intellectual conjecture could grip the imagination as much as this one does. In Hume's case, the active confirmation is similarly natural.

Admittedly, the type of illustration varies. A person of weak temperament will find an argument in Hume's text to nourish his prevailing melancholy, and this kind of reinforcement admirably points up Hume's trivial-principles thesis. A person of strong temperament, however, "will be the first to join in the laugh against himself" when the light dawns, the laughter then pointing up the trivial-solutions thesis. And if the temperament is very strong, we can even expect a desire to provoke laughter, to don the fool's cap in order to show that all's well with the world. Consequently, it is really no surprise to see Hume showboating as he does. He agreeably reveals the "whimsical condition of mankind" (E 160) in his own person. For the more the benignly skeptical point of view takes root in us, the less we shall be concerned about preserving the mere affectations of our dignity. An insistence on reducing to zero the phenomenological disparity between the person who is actuated by a passion and the person who surveys himself contemplatively is one such affectation. Our dignity, if we understand it aright, is not at all concerned if our right hand and left hand do not match—in contexts, that is, where hypocrisy or duplicity is not at issue.

The highlighting of inclination continues right to the end of the Conclusion. Hume utters no binding imperative to his reader (as the rationalist might wish him to do), compelling that reader to come with him on pain of irrationality, self-misunderstanding, or bad faith if he does not. If the reader has the same "easy disposition" as Hume, the reader will accompany; if the reader is of a different disposition, "let him follow his inclination, and wait the returns of application and good humour" (T 273). We thus unveil another dimension of the true skepticism: a higher tolerance of contingency, or ambiguity, in human affairs than either the rationalist or the prereflective can accept. If we pursue our philosophy "in this careless manner," as the variable lights of our many-sided constitution prompt or fail to prompt us, we shall have learned the larger lesson that Hume, on this interpretation, has taken such fastidious care to inculcate.

3

✻ ✻ ✻

The Sceptic's Version

As we leave the Conclusion of Book One of the *Treatise*, we should not forget the concluding paragraph of the essay of our intermittently companionable Sceptic (MPL 180), the consonance of whose views with those we have been canvasing will help to complete the union of these ideas, as well as to correct a tendency we may have to confine Hume's skeptical intentions to what he says about the understanding. The Sceptic's topic, the conduct and ethical improvement of our daily life, is a broader one than that which engaged Hume in "Of scepticism with regard to the senses," yet the Sceptic's thought movements in this more capacious field are similar, in various respects, to those we have already seen. I regard the Sceptic's thought movements as affording us a companion piece to those in the earlier set of movements, and explicating them is the subject of this chapter.

Like the conclusion of the argument in the *Treatise*, the Sceptic's conclusion does not stand alone, but presupposes the reader's therapeutic acquaintance with an earlier pretension-exploding argument. Unlike the version in the *Treatise*, however, this argument does not make us "torture our brain with subtilties and sophistries" (T 270). It is an easy argument, and "careless" up to a point, as befits the conversational style that is Hume's cachet in his later, more popular writings. So far are we from the torture chamber that we laugh when we read it; we have, indeed, a comic masterpiece, reminiscent of Sterne, which will perhaps be read (or be readable) with pleasure when the abstruse arguments of the *Treatise* shall be entirely forgotten. Yet we will try, as is sometimes our custom, to retrieve a few sober propositions from the mirth.

Since this last statement sounds like a remark about methodology, it would not be amiss to make our approach more explicit than it has been hitherto. I draw a certain sustenance from Shaftesbury's dictum that the true test for a serious topic of discussion is its capacity to endure laughter, whereas the test for an unserious is just the opposite, its capacity to endure a close examination.[1] Thus far, as we have moved through the *Treatise*, I have covertly tried to put our philosophy and its objects to the first test, and have inserted an occasional note of levity in places where others might discern the materials of tragedy; I am persuaded that reason and our Humean view of it have passed the test tolerably well. If this test seems unmotivated, we should perhaps recall a nice distinction that is also due to Shaftesbury: "There is a great difference between seeking how to raise a laugh from everything, and seeking in everything, what justly may be laughed at."[2] The risibility that extracts from everything a pretext for cheap laughter, and understands nothing, should be foreign to a truly serious purpose; to raise the rarer laugh that seeks the foible in the great and good only to confirm them should be an abiding hope. Nevertheless, I wish now to attempt the other test—that of submitting a lighthearted matter to examination—and hence the reader should not be too discountenanced by the gravity with which I treat the Sceptic's airy divagations, and even by the appearance of the moral sense, which will provoke an edifying pronouncement from time to time.

The Sceptic reviews the attempts of moralists or moral philosophers (the distinction is not sharp here) to remove disorder from our sentiments and practices by the presentation of order-promoting redescriptions of those sentiments and practices. These redescriptions might be thought of as

---

1. "Sensus Communis: An Essay on the Freedom of Wit and Humour," in *Characteristics of Men, Manners, Opinions, Times*, ed. John M. Robertson (Indianapolis: Bobbs-Merrill, 1964). Shaftesbury's deep idea calls for a discussion of its own. "Truth, 'tis supposed, may bear all lights; and one of those principal lights, or natural mediums, by which things are to be viewed, in order to a thorough recognition, is ridicule itself, or that manner of proof by which we discern whatever is liable to just raillery in any subject" (44). Do we know yet what this "manner of proof" proves?

2. Ibid., 85.

arguments because philosophers typically do not offer them merely as objects of attention or consideration (as artists do) but potentially as objects of belief. We are supposed to accept the redescriptions *as true*, and since their content is novel, neither learned at our mothers' knees nor picked up at the shop or at the tavern, we need solid inferential bridges connecting the notions we acquire in the humbler byways with those the moralist or philosopher should like to put us in possession of. Moreover, although the Sceptic does not expressly draw a distinction between the conclusion of a philosophical argument and the point of view it promotes, he is clearly more concerned with the point of view, and we perhaps have the feeling while listening to him that the point of view shapes the conclusion more than the conclusion does the point of view. Whether there is such a thing as a "philosophical point of view" we must of course decide, but at the outset let us simply note that it is the point of view that appears to attract the Sceptic's riposte. We can characterize this point of view as arising from theoretical intervention directed to a practical irregularity, and the intervention involves the use of what the Sceptic calls "refined reflections." There are, in the Sceptic's view, two basic problems with these reflections.

The first is that the theoretical intervention will either be redundant or impossible. If a refined reflection were "natural and obvious," it would suggest itself to the mind without the benefit of the theoretical apparatus. (We might call this the Philosophy Elimination Theorem, and proofs of alternative formulations are familiar post-Wittgensteinian philosophical exercises.) On the other hand, if we scale back the obviousness of the content bit by bit, we shall have something for the apparatus to do, that is, make the content worthy of assent, but then we are faced with the realization issue. How likely is it that the refined reflection will actually guide, or inform, practice? The more refined, the less likely: "A man may as well pretend to cure himself of love, by viewing his mistress through the *artificial* medium of microscope or prospect, . . . as hope to excite or moderate any passion by the *artificial* arguments of a Seneca or an Epictetus" (MPL 172, Hume's emphasis). Love for one's mistress comes bounding back, vigorous and undimmed, after one sees her from the physical or conceptual perspectives that deaden love, because these perspectives are so rare, so ephemeral—and so unhuman if they were less rare and ephemeral. This last plank puts us on the fast track to the Sceptic's second problem—that of the promiscuous effects that refined reflections would have on practice if they could be counted on to have effects at all. But since we should not be too forward in our address, we might halt a while in front of the Sceptic's examples of artificial media we rely on for the enhancement of perception so that we might better grasp the logic of the crucial transitions and so prepare the path for the more difficult topic of artificial arguments.

A visit to the microscope is a special event, passing in the twinkling of an eye, and the visit moreover *has* to be a special event. We could not live, as we do now, with such equipment annexed more or less permanently to our eyes. Unfortunately, making good on this claim, which sounds plausible, takes us into extremely hypothetical territory; but if we must go there, we cannot do badly in consulting Locke, whose historical, plain method we never have reason to associate with flightiness. In his discussion of substance, he concludes, a little sadly, that our knowledge of substances is very imperfect, and argues that it would be less imperfect if our vision were acute enough to let us see, say, the particles that constitute a piece of gold. We may suppose that we have an incipient complaint against the infinitely wise contriver of all things for not granting us vision of the particles, but Locke is eager to remove this piquant, epistemologically centered version of the problem of evil, and so he tries to show the reader what would happen if we had a more direct cognitive access to the microstructure of gold. Locke vividly expresses the disorientation we would likely feel if we had "Microscopical Eyes" that enabled us to "penetrate farther than ordinary into the secret Composition and radical Texture of Bodies."[3] Such visual penetration would be bad, to start with, because, if we had it, we would be unfitted for "the Market and Exchange" (Locke's mercantile imagination displaying itself, impromptu, to fine effect in this). We would also "see the minute Particles of the Spring of a Clock," but this sharp sight would cause us to lose the timepiece (that is, the visible motions of the hands that let us tell the time) as we gain the clock's particles. We have here a variation of the duck-rabbit phenomenon, except that we would presumably not be able to shift back and forth at will between the duck-particles and the rabbit-timepiece, our visual hardware not allowing us to be so protean in our perceptions. Locke, at least, seems to suppose that we would not be capable of shifting if we put clock perceptions on the gold standard. The yellow of the gold would "disappear" from view in the new perceptual dispensation,[4] and so we are to surmise that clock perception, and perception of the artifactual generally, would go the way of all secondary qualities. If we grant for the sake of argument that Locke is right about these

---

3. *Essay Concerning Human Understanding*, ed. P. H. Nidditch (Oxford: Clarendon, 1991), 303.
4. Ibid., 301.

visual extinctions, let us go on to inquire about the nature, and the reflective stability, of the horror he feelingly imagines.

Surely some of the disorientation can be attributed to mere unfamiliarity, to the shock of the new. It would make us giddy to be thrust perceptually into a sea of particles. But mere timorousness, or anxiety, in the face of the novel hardly warms us as a justification, and it would seem that if this were all that could be said about the grounds of the Lockean horror, a little reflection or a little adjusting time (which is usually more efficacious than reflection) would suffice to dissipate the sentiment. Suppose, for a comparison along similar lines, that our bodies, including our alimentary tracts, were transparent and allowed us to see every stage of the diurnal metamorphosis of our food into excrement. This scenario is similar to Locke's, except that we are not perceiving the world in a different fashion—the world has become different to our perception with the eyes that we in fact have. Our sense of social propriety would probably receive a cruel affront from the state of affairs in my imagined scenario, but we are a resilient race, and we revise our handbooks of propriety as circumstances warrant. Perhaps in this scenario we would retire to private toilets, as do characters in Luis Buñuel's *Phantom of Liberty*, to eat our dinners, and life would then go on much as it did before the arrival of the see-through esophagus. The sea of particles would be harder for us to stomach, I suspect, because of the extensiveness of the changes that a new perceptual apparatus would involve, but it is difficult to see otherwise why the Lockean horror would have to endure longer, or be more visceral, than the disorientation that obtains in my scenario.

Be that as it may, if we were given a *choice*, I do not think that we would know how to choose either particle perception or transparent digestion, and perhaps Locke's anxiety about microscopical eyes is best regarded as symptomatic of the vertigo that the possibility of choice would present to us, as being the endorsable result of an elective uncertainty rather than a (merely) causal reaction to the novelty of the scenario itself. The reason we would not know how to choose is that the effects on our lives of the proposed change would be so dramatic as to diminish most materially the resemblances between our once and future lives, and there would not be available to us a point of view from which to evaluate the two dispensations fairly. Furthermore, our inability to make a reasoned choice between the two types of perception would have repercussions for the intelligibility of the choices we would make with the second type, insofar as the first type remained vestigially active in our imagination and memory. But the main point to be insisted on is that choice presupposes some unchosen framework within which the choice is made.

For the making of these choices, the detection and extrapolation of resemblances has important work to do, as it did for our belief in continuing existents. Locke's microscopical perceiver would doubtless have a more complete knowledge than we do, at least on Locke's understanding of the matter, but we would be lost if this perceptual option were given to us. Richard Rorty has relatedly noted that pigs are much more intelligent than koala bears, yet we send pigs to the slaughterhouse and form societies to protect the koala, and he thinks that we do so because the koala looks more like us than the pig does.[5] In Locke's scenario, the microscopical perceiver is the pig and we are the koala. Although some might hold that our practice regarding pigs is just irrational, and then want to extend that verdict to our feelings about microscopical perception, it seems much more promising to say that the resemblance relations that the conditions of our embodiment make salient supply us with our only basis for making judgments of rationality or irrationality. Eating the koala *does* resemble cannibalism in a way that eating the pig does not, and it would be a rationalist prejudice to deny, antecedently and in principle, the relevance of the facial features we share with the koala in our arriving at this judgment.

In other words, it would be a mistake to think that even if the original, ostensible grounds for Lockean horror are inadequate, the new grounds I have proposed must be inadequate too. Where we have no resemblance that is both intuitive and felt, we have no grounds for choice; where we have an insufficient resemblance of this kind, we have an intrinsically poor sense of the outcome of the choice. A number of examples make this clear.

We are, and should be, often impressed with the argumentative rigor of philosophical discussions of personal identity. We admire the inferences drawn about the self on the basis of all these hypothesized fissions and fusions. Yet these arguments do not leave much conviction in their wake, and the reason is that the bizarre amalgams and clonings put us in a space where we do not recognize ourselves. We may recognize ourselves intellectually in these rarefied demesnes, but it is an error to think that intellectual self-recognition suffices to underwrite inferences about the whole person. It is not

---

5. *Philosophy and the Mirror of Nature* (Princeton: Princeton University Press, 1979), 190. Rorty makes his claim about the pig and koala in order to emphasize the importance that the imagining of community has in our judgments—a slightly different point from the one I am making, but in harmony with it.

clear that anyone baldly owns up to a view that reduces persons to their intellects, but it seems to me that the more hypothetical discussions concerning personal identity make sense only if this view is a premise. The fact remains that an amalgam or a clone does not resemble anything with which we are acquainted. All intuitions go on holiday when salient resemblances are absent.

For a like reason, we do not know whether a painting will be aesthetically a success before its execution, even if we are given a reasonably informative description of the plan for the work. We need to see how it resembles works whose status is already known, how it differs from them (which presupposes an awareness of resemblance), and what its resemblance relations are to objects in the depictable order of things. Similarly, we get reactions from reproductions that differ from actual paintings, no matter how splendid the reproductions are, and we would not trust an art critic who wrote a review after having looked only at the pictures in a book. Reproductions attenuate some of those aspects of the work which we need for our resemblance-based perceptions.

We are never sure about the "look" of the room we are decorating, the chemistry of the dinner guests we are inviting, the reflective sentiments we feel about a momentous ethical decision we could make, until we do the room, invite the guests, are confronted with the decision. (Some detection of these rightnesses can be done imaginatively, if we are imaginative enough, but then this means that we have to be good at re-creating, for our own consumption and in whatever fashion it is done, perceivable states of affairs.) The reason is that the pool of significant resemblances between things, or between people, is too unamenable to abstract codification for us to hazard, on such a basis, conjectures that will have a high likelihood of success. Mere intellectual awareness of the relevant facts and of our introspectible emotions in these cases is never enough. That we need to feel the relations that inhabit the logical space of resemblance is borne out if we reflect on what occurs when we make a bad guess, before the fact, about our reaction after the fact. We are often stymied if we try to explain the badness of the guess: we may throw up our hands, saying that a certain reaction made sense when we were revolving ideas around in our heads, but that the realization of the project gave us a surprise. Felt resemblance relations are invisible at the idea-revolving stage, and when we try to explain what went wrong at this stage, we come up empty because we cannot find anything.

Earlier we granted Locke his assumption that we would lose the clock if we gained the particles. We should now consider briefly what our position would be if we did not have to say good-bye to the clock. This reworking of Locke in effect gives us the scenario of Borges's "Funes the Memorious."[6] Ireneo Funes has, in addition to an exceedingly fine memory, extremely acute visual perception that roughly approximates Lockean microscopy. Unlike Locke's protagonist, however, Funes appears to have his feet still very much in our world. Yet Funes is not a fortunate man. He is flooded with the sum total of perceptual stimuli the world affords him at a particular moment, and he cannot part with a single experience. A divine languor is Funes's portion, and Borges informs us that Funes is also not very bright, because thinking presupposes forgetting and abstracting. We thus have a reversal of Locke's protagonist's intellectual powers. The microscopical perceiver still has many aspects of the world concealed from him, and so there is a need for his mind to make inferences, as well as for the room in which his mind can make them.

Having drawn our philosophy from a source that is not too profound, in the manner of Hume (who once drew his from *Don Quixote*), we should not have trouble appreciating Borges's characterization of Funes. It does seem right to say that our experience can be *saturated* (not, as in Locke, replaced) to such an extent that we would be disoriented, lose our bearings, lose our interest, or what have you. The mind needs a kind of shade, and we can attend to what is in the foreground only because there is a background. This broadly pragmatist thesis is a familiar one. I shall not seek to defend the thesis, yet I hope to regard it as acceptable scrip, for I should like to begin turning our view forward to our proper topic, the artificiality of a certain philosophical perspective.

Let us (while noting some of our results thus far) first bring the notion of perspective itself into better focus. A perspective properly does not constitute the content of what we perceive, but rather affects the *visibility* of those contents. (The microscope simply makes it easier to get at the smaller parts of things.) A perspective is therefore not the same as a vocabulary, a conceptual scheme, a paradigm, or a language game, as these are often understood. A perspective is artificial if it is not habitual. And finally, an artificial perspective would be malignly natural if we did not know how we, as whole persons, would occupy it, or if occupying it would redound to the disequilibrium of the whole person.

Now the Sceptic effects an ingenious identification of microscopes and arguments, tacitly uniting them under the rubric of (shall we say) "perspective-alteration devices," and it does seem that there is a tacit reference to an

---

6. In *Labyrinths*, ed. D. A. Yates and J. E. Inby (New York: New Directions, 1964), 59–66.

embodiment in a perspective, even when the perspective we occupy falls within our imagination. Consistently, the Sceptic shows a decided tendency to treat our mental maneuverings in such frankly naturalistic terms as the microscope-argument identification takes for granted. (He takes seriously the metaphor that philosophy is the "medicine of the mind," for example—so seriously that it is not entirely a metaphor.) If his naturalizing yoke is permissible, then we ought to expect that our preceding conclusions about microscopical eyes will be matched by another set about overly argumentative minds. We shall not be disappointed.

As with the microscope case, the interesting claim to be made out is not that the artificial perspective is rare and ephemeral. We know that looking at a candidate object of belief through the lens, as it were, of an elaborate argument is episodic and occasional, or that the result is. We think exquisitely nuanced thoughts about the obligations we have to future selves when we work through the proofs in our study or in the seminar room, but our minds are tuned to a high and exhausting pitch that we drop as soon as we leave these sublime halls of introspection and analysis for a cup of coffee: all the nuances blur and we merely sense that it is probably a good idea if we do not live ruthlessly for the moment, if we have a little concern for that hard-to-imagine self, psychologically continuous with us, who will be collecting a pension thirty years from now. This is the afterglow of the argument, and if we are philosophers, most of our lives are spent in this afterglow (and if we are not, almost all of it is). Of course, because the content of our relaxed thought is not especially sophisticated, we occupy a position that could be, and usually is, occupied by persons who do not peruse the proofs in the first place; and so we are back to the Sceptic's earlier observation about the redundancy of the philosophical intervention. But let us move on to the more interesting and more difficult claim that the rarity of the episodes is itself a good thing. The Sceptic's second problem with refined reflection concerns this claim.

The Sceptic gives us a counterfactual consequentialist argument that resembles Locke's animadversions on the marketplace and clock. Of philosophical arguments, the Sceptic holds that "commonly they cannot diminish or extinguish our vicious passions, without diminishing or extinguishing such as are virtuous" (MPL 173). This is implicitly the beginning of a moral-luck (or, again as I would prefer, moral-opacity) argument: whether our passions are good or ill is dependent on deliberatively opaque contextual facts, and thus if we silence a bad passion, we at the same stroke silence a good, passions without their contexts being indifferently or indeterminately good or bad. Yet it is not merely a moral-luck or moral-opacity argument, as we can see at once, because there is a feature of refined reflection that, in conjunction with the luck or opacity considerations, would produce the unwelcome consequences. This feature is *abstractness:* the reflections the Sceptic reviews do not carry a sufficiently determinate reference to this or that real-world context. Their abstractness gives these reflections the appearance of great power, a power akin to that of an explanation, which has an authentic deployment in many contexts indifferently. But the appearance of such power terns out to be spurious. For if we bring in heavy artillery of this kind to resolve a local problem of passion management (and the Sceptic appears to think, like Nietzsche, that the problems are always local, or more local than we realize), and if we allow the artillery to hang around, so to speak, to exert a systematic influence on our sensibility, then the presence of all that uncontrolled matériel will start to make mischief for us. The enduring presence of the argumentative artillery is the analogue of the permanently affixed microscope. Each case invites us to consider what our responses would be like if artificial influences on our responses became pervasively natural. Before developing this line of the Sceptic's thought, however, I want to make two comments about what the introduction of the notion of generality (via the notion of abstractness) does for us.

First, generality gives us one way—though only one way[7]—to begin making sense of perspective talk as it is applied to consciousness itself. The physiological examples we have considered involve perspective generators that lie outside consciousness, in the kind of optical hardware that a person might have (though of course the kind of hardware informs a person's perceptual consciousness). That being so, talk of perspective in these examples is unproblematically continuous with perspective talk in its home setting, which has to do with variations in perceptual consciousness that a person's physical location induces. But here, as we think about how an argument can affect one's sense of self, we are already well within conscious-

---

7. Another way concerns the notional, or virtual, physical movement that we can make in our imaginations. Hume thinks that in order to form a conception of anything that lies at a spatial or temporal distance from us "we are oblig'd not only to reach it at first by passing thro' all the intermediate space betwixt ourselves and the object, but also to renew our progress every moment" (T 428). One could say, without strain, both that this virtual movement involves (imagined) perspectival variation and that our making the movement itself represents one kind of purely intramental perspective on things. However, this imagination-centered way of unpacking intramental perspective does not help to explain the perspective shifts that refined reflections bring about.

ness at the outset, where we cannot appeal to our hardware or our location to explicate the applicability of the perspective notion. Generality can fill the void that threatens to make perspective illicit.

It is worth observing that the generality our consciousness can possess need not attach to our mental contents themselves. We can think about a chair, but we can also think about it as a representative of its class. I am not suggesting that these are two discrete and wholly separable mental operations. Identifying the particular without some reference to the class may well be impossible (as Hegel's account of sense certainty suggests), and vice versa. If so, we nevertheless attend with greater or lesser selectivity to more particular or more universal strands in our thought, and so we can speak of a continuum of generality, along which it is possible to plot perspectival differences.

Different people will occupy, at one time or another, somewhat differing perspectives on the generality continuum. The more unreflective our life, the more we respond to things in a particularistic manner. The more reflective, the more general, because reflection causes the mind to move in the direction of greater generality—a fact that Mill is perhaps unwittingly quick to exploit, in *Utilitarianism*, as he prepares the reader's mind for receiving a most generalized theory by drawing him or her into a protracted reflection on the nature of the good. It would be easy, however, to exaggerate the distance between the reflective and unreflective. The least reflective person reveals a wonderful talent for responsive generality upon entering the grocery store, and much of the increase we observe in the reflective is responsively confined to their imaginations. Outside the imagination, the philosopher is, as Hume said, lost in the man. (And just as we should guard against exaggerating the differences between people, we should take care not to assume that if the relative generality of reflectiveness is better than the relative particularity of unreflectiveness, an unrestricted level of generality must be good indeed for the mind.)

The second comment I want to make is that we have to confront the issues regarding the relationship between physical and mental perspectives—as I shall call the perspectives whose generation lies outside consciousness and the those that lie wholly within—and, in particular, we need to consider the feasibility of making neatly corresponding claims for each kind of perspective. If we return to the physical, there are complications it has that could give us pause and that could undermine our sense that we are talking about something similar to the mental.

In developing the physical account, I have resolutely, and perhaps injudiciously, restricted my gaze to the example of the microscope, which brings objects closer to us than they are for unaided vision. The alert reader will remember that the Sceptic spoke of "microscope or prospect" when he invoked the artificial media, and prospects do just the opposite of microscopes: they make ordinarily large objects appear smaller. A prospect is not a mechanical instrument, but a natural vantage point, and we might think that there is consequently a disanalogy between microscopes and prospects.[8] But the givenness, the nonartifactuality, of prospects is a wheel that turns nothing here, because the Sceptic could rightly insist that we do not spend the bulk of our time mooning about at scenic overlooks, and so nature readily admits of (in one by-now familiar sense) unnatural possibilities. And we could also imagine, if we so chose, an instrument that would take the place of the prospect, and for the sake of an opposite number we could call it the macroscope, which accommodatingly gives us the big picture (our heart's desire) and thus differs from the telescope (which is really just a microscope for distant objects). With the two extremes of physical perspective firmly in hand—the very near and the very far—we may well wonder whether the existence of the spectrum defined by these extremes tends to vitiate the legitimacy of my talk of mental perspective. Or if it does not vitiate its legitimacy, we may wonder where on the spectrum of mental perspectives we should locate the Sceptic's target, the refined philosophical point of view.

That there are mental perspectives is not in jeopardy, I would argue, but there is one striking difference between the physical and the mental. With the physical, but not the mental (at least insofar as we are considering those mental operations that—unlike the imagination—are modeled independently of physical relationships), we are able to mark a real distinction between the near and the far. The view we have from a prospect genuinely differs from that of the microscope, whereas in the mental order the language of near and far is so confounded that the terminal distinctions are otiose, and if we do retain these distinctions, we do so for a more picturesque purpose. One example should make this idea clearer. It is not uncommon for philosophers to resort to prospect talk in their descriptions of the understanding that, in the limit, philosophy is supposed to yield. We are told to expect the big picture, to see the world aright, to see the world *sub specie aeternitatis*, to have the God's-eye view (even if, as a special instance merely, there is no

---

8. As the *Oxford English Dictionary* informs us, there was once an instrument known as a "prospect glass," but in the passage from Hume's essay, we are plainly dealing with prospects as we know them.

God's-eye view), and to celebrate (or lament) the view from nowhere. But the inventory of prospect terms never stands by itself. We also have close reasoning, careful distinctions, deceptive first appearances, hidden realities, and (from Hume) the "*intense* view" of things (T 268). This equally common language is more in the microscopic vein. Now I do not think that we can ever have a reflective practice that does not nurture both styles of discourse simultaneously, insofar as the practice is sound, however much we dissociate the styles for particular purposes. No proposed God's-eye view has caught imaginative fire without a great deal of worm's-eye probing, and vice versa. Spinoza is perhaps the most intuitively persuasive illustration of this mutual dependency. Few systems have been as audacious in their aspiration as his, and few as rebarbatively attentive to minute detail. We are not really dealing with two different mental perspectives here, but two metaperspectives, and thus we do not have an analogue of the microscope-macroscope contrast.

The language of perspective need not fall into disutility in mentalistic contexts, however, even though the terminal distinctions of physical perspective do not occur. For we may just require another vertical-horizontal contrast in order to make sense of mental perspective, and hence of the differences between physical and mental perspectives. In the physical, we have the near and the far options spread out before us, horizontally; in the mental, we think more readily, instead, of progressively distant removals from our unreflective viewpoint, from that which is present to us to that which is not, and this suggests a vertical relationship between us and the condition to which our arguments escort us. To speak of the perspectives that philosophy induces is appropriate and far from exceptionable, and the notion of the artificiality of some of these perspectives is intelligible as well. The further up we advance on the vertical axis, the more artificial the perspective becomes, owing to the removal—just as greater artificiality obtains for the physical the further out we advance, in either direction, on the horizontal axis, owing to the heightened magnification or diminution of the objects we perceive.

Able now to rejoin the Sceptic, we can restate his second observation about refined reflections—concerning their malign naturalness, to use my idiom—as follows. If we were to occupy the artificially distant philosophical perspective habitually, then our relationship to the objects of concern to us in our truly habitual ("carelessly" nongeneral) perspective would either be so changed that we would no longer recognize our manner of life, because of attenuated resemblances, or else remain the same, but at the price of our having to undergo a broader affective discomfiture. That the objects change at all has something to do, as already noted, with deliberative opacity, but what is notable about the Sceptic's argument is the way the objects change. By attempting to choose our *intramental* embodiment (that is, the point of view our mind is to take), we in effect end up with an embodiment we would never choose. Our mothering nature, with her hidden parameters, insists once more on her crooked prerogatives.

The argument is quite abstract, as I have given it, and so let us look, in the spirit of particularity, at some of the flesh that the Sceptic himself puts on these bones. He discusses, or sketches, nine examples of how our philosophy would get out of hand if it got out of the closet. There is no need to review all of them, but it would be instructive to compare a few of those maxims which conform to each of the two patterns of malign naturalness. I would like to associate each of these patterns with a name, and Hume the resourceful essayist comes to my assistance.

We can read the Sceptic's remarks on his chosen philosophical examples as commentaries on the moralists who have come before him. Hume placed "The Sceptic" as the fourth member of a quartet of essays that attempt "to deliver the sentiments of sects, that naturally form themselves in the world, and entertain different ideas of human life and of happiness" (MPL 138). The other three essays are, in their order of appearance, "The Epicurean," "The Stoic," and "The Platonist." Now it is significant that all of the argumentative strategies the Sceptic considers have a tincture of either the Stoic or the Platonist about them. The Sceptic does not try to undermine the Epicurean (and he even deploys the Epicurean point of view in what is arguably his best sally). The Stoic and the Platonist recommend artificial perspectives for the pursuit of happiness, unlike the Epicurean, who is a pleasure seeker and represents the ethic of common life. We might say that the Stoic and Platonist represent the two poles, or moments, of the heroic, uncorrected ethical enterprise and that the Platonist favors a more radical disembodiment than the Stoic does. The Stoic corresponds to the person who, like Funes, has a foot in each perspective; the Platonist is more like the microscopical perceiver, who has left our wonted perspective behind.

The order of the moralists appears to be deliberate. Although it is possible to read the four essays merely as presenting four discrete conceptions of value (which just "naturally form" in the world), we have a philosophically more fruitful reading if we suppose that they exemplify a dialectical progression from common life through reflection back to a version of common life, a progression that mirrors the sequence in the *Treatise*. This is not to say that the Epicurean and the Sceptic are simply the same, any more than it is to say that the person who naturally returns to philosophy is identical to the person who naturally avoids it, but we will have to wait until the end before we can deal more satisfactorily with the issue of their distinguishability.

It may seem that presenting the four portraits as offering four points of view on the goods of life is merely, and objectionably, a formal characterization of these different "sentiments." After all, it could be argued that the Epicurean, Stoic, Platonist, and Sceptic differ in what they take the *content* of human good to be. I think, however, that this gloss oversimplifies, as well as conceals, the source of their disagreement, if we can suppose that they are disagreeing with each other. There is one substantive normative commitment that the Stoic and the Platonist share, which is that goods that are proof against contingency are the real goods, but this commitment would hold out great attractiveness only to a mind disposed to think that a very general perspective was the proper one for surveying goods in the first place. And so, it is not really a coincidence that the aversion to contingency is a commitment that the Stoic and Platonist accept, and the explanation for that acceptance lies with the point of view they reflectively adopt.

Let us now turn to the Sceptic's criticisms of refined reflections. On the Platonic side of the Sceptic's ledger, we have Fontenelle's palliative for an ostensible good, ambition (MPL 174–75), and Plutarch's remedy for an ostensible evil, exile from one's native land (MPL 175). Fontenelle advises us to consider the "true system of astronomy," which will make our sublunary antics appear contemptible and thus put a stop to the passions that actuate us. Similarly, Plutarch tells a banished friend to consider the earth a mere mathematical point in comparison with the heavens, and so going into exile is "little more than to remove from one street to another." Plutarch, dispensing a little extra encouragement, says that we are able to flourish anywhere, since, unlike a plant, we are not rooted to one spot. This extra touch is implicit in Fontenelle as well, because, if we are to appreciate the true astronomy as Fontenelle desires, we may have to think of ourselves as essentially not bound to our little sphere, as free-floating inhabitants of no particular spatiotemporal region. In both of these authors we are asked to revise our view about an object of concern by means of a recherché comparison that reduces the engaged sentiment to affective absurdity. Ostensible goods and evils cease to be goods and evils at all if we view them from a sufficiently disembodied angle.

Given this description of what Fontenelle and Plutarch are up to, the Sceptic's commentary is not too difficult to predict. To Fontenelle he replies that the true astronomy would destroy a desirable patriotism together with an undesirable ambition. To Plutarch his reply is much the same, though slightly more waspish: "These topics are admirable, could they fall only into the hands of banished persons. But what if they come also to the knowledge of those who are employed in public affairs, and destroy all their attachment to their native country?" Patriotism may truly be the last refuge of scoundrels, as Johnson said, but a modicum of parochial affiliation is necessary for the magistrates (and citizens) of any polity.

The Sceptic also says something else to Fontenelle, a saucy fillip that rewards the detour of the inquisitive. He notes that while "the same gallant author" holds that "the bright eyes of the ladies . . . lose nothing of their lustre or value from the most extensive views of astronomy," it is scarcely to be expected that philosophers would wish to restrict our concern to matters amorous. The Sceptic could well have had a cakewalk with this last observation. Why would philosophers be uneasy with the suggestion that sexual goods are the true goods? Fontenelle is right, truth to tell, once we subtract the window-dressing gallantry: no system of astronomy (or system of anything, for that matter) will silence the sexual impulse. Hence, it looks as though sexual goods should have a sturdy entitlement to prestige in the table of values, since they pass through the Platonist's crucible—the contingency test—so manifestly intact. Yet this is not so. Why?

The reason, it seems clear, is that our sexual urges survive the test through their sheer pertinacity and their imperviousness to intellectual considerations—not exactly stellar qualities for those who scan their minds for the signature of the demiurge. That these urges have these qualities is hardly to be contested. As Hume observes in his account of the origin of property, the "natural appetite betwixt the sexes" is "the first and original principle of human society," capable of bringing together our rude, not necessarily foresighted ancestors into social circumstances where they could acquire remoter concerns (T 486). Sex, not contract, is the original cement, and all foundations must be laid with the toughest materials so as to ensure that their superstructures last through the various vicissitudes they are heir to. We do not have to be in league with Freud to sense the preintellectual power of this "appetite," which is the chief psychological ingredient that takes us from the families of our birth to the families we construct.

The Sceptic could thus have reaped a second layer of commentary without having to do much work for it. That the sexual goods pass the Platonist's test is excellent evidence that we are more rooted than the Platonist thinks, and indeed the test itself could be better characterized, contrary to its framer's intentions, as a helpful device for filtering out, and identifying, those truer goods that presuppose greater degrees of embodiment. If the Platonist instead "feigns a fiction" to save his test, importing requirements that disallow the passage of sexual goods, then the Sceptic can adduce the feigning and the concomitant desire to avert the palpable reminders of our mammalian condition as further tokens of embodiment (or at least further tokens that the Platonist is embodied).

On the Stoic side, let us look at two strategies for dealing with misfortune, one from an unnamed author and one from Cicero (MPL 174). The unnamed author advises us to suspend before our minds "death, disease, poverty, blindness, exile, calumny, and infamy, as ills which are incident to human nature," so that if we are felled by one of these, we will be better able to handle it. Cicero supplies a therapy for deafness. There are many languages we do not know, and to these languages we are de facto deaf: "Is it then so great a misfortune to be deaf to one language more?" We should notice that these arguments have a different complexion from those of the first set. The Platonic-style arguments purported to show that local goods and evils fade to naught, given a universal perspective. In this, they were victims of their own success. But what I chiefly want to note here is that, according to these arguments, there is less to these local goods and evils than meets the eye. The Stoic-style arguments do the opposite. They purport to show that evils generally are much worse than they appear and that some saving remnant of the goods is, similarly, much better. (The Sceptic does not consider arguments that exhibit the Stoic's positive evaluative agenda, however, and so we must content ourselves with the negative.) If we suspend death and all the rest before our minds, it is owing to the *possibility* that these evils will befall us. Granted, death awaits us all, but we have no certainty that disease, poverty, and so on, are in the eaves. Some of these are highly probable; others are anybody's guess; others still are quite remote (though not impossible). Therefore, to have the assurance that the Stoic desires, and which is tantamount to *insurance*, we have to set the whole gamut of probabilities aside and count the evils as if they were all items to be reckoned in a census of certainties. This strategy clearly exacerbates our awareness of the evils of the world, despite official Stoic doctrine that these evils are not even evils. The same is true for Cicero's advice. We do not ordinarily think that the languages we have not learned are normative deficits. True, we might repine at our shoddy school French, but there is a special explanation for such a sentiment: we might be drawn to Gallicism on account of the elegance, the cuisine, the *joie de vivre*, of the French. But we do not extend our hankerings, omnivorously, to include every tongue. It requires a turn of mind that erases the distinction between the special cases and the general, making us feel the lack of all other languages in the same manner we feel the lack of French. And we thereby exacerbate the awareness of evil.

As before, my outline of the structure of the arguments makes the Sceptic's commentary predictable. To the unnamed author the Sceptic replies that omnivorous reflection on evils will not prepare us for them and that it is, moreover, "the true secret for poisoning all our pleasures, and rendering us perpetually miserable." This is the affective defeat. For Cicero we have only the Epicurean "repartee" of blind Antipater the Cyreniac, who reminds his well-wishing women friends that there are, after all, pleasures in the dark—the rhetorically implied moral presumably being that a known and cared-about good in the hand is worth an unknown infinity of evils in the bush. In both cases the Sceptic thinks we are happier without our magnifying glasses.

The Stoic is a better illustration than the Platonist of why the refined philosophical point of view should not become too habitual, and a good illustration of why, if the point of view were habitual, it would be better to be the Platonist. Although it requires real determination to look at the world as a nonepisodic Stoic would have to do, that is not the real sticking point. The problem is what would pass before the nonepisodic Stoic's mind. To see a parade of evils would be bad by itself, and the Stoic invitation to see the parade can be beneficent only if the person receiving the invitation is of a certain type and in an unusual situation. Someone who has just suffered a loss, but whose life is still very much in order, and enviably so, is the ideal candidate for Stoic consolation if this person is apt to wallow tediously in his or her local misery. ("How can you moan so over missing that train? You are still having a wonderful trip that not many people expect to take.") We should applaud the prescription of the Stoic anesthesia in this case. But the more we depart from this kind of case, the more questionable the prescription becomes. As the incurred evil becomes greater and more truly serious, the Stoic argument becomes heartless; as the sufferer's temperament becomes more cheerful, the argument becomes a counteragent to that cheerfulness, variously effective or ineffective depending on the settled strength of the temperament. And even in the optimal setting, we must be hesitant with endorsements. After the storm blows over and the person's emotions return to their former equilibrium, he or she would then do well not to take the Stoic recommendation too seriously.

The problem is that the Stoic darkens his vision of value-invested objects:

his perspective converts many innocent pleasures and many paltry vices into things that appear much worse than they need to appear. And there is a potentially worse effect of full-time Stoicism. Since many people do not taste most of the principal poisons in the world's cup, the Stoic ethic will also darken our vision toward those people whose vision is not as darkened as ours is. We will patronizingly regard them as naive, self-deluded, or otherwise not as enlightened, responsible, or realistic as we are. By starting with a refusal of the innocent goods of the world, "we may, at last, render our philosophy . . . only a more refined system of selfishness, and reason ourselves out of all virtue as well as social enjoyment" (E 40). If it is objected that this self-indulgent high-mindedness is an accidental consequence of the system, the accidents occur almost universally. We—many of us—do not accept the argument that handguns are only accidentally related to the murders committed with them, and the reason is that the probability of misuse is high; a similar conclusion is germane here. If there is a causal tie between a conception of value and an unamiable character disposition, the existence of this tie must count as an objection to the conception by our naturalistic lights. Not only the ethic but the high-minded stance caused by the ethic has bad causal implications. Hume noticed that "of old, the perpetual cant of the *Stoics* and *Cynics* concerning *virtue*, their magnificent professions and slender performances, bred a disgust in mankind," a disgust that extended to Lucian (in many respects "a very moral writer"), whose "peevish delicacy" ironized him out of virtue, or at least out of the praise of it, by the canting examples around him (E 242). Nothing makes virtue appear so repellent to a humane mind as an overrating of its importance.

Not that I would minimize the number of woes in our experience,[9] but a

---

9. Nor would Hume. In *Dialogues*, Part X, Demea and Philo seemingly seek to outbid each other in cataloguing the "innumerable ills of life" (Demea) and "the misery and wickedness of men" (Philo) (D 58), and what they say makes Cleanthes' brief contributions appear shallow and Panglossian by comparison. At one point Demea says that "were a stranger to drop on a sudden into this world," he would show him "a hospital full of diseases, a prison crowded with malefactors and debtors, a field of battle strewed with carcases, a fleet foundering in the ocean, a nation languishing under tyranny, famine, or pestilence" (D 61). For light relief the strayer would be treated "to a ball, to an opera, to court," which (Demea thinks) would only diversify the impression of sorrow. The Sceptic says something very similar: "It is certain, were a superior being thrust into a human body, that the whole of life would appear so mean, contemptible, and puerile, that he never could be induced to take part in any thing, and would scarcely give attention to what passes around him" (MPL 175). That Hume's own point of view is more in keeping with Sterne's than Swift's should not prompt us to overlook Hume's lively awareness of what Swift, too, was aware of.

consistently Stoic brand of reflection surely exaggerates the number beyond all plausibility. There are fewer mines and more mine-free fields than the Stoic allows. If the Stoic has a sanguine assessment of the world, it is because he forgets his ethic, and this forgetfulness is what endears him to us. If the Stoic responds that an awareness of problematicity is virtuous because we have to correct our natural tendency not to face up to problems, I believe that the Sceptic's best answer would be a simple denial that such an awareness has any independent virtuousness at all.[10] The proper method for dealing with an evil is to take steps to remove it, and thinking that has evil for its subject and that does not terminate in the taking of such steps is not pleasing. The best policy here would be to take the necessary steps while ignoring as much as possible that part of ourselves that might cause us to linger, for no good reason, over the reasons for our action.

Besides relying on the salve of forgetfulness, the Stoic could avoid the unhappy consequences of his recommendations if he disembodied himself more perfectly than his argumentative approach calls for, and arguably this is what he is aiming at. He would then naturally evolve into the Platonist, and this would have happier consequences because the darkening of the vision would disappear as his earthly preoccupations became weaker. Such a person would be more likely to view the world in such a way that "every event becomes an object of joy and exultation" (E 101). (This unselective joy could be the mindless good cheer of a person who has nothing at stake, but it is pleasant for all that.) The persons whom Hume adduces as having led "artificial lives," Diogenes and Pascal, perhaps conform to the Platonist model, albeit in strikingly different ways and despite their dearth of serenity (E 342–43). We might marvel at these men because they are self-contained monuments to the remarkable capacities of humankind. Nevertheless, such figures are wisely not thought to be models for our emulation, and we almost treat them literally as artworks, as characters that seem to have almost no lease on existence apart from the imaginative exercise they occasion.

I should like to offer a number of assorted remarks about the Sceptic's display of the philosophers' arguments, remarks intended to bolster the Sceptic's case. First, the Sceptic need not be taken to deny that *pro tanto* goods and evils sometimes lose their initial complexion. It might be thought that he does deny that this can happen, since his counterarguments are

---

10. And it can be vicious, as Nietzsche reminds us: "For the sight of what is ugly makes one bad and gloomy" (*The Gay Science*, trans. Walter Kaufmann [New York: Vintage, 1974], sec. 290).

always directed to arguments that putatively show that some goods and evils are not what we thought they were. Hence, the Sceptic can appear to be recommending a bland—and surely untenable—acquiescence in our first impressions. The hastiness of this inference becomes apparent, however, if we bear in mind that there are two ways we can be led to revise our judgment about a good or evil, one utterly innocuous, the other more suspect, and these are similar to the options we had when thinking about optical illusions. The innocuous path to belief revision involves learning about latent or more remote properties of the good or evil under review, the cognizance of which undoes, works against, or modifies the first impression. Thus, we may enjoy our cups immoderately at first, but as we learn about the coming hangovers, the lassitudes, the disruptions of our schedule, and (most important) the feelings we have about these things, we revise our judgment and correct the initial impression. To have both the factual awareness and a feeling for our feelings is a Humean requirement for the good critic, for the critic must be able to show us the hidden properties of the work, those which elude our casual, undiscerning inspection. The Sceptic would indeed be foolish to deny that this sort of revision occurs or should occur. But the Stoic and the Platonist are not engaged in this enterprise. Their path to belief revision involves nothing more than a perspective shift. We are not getting any new *information* about ambition, exile, blindness, and so on, when we make contact with their arguments. We do not learn, for example, that if we are duplicitous, we will fuel suspicions in the hearts of those persons whom we will have to trust. (This bit of intelligence is similar to being apprised about hangovers.) We are simply told to change the frame of reference, and are given some reasons for making that change. Interestingly, the goods and evils themselves hardly figure as actors at all on the stage of these arguments; all the important work concerns the stance we are to assume for surveying these items en bloc. The Sceptic's arguments are indeed directed against this kind of belief revision, but it is intuitively much less creditable than the other because we are not doing any thick, interpretive work with our evaluatable objects, not doing any genuine criticism (in the usual art-, book-, or film-review sense of the term). By the Sceptic's standard, the second kind of belief revision is the higher alchemy.

Second, we may wonder if the Sceptic is shooting his arrows at straw men. The arguments of Fontenelle, Plutarch, and Cicero are such easy targets that we are incredulous while we read them, before we even reach the rebuttal. If so, the Sceptic gets a good laugh, but purchases a victory that is more Pyrrhic than Pyrrhonic. This conclusion too would seem to be quick. Although the arguments are simple, they are emblematic of other philosophical positions that are considerably less so, and thus their simplicity is heuristically helpful for a conceptual investigation. If we begin with the relatively unphilosophical moralists of our day, we immediately find versions, or parodies of versions, of the Platonist and Stoic. And within philosophy we find them too, though the form is frequently so fantasticated as to preclude immediate recognition. In Kant we encounter the inference, redolent of Stoicism, from "X is abusable (can play us false, may perish)" to "X is not a true good," and the Kantian tradition generally is a continuation of the Stoic. The Platonist legacy appears in any ideal-world or ideal-observer theory of ethics, including the utilitarian, and the questions that typically arise regarding the relationship between the ideal and nonideal components of the theory mimic the questions the Sceptic poses. I do not want to examine these more sophisticated contenders, nor do I want to undercut them, except insofar as they may depend on the particular features I am criticizing, and these features can sometimes be found. The straw men, then, should not beguile us into supposing that all the men who resemble them must be straw as well.

We can moreover consider the Sceptic's opponents in a light that suggests they may be permanent interlocutors for the Sceptic. The Stoic and the Platonist are two moments in a single tendency, which expresses itself in the attempt to solve theoretical and practical difficulties through the disembodied self-ascription of preferred causal lineages. We utter injunctions to ourselves with an imagined voice that comes from a perspective we should like to embody. The theoretical attempt has a rough-and-ready clarity and distinctness; the ideal embodiment flatters some of our passions; and the nonrationalist rivals are unobvious and unassuming. It is therefore unlikely that the Stoic and Platonist tendencies would, and even undesirable that they should, disappear entirely from the imagination, however much they vanish in the heat of life.

Third, it must be emphasized that the Sceptic is not really inveighing against the making, the entertaining, or the authentic criticizing of these refined reflections. He merely charts what would happen if they were reduced to practice, or, to speak more precisely, were to have a consistent effect on practice. The whole of the problem is the failure of the reduction. The Sceptic implicitly demands of an ethic that it have a *concrete universality* in the agent's life, and this contrasts with Kant's demand that the relevant universality be intellectually perspicuous in such a way as to be statable as a rule. By concrete universality, I do not mean that the ethic has to be constantly before the mind; I mean instead that the point of view that the ethic nurtures should be such that it is causally sustainable in all the typical psychological contexts in which the agent finds him- or herself. And here we have one clear and authentic break with a rationalistic desideratum.

The Sceptic thinks that the "chief triumph" of philosophy, apart from its tendency to polish the temper, lies in its showing us "those dispositions we should endeavour to attain, by a constant *bent* of mind, and by repeated *habit*" (MPL 171, Hume's emphasis). The Sceptic, revealingly, is not saying that philosophy should dictate our habits to us, what we should do and not do habitually, but rather that philosophy should point out the "dispositions" (close to my "perspectives" or "points of view") that are *habit-compatible*, that flourish in the habitual nexus that defines a particular person's life. To be sure, in this passage the Sceptic seems to be speaking rather of the habits that are compatible with certain approved dispositions, but if we remember that he begins his essay with an admiring tour of the "vast variety" (MPL 159) to be found in nature, which includes the different human lifestyles, it is clear that the dispositions are not preselected for the habits. The Sceptic is speaking of the kinds of lives that can support habits, can become habitual. This is the right test, and the Stoic and the Platonist fail it.

The Sceptic's criterion is similar to one that is implied in a remark that Nietzsche makes. After saying that he abhors moralities that promote renunciation and deal in negative imperatives, he tells us, "But I am well disposed to those moralities which goad me to do something and to do it again, from morning till evening, and then to dream of it at night, and to think of nothing but doing this *well*, as well as *I* alone can do it."[11] Nietzsche could be intending a particular kind of virtuosic action here, and although that is not the Sceptic's intention, we have a shared commitment to that which can endure, that which can be repeated, in a number of dissimilar contexts. This type of commitment is crucial for understanding rationalism, and the idea of repetition (in place of universalizability) as a normative criterion is one that the serious nonrationalist must make explicit. But having shown the precise respect in which the Stoic and the Platonist are wanting in the Sceptic's eyes, and the implicit alternative to their way of thinking, is something of an achievement in its own right, and for now we must move on.

Finally, it must be emphasized that the failure of the Stoic and Platonist as

---

11. Ibid., sec. 304 (Nietzsche's emphasis).

philosophical moralizers does not mean, for the Sceptic, that they fail in other capacities. I earlier drew a contrast between representations that are objects of attention (or consideration) and representations that are objects of belief, a contrast to which I wish now to return. The paradigm of an object of attention is an artwork, since artworks are not aimed at getting us into a condition of belief. Nor are they aimed at producing the global sort of influence that the Sceptic requires an ethic to have; their influence is intermittent, and desirably so. Although the goods of our life are subject to the same sort of criticism to which artworks are, and although the distinction between the moral and the aesthetic is muted by the nonrationalist, there are differences between the moral and the aesthetic that need to be maintained, and one of these is the difference between local and global influencers of sentiment.

My view is that we need both global and local sentiment influencers, and productions that are mistakenly classified under one rubric may be successfully transferred to the other. Because the Stoic and Platonist perspectives are admittedly intermittent and their reflective benignity depends on their intermittency, we could conclude that we have lost an ethic only to gain a statement about value that is closely akin to an artwork, or to an artistic statement, and that such virtues as artworks exercise in the economy of our minds are the virtues that these philosophies possess. I believe that this is what Hume may suppose.

Hume has a seemingly intrusive footnote in "The Sceptic," which is the only intrusion of its kind in the essay quartet, for here Hume speaks utterly *in propria persona*. In this footnote Hume gently chides the Sceptic for "carrying the matter too far," and because of this trip to the woodshed some readers may be inclined to say that (i) Hume is putting distance between himself and the Sceptic and that hence (ii) only the footnote really represents Hume's views. This reaction strikes me as quite excessive. It is much more consonant with Hume's cultivated carelessness that we should expect him to give the Sceptic a little ribbing, just as he mocks, and mockingly confirms, his own antiheroic position in the Conclusion of Book One of the *Treatise* by giving vent to a little gentle heroics. Far from withholding endorsement from the Sceptic, the footnote can be read as establishing between Hume and the Sceptic a bond of intimacy that does not hold between Hume and the two moralists who precede the Sceptic, and that does not hold to the same extent between Hume and the Epicurean. The bond with the Sceptic is mirrored, however, by the conversational dalliance between the Epicurean and his inamorata (Caelia), which is another thread that ties the first and the last essays together (for there is no dialogue when the Stoic and the Platonist speak). Such conjectures apart, we can reasonably believe, given everything that we know about Hume's views, that "The Sceptic" expresses those views.

Now this footnote is presently important because Hume lists a number of reflections "whose natural tendency is to tranquillize and soften all the passions" (MPL 177), and these reflections look suspiciously like the stock in trade of the moralists whom the Sceptic derides. (For example: "Is it not certain, that every condition has concealed ills? Then why envy any body?") We need to read Hume's prefatory remarks carefully to make sense of this tricky dialectical counterpoint. Upon making the claim about the tranquilizing influence, Hume qualifies it by restricting the influence to those whose "tempers . . . are thoughtful, gentle, and moderate," adding that these reflections "fortify" (that is, reinforce) these tempers. That the recipients of the edification are those who are least in need of it is the Sceptic's point about redundancy once more, and fortifications are not the same as foundations. The persons who stand to reap a benefit from these reflections, then, derive their steadiness from a prereflective source, on the one hand, and apparently see through the pretensions of the reflections, on the other. (If they are truly "thoughtful," they will, as Hume says a little later, not expect too much from the philosophers.) This is therefore to say that they will stand to these reflections as we usually stand to artworks. And so, Hume's footnote is a gesture of courtesy to the defeated Stoic and Platonist, graciously allowing them a niche in the skeptically minded imagination, while archly moderating the Sceptic's own point of view with some of his own medicine.

To be sure, there is little reason to believe that Hume thinks that we should dogmatically occupy the Sceptic's point of view, and ample reason to believe that fluctuation among the four moral tempers is not a worry. But we can conclude that the Sceptic's point of view lets us explain the deficiencies in the other tempers, and thereby permits greater reflective stability than they do. In practice, the world is served well by a diversity of tempers, but when we reflect, the skeptical sentiment emerges as superior. The reflective problem with the Stoic and the Platonist, then, concerns the articulation of their positions more than the sentiments and moods a Stoic or Platonist starts from.

To suppose that a perspective affords us merely a form of aesthetic experience looks like a fall for the Stoic and Platonist, and it would certainly look like a fall *to them*, who would be loath to have their rationalistic theories functionally classified along with the *Divine Comedy*, *Middlemarch*, and other (according to rationalistic standards) less-than-circumspect mental modifiers. And apart from their own peculiarly intensified form of consternation, it is possible to feel the pathos of this reconception. We uncover much the same pathos when we hear the expression "the Bible as literature," for a text that was formerly Holy Writ has become a culturally more modest instrument for edification. Other examples of similar reconceptions spring readily to view: Mont-Saint-Michel as Significant Form, Paracelsus as the History of Ideas. We should be less, or more, than human if we did not imaginatively shed a generous tear at these spectacles. But let us mingle some light with these tears, and to that end, here are three quickly observed points.

(a) We are back to the issue of heroism again, and these examples permit us to make the following addition to our previous reflections. A culture will always accord reflective prestige to certain practices, persons, intellectual conceptions, and so heroize them, if we want to speak that way, in a relatively virtuous sense; but if cultural conditions change, the old prestige-invested items may retain their prestige only at the price of our becoming too self-conscious about our relationship to them, and so we might heroize in a relatively vicious sense. An honest person today cannot read Paracelsus or visit Mont-Saint-Michel with the same network of expectations that the first readers or visitors had, and the wish to recapture those expectations is literally unrealizable. That being so, we merely bring Mont-Saint-Michel down to earth, not down, when we reclassify. The object of pathos is the fact of historical mutability more than anything else. Our tears should flow, but they should be sparing.

(b) The Stoic and Platonist should not be too surprised at their classification. For the way of the world has always been to classify the philosophers with the mad poets and other garret dreamers whose unproductive brainchildren are largely confined to the fancies of a visionary few. Outside the university milieu people regard philosophers as vaguely literary types (distinguishable, perhaps, from the rest of the literati by the abstruseness of their favored topics), and this view has Aristophanes for its memorable as well as aboriginal spokesman. Doubtless, it rankles the Stoic and Platonist to hear the Aristophanic line coming from the Sceptic, who is a *philosopher* (albeit one who insinuates himself into the common-life perspective, which incorporates the Aristophanic line). But news the line is not.[12]

---

12. One might feel tempted to say that the verdict of the world is just wrong, but that seems just too pat. Aristophanes does see something that Plato does not. And conversely: the verdict of the world is not the whole story either.

(c) If the Sceptic can make out, within his system, a valued place for artistic mental modifiers, then the reclassification is arguably more of a coming up than a coming down for the rationalist. I think that this is right, but I take up the place of art (and the place of other primarily nonintellectual mental goods) in Chapter 5. Here I just want to keep the reader's eye open to this possibility.

Still, reviewing the merits of (a)–(c) is likely to leave us underwhelmed. What does the Sceptic really give us? An artistic, as opposed to moral, conception of rationalist moral philosophies, and his own laughter, it seems. (And those philosophies are a strange form of art, if they are art, since their makers presumably cannot think of themselves as artists while they make them.) We would like to know more about the nature of the true (nonrationalist) moral philosophy and the true art, at the very least, and regarding these he tells us little. This reticence is unavoidable, however, because of the content of the Sceptic's claims.

If the Sceptic is right, there should be no easy answers to the questions about which practices and dispositions are desirable, and by "easy" I mean "easy to formulate in theoretical formulae." Human nature is so complicated and so embedded in concrete historical situations that we can only get our answers by looking at our practices and dispositions on a cautious retail basis. This is what Hume does in the other essays. For example, we have immediately after "The Sceptic" (and the positioning may be significant) Hume's essay "Of Polygamy and Divorces," and here he unambitiously looks at a pair of practices in an information-gathering spirit and then draws a few conclusions about them, based on what he gathers, in conjunction with some general but fairly uncontroversial principles. This style of treatment is what we should expect the Sceptic to recommend and to practice, and unless we are truly dazzled by the non-self-sustaining rationalist vision, we should hardly be disappointed by this style. Nobody thinks that art criticism is impossible, or pointless, because we cannot state what Brueghel and Monet have in common and what distinguishes their works from the most forgettable kitsch. We exhibit the glories of Brueghel on his own terms, informed by patient art-historical research and mature, sensitive phenomenological critical interaction. (I have little doubt that the Sceptic, out of the constancy of his bent, would be pleased to show how a general theory of art either Platonistically encourages attitudes that would cause us to treat the Brueghel as we do the kitsch or Stoically magnifies the demerits of the kitsch. Both tendencies have been visible in the philosophy of art.) And yet we often are seduced into thinking that ethics, which—on one view—is the criticism of humankind, is impossible, or pointless, unless we have a rationalist theory of ethics. The hard work, the serious work, with Brueghel and with polygamy only begins when we turn aside from such a theory to what R. P. Blackmur simply but lucidly called "the substance of your chosen case."[13]

The Sceptic plays up the complications of our moral lives in the manner in which he brings his essay to its close. He observes not only that bad qualities can serenely coexist with the good in "the most worthy character" (MPL 178), but that the presence of the good can exacerbate the bad and even introduce badness into the equation. A sense of shame is a good thing for imperfect persons to have, and yet possessing it will make an erring person far more miserable than an "abandoned criminal" would be in the same circumstances. Similarly, a person who is capable of love but not friendship is apt to be better off than a person who is capable of both, because the generosity of the second person can easily make him "a total slave to the object of his passion" (MPL 180). This phenomenon of the excessively benevolent lover is particularly noteworthy because it shows how resistant to our blueprints and intentions human nature can be. If we are putting together a catalogue of virtues, in the hope of modeling an ideal character thereby, we might say, "A loving heart—that's capital. Let's include it in our catalogue. A loyal and steadfast heart—that's good too, so let's throw that in as well." But when we are done, we will have a catalogue of parts, all of which can be annexed to good effect to certain persons (though other nonblueprinted factors must conspire serendipitously with our selection for the desired effect to ensue), but which can never be assembled in a single person—except, perhaps, by reason of some highly unusual circumstances that display the assemblage advantageously, and that again cannot, owing to their irregularity, be incorporated into our blueprint. (This is also the point that the ideal character is inherently plural, and that its portrait is unlike a blueprint, which should not have multiple, nonequivalent compliance classes.) The craft of having a life, like that of evaluating lives, is not easy, in my quasi-technical sense. Just as the evaluator is in the shoes of the critic, not the abstract theorist, so too the person who longs for the true ideal, for a harmony between practice and reflection, must fashion it in a way that is similar to an artist's procedure, with attention to both the particular materials and the possible statements that the materials permit, adjusting each to each as the work proceeds—similar, but not identical, because an artist has far more control over his material than

---

13. In "The Critic's Job of Work," in *The Double Agent* (New York: Arrow, 1935), 302.

we do over ours (since we are the material, to a great extent). In other words, we should not expect intellectually clear procedures where our individual lives are concerned.[14]

Addicted as I am to parallels and recurrences, I cannot refrain from noting the parallel between the *Treatise* and "The Sceptic," and the recurrence of thought patterns in each. The Sceptic's review of moral arguments has a counterpart in the *Treatise*, Book Three, Part I, Section 1, where Hume criticizes the view that moral relations are susceptible of demonstration. If the odiousness of parricide consists in the demonstrable relation that holds between one being and another being whom the first kills and who is the cause of the first's existence, Hume asks whether the same relation does not hold between a sapling that overtops its parent tree (T 466–67).[15] The answer is yes, and the admission is as unwelcome to the defender of demonstrable moral relations as the discovery that the true system of astronomy would destroy both ambition and patriotism was to the defender of refined reflections. Both texts show how, in different domains, rationalistic standards go wrong.

Moreover, when we acknowledge the problem with rationalism, we simultaneously recognize the *seeming* triviality of the principles that do the work the rationalist thinks the august faculty of reason either does or should do. This awareness is evident in the Conclusion of Book One, and the Sceptic's penultimate reflections, those which concern the coexistence of the good and bad, makes this awareness evident in his essay. How can we not be brought to the view that "seemingly trivial" factors make our characters worthy or unworthy, happy or miserable, after we take the Sceptic's thoughts to heart? If we have the stuff of love and friendship in us, we might avoid becoming slaves to our intimates (and so be "saved from total skepticism" regarding our affective lives, as it were) if our intimates are similarly

---

14. This leaves open the possibility that such procedures may have more of a place in the public world, and for one useful account of that place, see Stuart Hampshire, *Innocence and Experience* (Cambridge: Harvard University Press, 1989).

15. Hume's argument about the sapling and the tree has been summarily dismissed by J. L. Mackie as being "more picturesque than cogent" because "there are further elements in the human situation which make them relevantly different from the non-human one with which Hume compares them" (*Hume's Moral Theory* [London: Routledge, 1980], 57). There are indeed further relevant elements, but I think that Mackie's criticism misses Hume's point. For we can read Hume as offering a challenge to the defender of demonstrable moral relations: if we say what the relation is, it will be possible to construct an example that exhibits the relation we name but that does not elicit our moral response.

constituted, or if they live too far away for our devotion to impoverish us or disrupt our other commitments.

And just as the Conclusion gives the rationalist one final stand, which yields the stalemate scenario, so too the Sceptic puts forward a dilemma that leaves no choosable options open to the reasoning mind, and the dilemma arises after the illusion-disabusing discovery vouchsafed by the Sceptic's penultimate reflections. The dilemma, at MPL 180, is as follows: The management of life, when we examine it closely, is a "dull pastime" rather than a "serious occupation," and this observation leads us to ask whether we should "engage ourselves in it with passion and anxiety." The Sceptic, speaking provisionally for the disappointed rationalist or malign skeptic, thinks not. The whole business is so paltry a thing that it does not merit such attentions. On the other hand, we are led to ask whether we should be indifferent to the pastime. Again, the Sceptic thinks not, because we would "lose all the pleasure of the game by our phlegm and carelessness." (Here the careless approach is a target for criticism to the extent that it becomes more of a principle than it should.) And so we are then left with the breathtaking reflection that any judgment about life will be flawed *just because* it is a judgment, and so our problem is on a new plateau, the flaw having become radical or intrinsic. That our metajudgment does not escape the infection of the radical or intrinsic flaw merely confirms the difficulty of the situation.

But the metajudgment has a peculiar and unreal flavor to it, a statement that only a spectator located outside of the defining constraints of the human order could utter, and speak truly as he did so. We speak falsely when we utter it, but not because we lack the appropriate assertibility conditions for the statement, as we do with the ordinary kind of falsehoods with which we are familiar. Indeed, the Sceptic has in fact provided us with ample grounds for that assertion. Rather, we err because we are so profoundly attached to the judgment-making that disowning the game in the manner that the radical critique indicates is tantamount to a self-repudiation, a condition that lies too deep for hypocrisy or duplicity and that puts us in the space of false consciousness. The person who holds that judgments of value fail merely because they are judgments is a person who denies the reality of evaluative distinctions, and is thus the evanescent figure Hume jousts at in the opening of the second *Enquiry*, a figure who is the value-theoretic cousin of the practicing Pyrrhonist. We must judge, as we must believe, and there is no other argument against the falsely conscious minds who think that they pass judgment and belief by.

Alternatively, if either kind of skeptic were exempt from false consciousness, we would consider them true aliens, with whom we could never find our feet. And so, we could say that the characters who profess the unreality of evaluative distinctions or who deny the tenability of all beliefs are pretending to be nonhuman. The pretense of assuming a nonhuman identity could conceivably be ingratiating and beautiful—we long, "Proteus-like," to change our form (MPL 168)—but the topic is difficult (since it is not clear that we could truly leave ourselves behind in an imagined incarnation). In any event, if these magic casements do open in our imagination, they should only open there. For the pretense is disturbing if we do not have the awareness that it is a pretense, and more profoundly so than other pretenses that we might mistake for the real thing.

The Sceptic, then, returns, as did Hume, to the natural perspective. Valuing "would be overvaluing . . . were it not that, to some tempers, this occupation is one of the most amusing, in which life could possibly be employed" (MPL 180). The inscrutable pleasure of making value judgments leaps into the breach left by reason, and we are restored to wholeness. We avoid false consciousness through a kind of divided consciousness, an awareness of the unavoidable incongruous oddity of our embodied practices; and the Kantianly unlegislatable pedigree possesses an incongruity (which reflection can magnify, as we have seen) whose comic possibilities are tonic if we but have the divided eyes, so to speak, to see the comedy. This detection is ultimately possible only if one eye sees what the careless vulgar see and the other what the Sceptic sees, which is itself possible only through a great care that is taught and mediated by rationalism. The first-order smiles of common life engender the third-order smiles of the extremely uncommon life that succeeds both the unreflective mode and its second-order rationalist response, and that resembles both without being identical to either. We see the resemblance to the unreflective mode most readily, with the least preparation, but a more discerning judge will also see the more elusive resemblance to the reflective mode. For the Sceptic, letting sophisticated amusement be his own criterion for engagement, has returned to the evaluative stance of the Epicurean, "the man of elegance and pleasure" (MPL 138)—but in such a way that we can only speak of him as the higher, or reflectively reclaimed, Epicurean. In a similar spirit we could relabel Hume at the end of Book One as the higher commoner. And at this point, with unifying parallels crowding upon us, we may be able to sense how unobvious the apparently superficial Humean position finally is.

4

※ ※ ※

Irrationalism

The criticism of rationalism in its two versions concluded, I now pursue a few of the consequences of benign skepticism, and begin by devoting some attention to the topic of irrationalism. I wish to advance two theses in this chapter. The first is that the Humean view of reason, or reasonableness, is not an irrationalist position. The second is that the Humean view lets us diagnose a deeper malady than irrationalism, a problem that we find, in a sophisticated form, in rationalist philosophy, but that is more visible, and more distressingly so, in monotheistic religion. This problem is the false-heroic tendency we have already detected, but I hope to show that this tendency has sturdier psychological roots than we might have realized; and by showing this I intend to heighten the overall plausibility of my account of rationalism and its alternative, which are my main topics.

My two theses taken together show also that our situation with regard to our self-corrective powers (and our self-esteem insofar as it derives from the exercise of these powers) is more complicated than the rationalist allows. On the one hand, human beings naturally criticize themselves in ameliorative ways, even though their criticisms are not really susceptible to rationalist codifications. On the other hand, we can never be very confident, in an intellectual sense, that our minds are so constructed as to guarantee that we shall make the right corrective turn at the right time (and we have some reason to fear that, relying on intellect alone, we can make the wrong one). Consequently, our prospects for reflective correction are worse than the rationalist thinks, but our prospects for collective correction, particularly as assisted by occasional warnings from skeptical critics, are better.

Let us begin with the thesis that the Humean is not an irrationalist. Hume's benign skepticism generated suspicions on two fronts early on, before we gave it its name, and these suspicions have possibly gained force as we have proceeded. First, there was the worry that this skepticism was friendly to irrationalism, if not explicitly irrationalist itself. Second, there was the worry that this skepticism was supportive of social, political, or cultural conservatism, of the business-as-usual way we do or have done things. These are different sources of suspicion, but such is our good fortune that a single set of considerations usually serves to answer, or at least allay, these worries. The worries arise, I believe, because it is thought that the Humean skeptic assigns a lowly place to reflection, and it is feared that unless we assign a higher place to it, we succor those harsher minds who, for their other, less praiseworthy reasons, would join us in our gentle aspersions. To reply to this claim we have to be clear about what we mean by reflection, and I want to offer two clarifications of the notion that will help to establish a desirably normative place for reflection in a Humean account of the reasonable person.

First, there is a species of reflection that is intrinsically normative and generically applicable. In both the *Treatise* and "The Sceptic" we have seen Hume rely on a point of view that corrects other points of view, and it seems apparent that the correcting stance is the same in each domain. We can say that Hume is merely exercising *good sense*, a label that puts the normativity of the point of view on display. It is difficult to conceive how a self-conscious animal could find its way about the world without having some inarticulate feeling for what counts as the sensible thing for it to do; and this feeling is the most primitive, and the least escapable, instance of normativity. And this feeling accompanies an animal everywhere, however sophisticated its projects become. The good sense that prompts us to leave the disappointed epistemological rationalist to himself is the same good sense that prompts us not to expect too much from the rationalist moral philosopher. This observation seems insignificant enough, but it is similar to—and arguably an extension of—a more dramatic conclusion Hume reaches about necessity in Book One, Part III. He says that "there is but one kind of necessity . . . and that the common distinction betwixt *moral* and *natural* necessity is without any foundation in nature" (T 171, Hume's emphasis). Necessity is the same whether it occurs in a physical or psychological context, and this identification of sameness, if Hume can make it out, is a signal antidualistic achievement for the naturalist. Likewise, good sense is as important when we are thinking about our general beliefs as it is when we sort through our emotional responses. (Covertly, I have tried to reinforce the seamlessness of good sense by occasionally blending philosophical and literary remarks, so as to reveal the sameness of a single mind under different aspects. But this is to digress.) This picture of an intrinsic, generic brand of normativity introduces my second clarification, which is, for present purposes, the more important of the two.

The interesting distinction within reflection is not between the normative and the nonnormative, but between the natural and the refined. Hume implicitly makes different claims about each, and so there is no single answer to the question about the "place of reflection." Let us then consider what Hume says about each variety of reflection in turn.

How natural is the normativity of reflection (to begin with)? Readers of the *Treatise* have noted that although Hume has sections on the reason of animals, the pride and humility of animals, and the love and hatred of animals, he has no section on the morality of animals, or (as we might say) the normativity of animals. In one respect, the omission is utterly unremarkable: the other animals provide us with no articulated normativity to discuss. But in another respect, the omission should incline us to seek out an explanation. If we are as continuous with the animal order as Hume thinks, then we should be able to explain why, and how, the "normative sense" arises. If we default on this obligation, the door is open for the postulation of vacuously higher faculties that the naturalist must regard as obscurantist and retrograde. Hume, however, nowhere tells us such a story. But we should not despair too soon over the tellability of a story, for I think the necessary materials for a Humean explanation are ready to hand.

When Hume is laying out his model of the human mind, the principal point of difference between the human and the other animals to emerge concerns the looseness of the imagination. We have seen that our minds do not rest in the "narrow circle of objects" that preoccupy the beasts, and Hume moreover likes to play up the fact that we can mentally race from one corner of the universe to another. For the bare mechanism of mental movement to work, an animal has to be capable of causal inference: "By means of it I paint the universe in my imagination, and fix my attention on any part of it I please" (T 108). But that which differentiates our racing powers from those of the beasts would seem to depend on the relative freedom of the human mind to entertain fanciful and unendorsed causal hypotheses (including those that are merely hypotheses, not candidates for firm belief), since the other mammals are capable of tracing cause-effect relations. We cannot form any idea that has no reference to causation, in the merely hypothetical sense: if I imagine a winged creature of romance, I imagine how it causally behaves in my make-believe world. These cause-effect relations are not endorsed, but elaborate causal hypotheses that we do endorse would seem to start in life much as our fictions end, as merely entertainable objects of consideration.

And here is how normativity can enter the picture. If a mind is so loosely tethered to its perceptions that it can merely entertain some of them, then we should expect a kind of cognitive pressure to develop. We should like to banish some of our floating ideas and to retain others. The very "loose and unsteady texture" of our minds (NHR 348) creates a need for selectivity, which is the basis of the normative sense. We are required to think that some ideas are more retainable or acceptable, more banishable or unacceptable, than others, and the occurrence of this feeling fortifies the retention or acceptance, the banishment or unacceptance. To be sure, acceptance or rejection is not simply a thumbs-up or thumbs-down affair, especially as the mind becomes more sophisticated in its operations, but we can paper over niceties for the present. To be sure, we have only pushed the explanatory problem back a step, since it would be interesting to know why the human mind lost its tight tether in the first place. That question, intriguing though it is, is more difficult to answer, for empirical reasons, but it is a question for which a naturalistic answer would not be too difficult to imagine.[1]

The point of these moderate armchair speculations is to suggest that normativity strikes, and must strike, a deep root in the human mind, and that it therefore arises naturally, even in those whom we do not ordinarily think of as being specially reflective. As a species, we are, and have to be, obsessed with having the sense that things fit. We believe—we have the feeling—that the sun will rise tomorrow, but we also feel that this belief is all right for us to have, though it may take a question or two to bring this second feeling to the surface. A similar demand for coherence characterizes our value judgments.

All of this is to say that Hume does not, and should not, assign a lowly place to reflection in any uncoached, natively arising sense. We constantly

---

1. The ideas of this paragraph are themselves loosely tethered to some found in Book One, Part III, Section 10, "Of the Influence of Belief," but I am not claiming to offer Hume's views here—just Humean views.

rely on nonintellectual normative feelings and turns of mind so as to avoid assorted informal contradictions that a less selective mind, or groups of minds, would continuously run into, and we can, following Hume, call these sets of feelings and turns "*steady* and *general* points of view" (T 581–82, Hume's emphasis). Given the suspicious turn we have accorded abstract generality, this term is apt to confuse, but Hume's meaning is innocuous, and consistent with the views of the Sceptic.

These points of view are not general in the sense that those who occupy them regard particulars as instances of the more general, nor do they involve the adoption of a peculiarly impersonal or self-denying stance. They merely involve the selection of a particular perspective that we deem to have a normative authority. Hume writes that a "beautiful countenance cannot give so much pleasure, when seen at the distance of twenty paces, as when it is brought nearer us" (T 582); but if we happen to be twenty paces away, we do not let our judgment about the beauty of the face be dictated by the appearance that the face, from that site, has for us. If we did take our cue from the twenty-paces site, we would be victims of a "momentary" appearance, but there is no reason to suppose that we would ever be so victimized: perhaps if we were sessile animals (like sea anemones) our risks would be greater. The kind of "reflexion" (T 583) that corrects a "momentary" appearance is similar, then, to the corrections that we make when we are taking in the appearances of Descartes's towers.

To occupy a general point of view is to refuse to let our evaluative judgments be guided by the momentary appearance that our interests can create, and our occupation presupposes a capacity to look at things with the eye of the imagination as well as with our ordinary eyes. When we excuse ourselves from evaluating, for professional purposes, the work of a loved one, we do so because we are too close to the person whose work we are evaluating and so the risk is high that our affection will outplead our calm judgment. The tether between us and the person is too tight, and we need to step back in our imaginations just a bit to get the better angle. Other noninterested evaluators are at the right imaginative remove, and their stance automatically makes them qualified evaluators (they may be disqualified on other grounds, of course, such as incompetence, but here I am just talking about stances). Once we step back, those "desires and inclinations, which go no farther than the imagination, and are rather the faint shadows and images of passions" (T 450) come into operation and determine the judgment. This noninterested stance is all that I think Hume means by a "distant view or reflexion" (T 583). We merely have a normative response in our imagination, where such irregularities as our personal situation may introduce retire into the background, and we are thereby able to explain—as it was Hume's primary intention in this passage to do—why variations in our occurrent feelings for X (which may reflect the closeness of our association with the object of the feeling) are not necessarily accompanied by variations in our esteem for X. The "distant view or reflexion" is itself hardly less momentary than the impressions it corrects, but its normative authority is not captive to the moment. And it is also worthwhile to stress that a general point of view is not a severe disciplinary device for maintaining order among sentiments that arise much more spontaneously by comparison. As a rule we occupy a general point of view effortlessly, even though the passions of the moment can subvert its influence on our judgment.[2]

Hume's "general points of view" pose a double set of implications for the issues regarding irrationalism and conservatism. What unites the irrationalist and the conservative is a certain opposition to self-criticism, and with respect to the beliefs we ourselves hold or advance, we can indeed say that the influence of general points of view on us is to make us uncritical. However, with respect to the beliefs that others hold or advance, their influence on us is to enhance our critical disposition. This difference is important because a critical tendency should operate selectively in order to be benign. When we come up with a novel idea, we rely, as much as we are able, on general points of view for our sense of fit, for the feeling that our novel idea is of some value or merit. It is the voice that urges us forward, unlike that internal prompter that always dissuaded Socrates. (I do not think that this forward-urging feeling should be called an irrational or conservative influencer—it is rationalism again that might bid us to apply these labels—but I shall return to this in a few moments.) But when we are considering the ideas of others, the same general points of view have the opposite influence: they lead us to examine their ideas with the utmost criticism. We collectively have a better grasp of the different sorts of fit than the originator does, and since we do not have his prepossession in favor of his ideas, we are in a position to subject them to a multifaceted scrutiny. This is the kind of criticism that matters, and

---

2. The possibility of subversion does indicate a point of difference between sense perception and emotional response. We do not have "temptations" to succumb to momentary visual promptings as we do to momentary promptings that involve our interest. But this difference does not give us any reason to suppose that the correcting device has to be formally different in the two kinds of cases, that sentiment correction has its own special constraints.

the Humean view has the consequence that the making of this criticism is an activity internal to our psychological makeup.

It might be objected that general points of view, as I have described them, lack determinate content (the selection of the point of view seems to rest on nothing more that historically shifting intuitions about what is regarded as acceptable) and that they do not perform any determinate critical office (the noninterested imagination is merely left to play, it seems). I agree that they lack determinacy, in each of these quite different varieties, but I think that this fact is a great and empowering virtue. We do not need to suppose that there is a specific body of truth, concerning either our general beliefs or the values we hold dear, that attaches, or should attach, to the natural reflective stance. For one thing, there is no such body: an affluent eighteenth-century white male will have a normative sense that will not square with that of an indigent twentieth-century black female, unless we propose the most banal questions to each ("Is virtue good?"). But general points of view do not require that sort of content to do their work. What is important, what is essential, is that we think that these points of view are available and that we are aware that others think so too. The actual content of a particular person's noninterested imagination, at a particular time and place, will be determined by a great many things—the person's temperament, self-descriptions, life experiences, education, and so on. The variety of sources by which our imagination gets stocked is quite remarkable, and it would be an error to think that this is bad and that we should get our contents from one type of antecedently approved source (much as it was an error when Descartes supposed that only a God could sustain his thinking—and not a constellation of finite, and more easily recognized, intelligences). General points of view are fluid, but because of their naturalness and lack of sophistication they are not too fluid. They continuously redefine themselves as the history of a culture continues.

And what of the work that general points of view are called upon to do? It seems to me that our simply having these points of view is more important than any particular office we might expect of them. Just as the imagination gets its material from many sources, so too the normative sense exerts itself in ways that are desirably unpredictable. The *progress* of the normative sense in the history of a culture has not usually been one of the central explananda for moral philosophers; but an argument can be made that it should be, and the relative functional indeterminacy of general points of view helps, I would argue, to make the occurrence of progress intelligible.

This interpretation of general points of view as effortlessly occupiable and only uninformatively specifiable will probably not satisfy Kantians and others who may long for autonomously generated imperatives, but it should surely satisfy the more historically aware who think that moral judgments must reflect the actual situations in which agents are placed. Hume sounds quaint and indefensible if we regard general points of view the other way. For example, when he says that a man who uses the terms "vicious," "odious," or "depraved," "speaks another language, and expresses sentiments, in which he expects all his audience to concur with him" (E 272), we are apt to be incredulous if we think this "other language" has a certain content that intellectual application can bring to light and that others, by dint of their own intellectual applications, can appreciate. But on my view, Hume's man simply has the expectation that his sentiments will be facilely entered into, and seconded, by an "audience" that will not have to think very hard or very long in order to enter into his sentiments and second them. We should have no grounds for incredulity here, and we moreover should appreciate why general points of view, so understood, are important to us. For we need the expectations and interpersonal facilities that they make possible if we are to avoid a kind of Sarajevo of our sentiments when they collide.

If we go to back to our forward-urging voices, the fact that there is no determinate content should remove much of the concern that we had about bad effects. Their naturalness helps to undercut the worry about irrationalism; their fluidity, the worry about conservatism. A nonrational action- or belief-influencer is not irrational or conservative by itself. It becomes irrational or conservative only in conjunction with other influences. Moreover, if we take the strenuous rationalist line, we shall be taking steps to institute, psychologically, the most uncritical sort of conservatism. There is, as Nietzsche insightfully discerned, a strange introversion, almost a death wish, in the dissuading rationalist voice: here instinct is taking us out of action, rather than putting us into it, and it does not take much effort to see that this instinct would tend to have an inhibitive effect on us, since our plans and projects, hopes and fears, are seldom extremely plain to us, and so the rationalist voice will have much to lament. The dissuasion should come indirectly and inconclusively, from other people more than from our own heads. We in part elude their influence, because their presence is intermittent, and in part cannot avoid it, and would not want to, because our own convictions falter if we are alone. And so, there is a desirable half-shade thrown over the critical dissuasions that originate in others, strong enough to give us pause but weak enough to be redescribed and resisted. There is also critical *encouragement* that comes from others, and very little of this is to be found on our own side: we know our uncertainties and anxieties only too well, and will seize upon them as dissuading arguments, but others see our exterior, and for them we are seldom the ungainly creatures we see in our private mirrors. (The different reactions of lecturer and hearer to the selfsame performance offer a case in point: what may be felt, from the inside, to be a disastrous delivery can appear to witnesses, on the outside, to be carefully controlled.) Psychologically, then, we should take care to avoid acquiescing in those critical self-interpretations that "sink the ardour of the generous youth" (MPL 136)—the generous youth of our souls, from which venue alone we may expect any important changes in the world.

Natural normative reflection affords us more protection than we may realize from irrationalism and conservatism. We need to consider the place for refined reflection, the activity that can take us far beyond our accustomed paths and that includes both rationalism and the Humean critique. Hume does assign a lowly place to this kind of reflection, but the reason is not one that should undermine it: this reflection simply has a causally very circumscribed theater of operations, and this any candid person should admit. This consideration should not be undermining, because thinking that our causal influence is more marginal than we should like will hardly dampen the spirits of a person who is truly attached to what he or she is doing. Nevertheless, it would be useful if we could extract a few positive, bolstering reflections on behalf of reflection from Hume's text, and I think that we can do this. I want to present three broad reasons for thinking that our benign skepticism does not discourage refined reflection as such. These reasons will give us further light by which to distinguish the benign skeptic from the irrationalist and conservative, for they are intended to show that while refined reflection is not as important as the rationalist takes it to be, it is not unimportant. (In what follows I generally use "reflection" to stand for "refined reflection." Also, discussions of reflection can easily become metaphilosophical expositions—a disappointing genre, admittedly—but I think most metaphilosophical claims that I make here could be recast, if desired, as claims about reasonableness.)

(1) *Reflection arises naturally.* This should be a truism, but sometimes one has the impression that it is widely denied. When Hume parts company from the rationalist, he plays backgammon, but he also returns to his study. There is a double return to common life and to philosophy, and the return, as we have seen, is accomplished through natural inclination. And by "philosophy" I have in mind a liberal, Humean conception of a highly reflective practice that is naturalized through and through. That is, philosophy, in order to

evaluate practices, causes all practices, itself included, to pass before us at one imaginative remove from our actual engagements with them. It is criticism in the widest sense, and though it might occur within academic philosophy, it might not. Still, philosophy as we know it is an academic subject, and it may be helpful for us to distinguish the naturalness of reflection from the (unproblematic) artificiality of the academic version.

Outsiders often denigrate academic philosophy on the grounds that it is merely scholastic, and so it often is, but we should bear in mind that there is no obvious, strain-free habitat for serious reflection. Although Hume's *Treatise* is an unlikely academic text (particularly if it were one written by a fledgling academician), we should not infer that Hume's conditions of authorship are the normatively proper ones for philosophy. The great point to be made is that it is always a surprise when explicitly reflective activity, pursued under any conditions, institutional or noninstitutional, proves itself to have anything more than the most ephemeral interest.

Yet academic philosophy does have a habit, it should be noticed, of domesticating marginal thinkers (for instance), just as modern art has had a genius for exploiting "discredited" areas for its purposes. That the academic form of philosophy eventually domesticates many of the right people is a sign that academicism pays for itself, modestly but truly, and there is moreover always the slight chance that some nonephemeral work will be done. If the self-image of philosophy is sufficiently domesticated itself, complaints against academicism should become self-effacing to a great extent. (The complaint against academicism is not the same as the complaint against hardness, though the two can be run together. The second complaint, which is not disarmed by naturalizing our expectations, has no answer, and that is as we should expect.)

Of course, many cultures have not had academic philosophy, but that is not to say that explicit reflection as such is artificial. We can look at support for reflection in two ways, by considering the conditions that originally make it possible and those that preserve it. The conditions that are necessary for the initial flowering of this reflection are, to be sure, somewhat unusual: a certain degree of material well-being, a relaxation of traditional normative practices, a spreading sense of non–physically describable endangerment or uncertainty. I am thinking of ancient Greece here, but I suspect comparable lists could be made for the other known places and occasions of reflective fertility. And perhaps the delicacy of these conditions can best be demonstrated if we note that these same conditions, in conjunction with other factors, can produce, among other things, stultifying neotraditional nationalisms. The ground needed for the clear head is always rare; for a benign and causally efficacious clear head, even rarer. But once reflection is in place—and here we turn to sustaining conditions—it has a tendency to stay in place, in part because it is hard to turn our back on reflection after we make its acquaintance (as Bernard Williams has observed),[3] except by brute force, which is not so easy for us to accommodate (even from the prereflective point of view). Our Humean galley glides easily enough over the waters of reflection, avocationally and casually, if not on a robustly habitual basis; and the exposure we do have to it is sufficient, usually, to make us respect it. We could claim for it what Hume claims for justice: although it is artificial in one respect (because it is made rather than found), the sense of it is natural. But reflection is not artificial if we think of artificiality as involving a strained imposition on the way we think about our lives.

In drawing a contrast between precipitating and sustaining conditions, I am borrowing an idea from Hume's essay "Of the Rise and Progress of the Arts and Sciences," one of whose burdens is to show that the "civilizing arts" arise in republics but flourish under monarchies. Philosophy is an odd creature that does not really fit neatly into Hume's story, owing to its high degree of self-reflexivity, but it is surely possible to tell some such story, with greater elaboration than Hume's essay displays, and that story would be plausible. Uncertain origins apart, the difficulty of giving up reflection alone should make us reluctant to suppose that reflective practices are not congenial to our natural inclinations.

That we do not have a natural inclination to reflection is interestingly denied by both the irrationalist and the conservative. The irrationalist, such as Callicles, thinks that reflection is put upon us by whatever superior power for whatever reason, and that we return to our proper station if we throw off this supposed yoke. The conservative thinks that the old folkways stand on their own, do not produce fissures in which reflection can grow, and so critical surveys of the folkways inevitably have for him an aura of mendacity. On this issue, the irrationalist and conservative are siblings, one merely more rambunctious-sounding than the other.

Unluckily, the Humean position has perhaps been tarred with the reflection-as-artificial brush because of a partial misunderstanding of the views of Richard Rorty. The language that Rorty uses often suggests reflective artificiality (as when he attributes "the invention of the mind" to Descartes). Strictly speaking, however, what Rorty attacks is the idea that reflection has

---

3. *Ethics and the Limits of Philosophy* (Cambridge: Harvard University Press, 1985), 163–64.

a determinate structure or content that is not historically determined, which is not the same as the idea that reflection itself is historically determined. So this is a misunderstanding. But there is another element in Rorty's thought that is more problematic for the Humean. Rorty apparently divides all cognitive practices into two categories: the sciences, which predict and control, and the arts, which edify. Given this division, philosophy belongs more with the arts, and this affiliation may make the more explicit forms of reflection look more self-deceived than they should look. I was happy, on the Sceptic's behalf, to consign rationalist theories to the arts, but doing so implied a contrast with a nonrationalist Humean theory, which was not to be so consigned. Now in the fullness of time the Humean theory might acquire this status, but if so, it seems to me that we would need another theory, which we would not regard simply as an artistic expression, in order to make the relevant identification. Criticism, as I broadly understand it, is neither an art nor a science (though it combines elements of both), and reflection is nothing if not critical. If we resist the wholesale attempt to understand criticism on the model of artistic edification, we shall be more inclined to think that reflection is natural.

But to acknowledge the naturalness of reflection is of course not to advance the cause of reflection to any material extent. I am not convinced that we have here anything like a *cause* to rally around, however. If reflection is truly natural, then people who are fortunate enough to live in the right cultures will find their way to it relatively unselfconsciously. It is a curiosity that so many philosophers seem to think that if reflectiveness had a merely affective claim on us, then almost nobody would be reflective. (One wonders if they really might have come to philosophy as the lackeys of an inclination-restraining pain, the pain of irrationality.) Moreover, Hume's benign skepticism heightens rather than diminishes this intuitive feeling of appropriateness. What could be more natural than Hume's treatment of rationalism? The kind of critical engagement Hume demands of his reader is of the sort that strengthens the reader's commitment to what he or she is doing, because Hume is trying to get the reader to find increasingly occupiable reflective positions. This game is not a dull pastime, but can be played anew with passion.

(2) *Reflection is necessary for showing the frailty of the prereflective order.* To put it crudely, we have a tension between the strength and durability of our practices insofar as they occur unreflectively, on the one hand, and their weakness and recalcitrance to intellectual codification, on the other. Consequently, our practices are simultaneously strong and weak, but in different

respects. Their strength is immediately apparent, we might say. Until we do philosophy, we are not bothered by why we believe that the world did not come into existence fifty years before our birth, or by how we perform the action of lifting our arm. We believe, we act: and the fact that we do these things at all is proof of our prereflective strength of performance. Their weakness is not so readily open to our view. Indeed, their prereflective power helps to conceal their reflective weakness, to make it easy not to notice (and of course many persons never do notice this weakness). Philosophy leaps into this space, showing us that our practices become vexingly uncanny the more we probe them. We would never have dreamt that the tendency of the mind to continue on its course was what accounted for our belief in continuous existents if we had not had Hume's very refined argument to disclose it.

The invisibility of this frailty is akin to the invisibility that, according to Hume, awaits us for those causal connections of which we have not had adequate experience. "Adam, though his rational faculties be supposed, at the very first entirely perfect, could not have inferred from the fluidity and transparency of water that it would suffocate him" (E 27). Adam would need constant conjunctions of fluidity with suffocation in order to see that a lake was a potential suffocator. So too we need philosophy in order to see what the justifications of our practices come to. There is an interesting complication in the second case, however. The weakness is before us all the time, just as the causal relation is, but we do not make it visible through experienced conjunctions. The disclosing "experience" is the nonrationalist argument itself, and we might then think of the manner of disclosure as a pragmatic verification of the frailty it discloses: we do not bring secret causal relationships to light except through repeated viewings of objects, but here we have brought a secret justificatory relationship to light through a markedly irregular channel.[4] Or is it then even a secret at all? Could we have "discovered" it merely by scrupulously introspecting? The questions do not seem to admit of answers that we can give, or know how to give.

Given the special character of this advance in our knowledge, given its surpassing refinement, the desirability or importance of procuring it may be somewhat mysterious, particularly on refinement-wary Humean grounds. One reason it is important is that our minds tend to move heedlessly in their paths when they are animated by a great idea or by a powerful passion in

---

4. My word "secret" may be misleading. The secret that Adam unearths is the constant conjunction, not a more hidden "tie," which for Hume will always be a secret, save insofar as we trace the tie to the feeling of determination in our own minds.

consort with a great idea, and such heedless movement can produce quite a bit of harm, much of it as invisible to the agent as the frailty itself. A lively awareness of the seeming triviality of our mental operations tends to check this movement, thus leaving a space for less tutored, less coached natural inclinations to insinuate themselves and determine the will. Where there is no proclivity for the mind to embrace refined thoughts and become enamored of them, the cogency of this reason accordingly declines; nevertheless, our minds are often attracted to refined thoughts. I am not simply thinking of sophisticated refinements, the sort that intellectuals (in the narrow sense) retail. Many refinements are exceedingly crude, as paradoxical as that may sound. The demagogue who cannot get through a tirade without delirious, hackneyed appropriations of capital-letter words (such as "Family Values") reveals a tropism toward refined thought, since these words do not refer to palpable objects of experience. All ambitious members of our species love to think that they have a special relationship to arcane but practice-transforming reservoirs of knowledge, and this idea is difficult to disabuse, or even moderate, without a change in their self-conception that brings them back to earth.

Much evil has been either perpetrated or excused for the sake of ideas, by people too complacently attached to the dictates of their heads and too easily detached from the calmer promptings of their hearts. Habitués of the airier chambers of the mind are better equipped to cozen themselves than other people are. Our century affords abundant examples. Heidegger was able to give reflective reinforcement to the Third Reich while overlooking its darker sides, but such a reflective person should be better able than the fearful burgher to see the direction the nation is taking. To whom much is given much shall be required. Sartre and other refined Frenchmen pretended not to see, and perhaps really did not see, the inhumanities practiced by the Soviet Union, but rendered their approval or acquiescence because their theories either silenced their sentiments or allowed them to conceal the irresolution of their characters. Such people furnish us with shameful examples, simply put, and they bring vastly more discredit on the life of reason than any ironical Humean deflation ever would. Cruelty smells sour under any name, and letting a name conceal an odor is perhaps the least agreeable consequence of an uncorrected rationalist disposition.[5]

5. The responsibilities that intellectuals bear for what they say and write in a world inhabited mainly by nonintellectuals, who often do unsavory things that are reflectively reinforced, is a large and frequently disturbing topic. Tony Judt, in *Past Imperfect* (Berkeley and

It is striking, incidentally, that uncorrected intellectuals are often so massively ironical about the schemes, passions, and concerns of ordinary life that they have no irony left for their own schemes, passions, and concerns. This phenomenon plainly shows the incompleteness of their reflection. For we are dealing with conservatism in a new key, insofar as the uncorrected viewpoint merely reprises the thoughtless self-assurance we routinely observe in the unreflective, together with their facility in proffering nuance-free dismissals of persons and practices that do not precisely conform to their own evaluative postures. We have much of the bad side of the unreflective life in evidence here, with very little of its good (which is its tendency not to take itself, and its muddles, too seriously). This observation gives us another case study for the benign skeptic, since a headlong desire to separate ourselves from ordinary practice, far from being satisfiable, results in a ghostly caricature of that from which we would distinguish ourselves. And thus the Humean critical turn represents a more perfect reflection. When we taste the tang of the common cask in the wine we make, we begin to neutralize the self-deceptive impulses that lead unto caricature, and begin to cultivate a genuinely more enlightened appreciation of humankind.

There is another reason for thinking our refined self-discovery is valuable, though at first sight it appears to be at right angles to the reason that we have just considered. When we see the basis on which we believe and act, we are surprised that we *can* believe or act at all, that our elaborate conceptions and sophisticated performances do not collapse under their own weight. For we seem so little different from the perishing brutes that never think about quantum mechanics or that never undertake commitments to fulfill myriad obligations to their families, friends, colleagues, and governments, that we dimly suspect we shall psychologically relapse into a lower rung of animality as a consequence of our making the discovery. But the naturalistic conception has a great advantage in the long run, despite a possibly bumpy start. When we consider how similar the operations of our minds are to those of the lower animals, we should eventually be struck by how much more successful we are at doing things than they are. We start with little, but end, comparatively speaking, with so very much, and hence we should come to feel pride in our capacity. Indirectly, our self-discovery is a mighty confidence builder; and, as we know from experience, confidence begets achievements

---

Los Angeles: University of California Press, 1992), examines the public record of French intellectuals in the 1944–56 period, and that record should give us pause.

that further secure our confidence, which begets other achievements, and so on. "Nothing carries a man through the world like a true genuine natural impudence" (MPL 553), and the same can be said for collections of men and women, who are able, "tho' subject to all human infirmities," to produce a "composition, that is, in some measure, exempted from all these infirmities" (T 539).[6]

Hume advances the empowerment line of thought in a few places. The Sceptic holds that there are two important effects to be expected from philosophy; and although he says "books of philosophy," which may indicate some distance on his part, the effects to be had from these books are ones that he to some extent endorses. (The true philosophy can be extracted from the false.) The first is that we notice "how despicable seem all our pursuits of happiness . . . how frivolous appear our most enlarged and most generous projects" (MPL 176). This corresponds to the first reason, the disabusing we undergo. The second effect, which concerns me now, is that philosophy corrects our "natural infirmity" of comparing our situation with that of beings more perfect than we are by making us compare it with beings less perfect: philosophy, by properly making the eye turn downward, secures us in our feeling for ourselves (MPL 177). The Sceptic does not say why the downward gaze occurs as it does, through philosophy, but I have tried to provide an explanation in the preceding paragraph, and we can also detect within the Sceptic's essay the reasoning that makes the thought appropriate. The failure of rationalism, with its perpetual upward gaze, only brings the Sceptic's and the reader's attention more forcefully back to the animal kingdom, and so we in fact arrive at a downward comparison. (The way up is the way down, as Heraclitus sententiously says.) Nor does the Sceptic say why we are secured, apart from a suggestion that the downward gaze affords us an opportunity for a rather empty invidious comparison, a little *Schadenfreude*. If this were the sum of the securing, it would be a hollow triumph, but that it is not the sum is apparent from Hume's essay "Of the Dignity or Meanness of Human Nature."

The essay concerns that once-popular topic, whether human nature is more depraved (or deprived) or more divine, a topic not without twentieth-century echoes or relevance. The opposition is independently intriguing because we do not typically encounter a specimen of a pure view, an alignment solidly in one direction or the other. The theologians who are

---

6. Hume is talking about government at T 539, but the point he is making is general enough to cover all instances of collective human achievement.

most apt to stress depravity are also among the most insistent that we have a divine affiliation (though we have to go through the right spiritual exercises to make the affiliation a congenial one). Similarly, the secular counterparts of these theologians, the Hobbists and the Mandevilleans as well as our rationalist friends, stress our natural blindness and ineptitude, but their critiques presuppose a more elevated standpoint from which the critique is delivered, and so the blindness and ineptitude cannot be entire. Hume continues the mixing of the two sides, but with him we have the gentlest shadings of the two components. Yes, we bungle things, but that is no justification for indignant moralistic harrumphings, and, yes, we improve upon our arrangements here below, but we shall never so improve upon them that we will have any grounds for thinking that we are angels in disguise. Hume mutes, at both ends, the bold colors the theologians (and their only slightly paler secular brethren) go in for, and he implicitly recommends that we enter what Nietzsche called the temperate zone of culture.[7] As such, all these pairings of the high and the low can fund either pro or contra attitudes toward ourselves, and Hume's is no exception (although the bolder emotions of exhilaration or despair would seem to be ruled out).

Given the option, Hume recommends the pro attitude, and he bases his recommendation (MPL 82) on the kind of grounds I have suggested, the panoply of things we can do in comparison with the other animals. Here, in this essay, he seems to think that this comparison is the natural one to make, and that special (and more dubious) considerations must be brought to bear in order to defeat it. As for the naturalness of the comparison, Hume is right: we only have the other animals to keep us company (barring developments in artificial intelligence or contacts with extraterrestrials), and we look ravishing next to them. As for the special considerations, Hume is also right, though, if we go by this essay alone, it is a little difficult to see why. Apart from offering the well-taken but limited point that we should not evaluate the class of human beings by its most illustrious exemplars, Hume says that we should not disallow the comparison by "forming a new and secret comparison between man and beings of the most perfect wisdom" (MPL 83). But why should our reach not exceed our grasp? Hume's unexpanded remarks make it sound as though we determine our point of comparison through a voluntarist

---

7. In *Human, All Too Human*, section 236, Nietzsche contrasts humankind's more "tropical" past, where contrasts were more sharply drawn and keenly felt, with our present culture: "a light, though not brilliant sky; pure, rather unchanging air; briskness, even cold occasionally" (trans. Marion Faber and Stephen Lehmann [Lincoln: University of Nebraska Press, 1984]).

choice, and this impression is unfortunate because Hume has the resources, from his naturalism, for making the choice nonvoluntarist (if there is a choice at all). It is because we are ontologically continuous with the animals that comparisons with them are more appropriate. The other comparison entails an egregious appeal to ignorance, since, as the skeptical arguments point up, we have no good idea of how our manner of existence could be continuous with that of a "being of the most perfect wisdom."

This naturalism-based reason for thinking the self-discovery salutary appears to cut against the grain of the first, but in fact it does not. We must distinguish between a false pride, whose causal foundation is too modest to support the feeling (except in effigy, which accounts for the falsity), and a true pride, whose causal foundation supports the feeling. Our reflective self-discovery enfeebles the false pride while strengthening the true, and so there is no informal contradiction. The pride we have in a faculty that corrects itself, or that we fancy gives us access to recondite truths via self-aggrandizing reliance on it, is a house of cards that begins to totter under the pressure of Humean reflection. The pride we have in those faculties which allow us to redress our animal infirmities, and which therefore make something new possible under the sun, is augmented because we see how much our achievements cost. As my contrast shows, there is a difference in the causes of these two forms of pride, a difference that in large part explains their complexion. The first cause evaporates upon a closer view, produces no fruit, and can only be sustained by increasingly desperate metafictions. We are in the position of the plagiarist who tries to create applause for himself so that he can counterfeit the feeling that honest achievement brings (T 324). The second cause is honest because the achievements are shareable and not destabilized by reflection. Our social self-corrections are unheroic because the achievements we offer to the race require patient and multiple assessments by our fellows; this pride in the "dignity of human nature" cannot be traced to the luxuriations of a single person, or to a single group of illustrious exemplars. The Humean moral valet must see the genuine achievements of the master he serves if the debunkings that his intimacy makes possible are to stand innocently.

And another difference between the two prides is worth noting, though it should not be surprising. The pride that is born of patient achievement arises generally as a by-product. We do our work, and the pride then creeps in unawares. With the false sort, this element of indirection is difficult to discern, at least in a pure—that is, unpremeditated—form. To be proud of an imagined supramammalian prowess seemingly requires, at some node in the generation of the pride, a direct intention either to procure or to retain the feeling. We have the need to *prove* our worth to ourselves or others, and this need speaks against the object to be proved. Pride grows best in the dark, and coaxing a growth raises skeptical questions that are difficult to dismiss, unless we, returning to the plagiaristic approach, feign unpremeditatedness. Hume, too, is uncomfortable with semiconscious pride mongering, and a concealed intention is the problem, it seems, with persons who have "an ill-grounded conceit of themselves" and who consequently seek out "some person, that is more foolish," to keep up their spirits (T 596). This discomfort is also apparent in the Sceptic's reluctance to grant the downward gaze a complete endorsement, in that "a very good-natured person" will not be elevated by what he sees (MPL 177). But I suspect that the Sceptic really means that a good-natured person will not *want* to be elevated by the downward gaze. A virtuously proud, good-natured person can hardly avoid these comparisons (which, in the usual course of things, are made between him and other persons), but making the comparison is not a motivator.

This examination of the false pride and the true lets us make an important observation about conservatism and irrationalism. The conservative generally denies that our practices have the pride-scotching frailty that the Humean insists upon. Our practices stand strong and secure for the conservative, and often with, or because of, supernatural backing. On the other hand, the irrationalist recognizes the frailty and celebrates it, but tends to be averse to recognizing the pride-supporting strength the Humean equally insists upon. The irrationalist will not listen patiently when the history of our collective, constructive groping is set before him, and (not unlike the rationalist) supposes that if he individually cannot perform an action, it cannot be done.

A final comment before leaving (2): That benign skepticism seconds a desirable form of pride should remove many of the misgivings that some of us have about our ability to maintain our sense of social conviction in the face of a naturalized self-understanding. Bernard Williams calls this sense of conviction *confidence*, and we should agree with him that "philosophy cannot tell us how to bring it about."[8] Williams seems to be disappointed, however, by the silence of philosophy, and seems to think that philosophy amplifies the silence, making confidence less available than it would otherwise be. As for the silence itself, I do not see that there is any reason for disappointment. The confidence we have in our practices can only derive from natural inclination,

---

8. *Ethics and the Limits of Philosophy*, 170.

and it is unlikely that the reflective detachment from practice could ever be so great as to make us lose confidence in the whole. (We can of course lose confidence in parts of our practice, and that is frequently a good thing.) It seems, therefore, that we have to worry much about losing touch with who we are and what we do. And as for the hand of philosophy in the matter, I strongly agree that rationalism can produce loss of confidence—the malign skeptical arguments conduce to that very end—but rationalism, as I have said before, is incompletely reflective, and its incompleteness is, or should be, accessible to us. The more naturalized philosophy should not have this effect, since it discredits all projects that try to implant or remove confidence from above.

(3) *Not only should reason accord with natural propensity, but natural propensity should accord with reason.* In my zeal to chasten the rationalist, it may have passed unobserved that I was assuming the rationalist's defaulted obligations. When Hume says that reason must "mix" itself with natural propensity in order to be credible, he was also imposing a requirement on the propensity: it needs to be such that it can mix with reason. The relationship Hume envisages has to be symmetric, since neither reason nor nature stands by itself. Our prereflective nature provides the test for reason: if a point of view can be consistently embodied, have concrete universality, then the test is passed. But similarly, our reflective (second) nature provides a test for the propensity: if a propensity cannot be endorsed by naturalized reason, then we should strive either to curb it or, better, find an endorsable outlet for it. A necessary condition for nonendorsement would be realized if the propensity were such that we could resist acting on it, or resist expressing it in a certain way. (Humean reason always bends its judgment in favor of those ingrained dispositions we cannot resist.) A sufficient condition for nonendorsement would perhaps be the unmodified propensity's destructiveness to the basic social preconditions for individual flourishing. (This may sound like a weak condition—surely many propensities are compatible with the maintenance of a society—but we should not want our skeptical position to have too many first-order normative teeth in it.) Let us consider examples.

By the end of "The Sceptic," the Epicurean stands higher than the Stoic or Platonist because, I would argue, his life is more livable than theirs (where livability encompasses compatibility with undistorted, self-aware reflection). The sentiments that variously make a person an Epicurean, Stoic, or Platonist are thus not on all fours. The Stoic and Platonist are not simply condemned (they are not dangerous), but they are not allowed simply to get away with their grandiloquent speeches. The Epicurean, too, is not simply accepted (his rhapsodizing about his frolics with Caelia, while heartwarming, bespeak a greenness of sensibility that is foreign to the more jaded Sceptic), but his track is a better one. Of course, I am going beyond anything the Sceptic says, since he does not line up his companions and give us reviews. But the Sceptic is a critic more than a performer—the title of his essay, alone of the quartet, does not have a footnote telling us that the described figure is a "man of X" (where X indicates a manner of life)—and we can safely hazard the reviews he would give. These attributable evaluations can be regarded as the deliverances of Humean reason.

The Sceptic would discuss his companions, I believe, in much the same way that Hume's ideal critic in "Of the Standard of Taste" discusses literary productions: partly in their own terms, with an eye to their distinctive particularities, how they achieve their effects, and the audiences to which they are addressed, and partly in the terms that our all-things-considered reflective normativity specifies. A literary production should not offend our moral sense, and this requirement is not so Mrs. Grundyish as it sounds, because Hume's moral sense is not, as we have seen, a punishing, censorious internal voice but merely the voice of the world that speaks, unexcitedly and with urbane indulgence, after all the evidence is in.[9] Such a voice is necessary because we need a stable point of view, and the moral sense we bring to the appreciation of a work is a component of, and is sharpened by, the standard of taste that the reflective critic exemplifies. This standard does not certify itself, and although it presupposes the relevance of various points of view, it does not rubber-stamp them. We begin with a taste for what we like in both works and persons, and as our experience grows more extensive, we find that our taste and our capacity for causally explaining it become increasingly bound to each other—so much so that we may not be able to identify our taste very well without the causal explanation. But then these judgments should stand up when the omniperspectival eye of the world looks upon them, an eye that a judicious critic imaginatively instantiates. And this is just another way of characterizing the seconding of reason.

9. Toward the end of "Of the Standard of Taste" Homer nods, unfortunately. Hume writes that when the moral notions in older literature differ from our own, the difference constitutes a "real deformity" in the work. "I cannot, nor is it proper that I should, enter into such sentiments; and however I may excuse the poet, on account of the manners of his age, I never can relish the composition" (MPL 246). I argue elsewhere that such a judgment is out of alignment with the rest of Hume's philosophy; see "False Delicacy," forthcoming in *Feminist Interpretations of David Hume*, ed. Anne Jaap Jacobson (University Park: Pennsylvania State University Press).

Since I have expatiated so much on heroism, I might conclude this discussion of my first thesis by considering Hume's explicit criticism of the more familiar kind of heroism, treating his criticism as an example of the kind of stance open to the benign skeptic. Hume relies on naturalized reason when he disparages military glory late in the *Treatise* (in a passage where the vocal practical moralist makes his last appearance), though he also shows, as we might expect, considerable generosity toward the natural propensity to admire this glory, and so his brief account yields an elegant example of the preferred interrelationship of spontaneous inclination and reflection in the seasoned mind. "Men of cool reflexion are not so sanguine in their praises" of military derring-do as the larger population is, and the cool reflectors withhold their accolades on account of the destruction these heroes cause (T 600–601). This destructiveness is so discernible that there should be no difficulty mixing this reflection with our natural propensities. Nevertheless, when we cool reflectors look directly at the hero whom the populace acclaims, "there is something so dazling in his character, the mere contemplation of it so elevates the mind, that we cannot refuse it our admiration" (T 601). Even though we should correct this judgment, one suspects that Hume thinks that something would be a bit amiss if we did not feel the less reflective sentiment, that "he must be more or less than man, who kindles not in the common blaze" (E 275), and that a critic who did not so kindle would not be a critic we should trust. We should definitely oppose the popular sentiment, but not unless we also hear the sometimes terrifying bells that ring for us and for those whom we would correct. This is the most difficult kind of criticism to do, since our natural propensities to accept and to reject are aroused simultaneously, and it requires much good sense to cast a philosophical vote against the military hero and the military virtues.

Since we can be reasonably assured that critical reflection is both possible and desirable on Humean grounds, let us turn to a darker side of our self-portrait, where we shall uncover some Humean grounds for pessimism, though not about reflection in general but about the kind that rationalism itself, in a more intellectualized form, exemplifies. As I intimated earlier, rationalism does not even help to apprise us of these grounds. To show why, I want to comment, tendentiously, on Hume's *Natural History of Religion*, an unfortunately neglected text that has much to offer the philosopher of mind and moral psychologist (as well as the reader of Hume who wishes to see what may be the remoter sources of Hume's discontent with rationalism). To motivate this excursus, however, I first need to say a few words about religion and philosophy, and about some different styles of each.

The historical and thematic connections between religious and philosophical practices are profound, as we are well aware, and it is possible for us, as observing naturalists, to compare the two kinds of practice with an eye to teasing out whatever interesting cultural resemblances obtain between them. If we countenance the propriety of this procedure, we can then examine an especially interesting resemblance, one that holds between the monotheist and rationalist on the one hand, and the polytheist and nonrationalist on the other. Like rationalism, monotheism is a late development, arising from an intellectually more inscrutable host practice, which it then transforms. Like rationalism, monotheism is superior to its host on *merely* intellectual grounds. But also like rationalism, monotheism is ultimately inferior if we take a suitably and defensibly broad—that is, more than intellectual—frame of reference from which to make our evaluation. To see how monotheism goes astray is arguably to see, at an ur-level, how rationalism goes astray.

If we are in doubt about the parallelism of the two pairs, we might, in the light of my earlier discussions of disembodiment, compare the representations of the gods before and after the theologians get hold of them. We listen to the exploits of craggy, irascible old Zeus, and we are entertained; we recognize in him a type of character, and we imagine a life for him. That life is certainly larger than ours, and not just in the sense that Zeus can do a few more physical tricks than we can. Even though Zeus must have the blues or become bored from time to time, we do not suspect that he is blue or bored for long. (Of course, his more expressive, and expressively expansive, temperament may be, and probably is, connected with his greater physical capacities, but they are still not the same thing.) And if Zeus strikes us as being a limited character (as all characters are), we can shift our attention to Athena, or any of the other members of the pantheon.

By the time we reach the Christian era, we notice a certain evisceration. Jesus is a rather epicene shepherd whose seemingly inexhaustible fascination with counting his flock makes him a little mysterious, a little harder for us to grasp as a complete person. In this diminished recognition, this newer inscrutability, we detect the influence of an ordering theology, but we do have a visible character nonetheless. But by the time the god of the philosophers is fully on board, we do not have an embodied person at all. Instead, we have withering theorems that demonstrate his existence, with many complicated steps and obscure inferential principles, and nobody has any idea what his (his?) manner of life could be like (or even knows if the language we use to describe persons is appropriate any longer for describing the divine). And if we do not have the theorems, we have fairly misty talk about the object of our ultimate concern, often accompanied by some morally earnest hand-wringing and furrowed brows. In these forms, this god appeals only to bookish folk who are high-minded or to social activists who are high-minded, and one suspects that a deep emotional attachment to some ethical conception of the world—an attachment that argument alone is powerless to produce—is what propels the imagination in the absence of a discernible person. (The raising of a moralistic tone that we encounter as we advance to a more perfect monotheism, and the factitious seriousness of that tone, are characteristic of rationalism also.)

Still, the superiority of polytheism must be argued for, and the unobviousness of this superiority counts as some evidence in favor of the claim that primitively rationalistic tendencies in the mind help to cloud the waters. To exhibit this superiority we can rely on Hume. Now the *Natural History of Religion* is a difficult work to interpret, with regard to at least some of Hume's intentions, because its topic is religion, and Hume's methodology makes a touchy topic even touchier. Hume's antipathy to Christianity is of course very familiar ("The Church is my aversion," as he once declared),[10] yet it can be difficult—more difficult than it at first appears—to find a principled basis for an objection to religion in Hume's account of human nature. Against those who would claim that our moral sense results from "the artifice of politicians," Hume argues that the "materials" for moral notions are already present in human nature, before the politicians ply their trade; if the materials were not already there, it would be "vain" for the politicians even to attempt to govern us through the alleged art (T 500).[11] A similar type of argument could be advanced for our "religious sense"—no amount of priestcraft alone could explain the priests' success—and yet Hume does not advance such an argument.[12]

---

10. Quoted in Ernest Campbell Mossner, *The Life of David Hume* (Austin: University of Texas Press, 1954), 234.

11. Terence Penelhum has discussed a closely related issue for Hume in *God and Skepticism* (Dordrecht: Reidel, 1983), chap. 6. The issue concerns what Penelhum calls the Parity Argument, which holds that "many of the secular beliefs of common sense or science with which faith is contrasted are themselves beliefs which we cannot justify by reason either, so that the contrast is a bogus one for that reason" (30). Fideism and benign skepticism have a great deal in common, on formal grounds, and so one type of critique of religious thinking—the intellectualistic—is not obviously available to this type of skepticism.

12. He even disallows such an argument in the second *Enquiry*. We are told that the power of "the principle of precept and education" is such that it "may even, in particular circumstances, create, without any natural principle, a new sentiment . . . as is evident in all superstitious practices and observances" (E 214). Hume became increasingly pessimistic toward

Questions of Hume's methodology aside, we also have to deal with the very guarded theistic pronouncements in the text. Hume speaks of something he calls "genuine Theism" (NHR 309) and apparently endorses. I assume, without argument, that "genuine Theism" is little more than an empty phrase, largely put in for camouflage—though probably indicating a topic that Hume, by his own lights, must sincerely regard as "a riddle, an aenigma, an inexplicable mystery" (NHR 363).[13] More controversially, I want to say that Hume sees things my way on the issue of the superiority of polytheism (I will argue a little for this). My intention, however, is not to offer a detailed interpretation of this work; I shamelessly want to raid it for a gem that I desire.

Polytheism arises "from a concern with regard to the events of life, and from the incessant hopes and fears, which actuate the human mind" (NHR 315). We survey the operations of nature, not with a dispassionate eye, but with our well-being firmly in view. (Pragmatism is the most ancient philosophy, as well as the newest.) Our emotions affect our perceptions through our tendency to personify things: "We find human faces in the moon, armies in the clouds; and by a natural propensity, if not corrected by experience and reflection, ascribe malice or good-will to every thing, that hurts or pleases us" (NHR 317). The beings we project onto the natural order are "like ourselves; only somewhat superior in power and wisdom" (NHR 328); and we seek to propitiate them by periodic pious observances, expecting thereby to win their favor and lead happier lives. Typically, we populate the pantheon "with continual recruits from among mankind," with historical figures who receive their apotheosis after death (NHR 327). We could say that this elevation involves an augmented personification of beings who are already persons, but the augmentation is continuous with the ex nihilo personification of seeing faces in clouds.

---

the end of his life, however, about the prospects for the demise of the Christian religion: the more inveterate the religious impulse, the harder it is to maintain, on Humean grounds, that the impulse is *merely* "created."

13. As with the evils that afflict our existence, here too we have a convergence in judgment between Demea and Philo, in *Dialogues*, Part II. Demea maintains that God's perfections "are covered in a deep cloud from human curiosity; it is profaneness to attempt penetrating through these sacred obscurities" (13)—while Philo says that "just reasoning and sound piety . . . establish the adorably mysterious and incomprehensible nature of the Supreme Being" (15). One might suppose that Philo is playing to the galleries. But, then again, if it is *truly* the case that God is "adorably mysterious," then silence on sacred subjects would evince a truer piety than Demea's orthodox religion, which in garrulous bad faith actually rolls aside a most generous portion of the "deep cloud." So which of the two speakers has the greater levity?

Two comments about this personification: (i) It relies on the projection of resemblances, and since I have laid great stress on the resemblance-extending powers of the mind, Hume's criticism of it here needs to be explained. The extension in this instance is not just a continuation of a mental motion along resemblant perceptions; it is definitely a projection, where we impose, say, the psychological structure of a deceased person on an inanimate object. If we ask how a projection differs from an exercise of Humean sympathy, we might not be able to tell the difference if we are consulting the narrowly phenomenological reports that sympathizers and projectors can give us. But with a person, we have independent evidence, beyond the feel of the projection, that we are dealing with a mind-bearing organism. We do not have this with the face in the clouds, or the hero in the grave, and we need that evidence before we can acquiesce in our mental motion. Once we have that, our sympathetic responses are to be trusted rather than distrusted. (ii) Hume immediately goes on to say that personification occurs regularly in the arts, but that its influence is restricted to the imagination, where the personification does not induce belief. Hume's remark is interesting because it shows the proximity between ancient gods and modern artworks in his thinking. We even have a basis for calling the gods art-entities falsely accepted as real entities.

The chief problem with polytheism is the ignorance that envelops the projection and that makes polytheism descriptively false of the world we live in. The ignorance is of two kinds. The first is just simple ignorance of connections in the causal order. Our ancestors, like other animals, witnessed an unending pageant of natural events, some of which our ancestors thought quite marvelous—a term I neutrally use for any imaginatively arresting unusual event. As Hume's discussion of alleged miracles in Section X of the first *Enquiry* shows, the marvelous events are those which demand patient causal explanation, but this explanatory patience is what our ancestors were incapable of, and so the projective causal explanation leaps into the felt vacancy, at once an effect and a cause of ignorance. I suspect that an awareness of the marvelous is inseparable from this kind of ignorance and error. Although Hume elsewhere freely speaks of the reason of animals, he does not speak of the superstition of animals; and if superstition were truly primitive, then we should expect to find superstitious habits of mind among our mammalian cousins. When Hume speaks of the causal inferences of animals, his examples are always of the most orderly and respectable kind: horses learning by experience how high they can leap, dogs knowing what a raised whip portends (E 105; cf. T 178). Their minds are less likely to be derailed, I conjecture, because they do not perceive an event as marvelous (a perception that would seemingly require that the perceiver's mind not be confined to a "narrow circle of objects"). The mind attuned to the marvelous creates a special ignorance for itself that only laborious, protracted future causal inferences are capable of dispelling.[14]

The second kind of ignorance is causal as well, but it is also self-directed. Our ancestors were presumably not aware that they were projecting (otherwise they would not have believed their projections), and this sort of knowledge about the self must arrive very late to consciousness. The patiently acquired knowledge that dispels the special ignorance is hard enough to come by, but the knowledge that we are the source of the marvelous (a discovery that reimplants the marvelous, aesthetically tamed, in our own breasts) is even harder. We could then say that the polytheist produces his distinctive mental constructs through an underinterpretation of his experiences, but this failure to interpret far enough is exceedingly likely because of his unpropitious epistemic circumstances—so likely that I am inclined to think that an intelligent animal species could not occupy higher conceptual ground without first stocking its mental cabinet with the superstitious curiosities we find here.

Apart from this enveloping ignorance, I do not see much else, on Humean grounds, to condemn in polytheism. The propitiatory rites furnished our ancestors with a festival atmosphere and reinforced seasonal rhythms, and these offices are hardly unwholesome in themselves. Moreover, the gods who are "like ourselves, only somewhat superior," heighten our sense of self-worth because we feel that their magnificence is within our grasp at the same time that their foibles prevent them from becoming oppressive. (A similar dynamic is visible in the influence of literary models, as described by Hume in "Of the Rise and Progress of the Arts and Sciences.") This heightening of self-worth is incidentally also the explanation for Nietzsche's metaphor of the transfiguring mirror, which appears in his description of the Greek art-religion: "In order to glorify themselves, its creatures had to feel themselves worthy of glory; they had to behold themselves again in a higher sphere, without this perfect world of contemplation acting as a command or a

---

14. Hume also does not attribute to the animals "curiosity, or the love of truth," which is "an affection of so peculiar a kind" that he was not able to treat it under any of the passion headings in Book Two of the *Treatise* (T 448). Intuitively, the love of truth seems to presuppose a capacity for appreciating the marvelous: if so, barbarism and the exposé of barbarism are fruit of the same fey tree.

reproach."[15] An aesthetically perfect god would be a human, all too human god with a host of nonaesthetic imperfections, blind spots, points concerning which we would feel free to criticize her (or him), but whose aesthetic perfection would be unveiled in the recognitive invigoration that our imaginative engagement produces. This idea is not foreign to Hume either, as we will find shortly.

But let us first introduce monotheism to our scene. Monotheism emerges from polytheism when believers "represent one god as the prince or supreme magistrate of the rest, who, though of the same nature, rules them with an authority, like that which an earthly sovereign exercises over his subjects and vassals" (NHR 330). The god who is favored by this strengthening is of course a god with whom we have some sort of friendly relationship (we do not strengthen the gods of our enemies), and so we strengthen ourselves indirectly, but at a certain cost, for by making our god a cosmos-bestriding colossus (for we now have the first associations between a god and Original Causation) we expose ourselves intimately and inescapably, as we had not been exposed before, to the consequences of incurring the god's displeasure. We can run but cannot hide from such a god, and the mind is increasingly attracted to pacification techniques. There is an element of this concern in polytheism, too, but the monotheistic turn brings in divine sanctions whose scope extends to the penetralia of the mind; concomitantly, where polytheism promoted more familial relations between gods and mortals, monotheism is more contractual. We must do, and increasingly must think, what the god prescribes, or else the breach-of-contract clauses go into effect. Thus, while we enjoy an enhancement of our stature owing to our cliently affiliation with the colossus, our new servility shows that the cost of empire is high.

Hume says that "adulation and fears" (NHR 330) carry the mind to the colossal god, and these mental dispositions are not the same as those which carried us to the polytheistic bevy of competing and mutually influence-modifying divinities. There were many sources of fear in the original scene, but the fear was directed at the prodigies of nature. Here the fear is aimed at the god who from behind orchestrates the entire natural show. Since fear is hardly a comforting passion, one that we wish to nurture and to keep, we cannot suppose that the mind is attracted to a single god by fear, however much the mind's attachment may be sustained by it. So we must look to "adulation" as providing the initial gravitational pull.

Polytheism resulted when our unbounded fancy was hoist with its own

---

15. *The Birth of Tragedy*, trans. Walter Kaufmann (New York: Vintage, 1967), sec. 3.

projective petard. The false inference depended on a failure to separate causes and effects, horizontally within the world and vertically from us to the world. Monotheism results when our more bounded fancy (bound, that is, to one god) succumbs to adulation. As my review of the origin of polytheism is meant to make clear, this adulation has to involve a very different mental miscarriage. The adulator is not confounding causes and effects. So what do adulators do when they transform, say, Bacchus into Christ? It seems, to speak conjecturally, that two things happen. First, the adulator acquires an "ill-grounded conceit" of himself in some respect.[16] Bacchus is no longer acceptable just as Bacchus; he must be a world-historical Bacchus in order to ground the believer's relationship. Second, the adulator engages in what I can only think of as a great deal of intense peering at the god, in his imagination (to be sure): looking very closely at Bacchus to see what nonobvious features he possesses that could entitle him to a world-historical inflation of his status. He who looks generally finds, and once the privileging features are selected, they furnish a standard by which to extrude, as anthropomorphisms, those which do not elevate Bacchus above his fellows. Monotheism would then be the result of subjecting a polytheistic projection to a scrutiny that seeks a better grounding for both projection and projector.

The monotheist's scrutiny is falsifying, but as with the polytheist's confused projection, the falsity is not necessarily apparent to the occasioning mind. I said earlier that the polytheist did not interpretively do enough with his experience; I wish to say that the monotheist does too much. We slide into polytheism passively, but we move into monotheism actively, with our hands, if not our eyes, much more open. Hence, the monotheistic metamorphosis is the result of what we might call an overinterpretation of the god. It is a more intriguing phenomenon than the passive slide, for its occurrence presupposes a certain measure of reflection, or inwardness, which is more difficult to uncover; and this inward view requires correction just as the outward view that gave us polytheism did. And even more correction: for the monotheistic turn actually destroys those goods which polytheism promoted and secured.

That the overinterpretive attempt to ground shaky emotion-invested projections accomplishes this destruction is made evident in four extraordinary sections (9–12) of the *Natural History*. Hume compares the social effects

---

16. I do not mean to imply, as my tag from Hume may suggest, that the believer's shakiness is necessarily a psychological phenomenon, due to an unsound temperament. On the contrary, I suspect that the ill-grounding is probably more the result of sociological developments: material prosperity, increased contact with neighboring cultures and their gods, and so on.

of the two kinds of religion in four areas, and on every count monotheism comes out unequivocally the loser. By juxtaposing mono- and polytheism, and by displaying the evident disparity in their effects, Hume is tacitly exhibiting polytheism as the worthier vehicle for the religious sentiments (within, to repeat, the nonendorsable framework of error that overarches both).

Before we look at the comparison, it may help to clarify the import of the polytheistic win. By Hume's own nonrationalist standards, the various effects he cites, which are effects on the imagination and sensibility, should outweigh, in our reflective evaluation of the two kinds of religions, considerations of mere abstract intellectual perspicuousness. Monotheism does have the upper hand (slightly) on intellectual grounds: we have a philosophical tendency to favor a single-god account if we are to have any theistic account at all (and the attractions of that tendency are handsomely apparent in Descartes's *Meditation Three*). But if our Humean philosophy is sound, this recommendation will be feeble if there are, at the reflective level, imaginative and emotional considerations that counteract it. This is my principal argument for thinking that Hume, under the uncertain layers of camouflage, is really plumping for the polytheist.

For supporting evidence, it is possible to draw parallels between the monotheism-polytheism pair and the pair of "false religions" that is the subject of Hume's essay "Of Superstition and Enthusiasm." The two pairs are not the same, but they do have notable similarities. Hume observes that enthusiasm, by which he means the imaginatively exuberant religion that confident, rapturous minds embrace—the religion of the Quakers, Anabaptists, Levelers, and Covenanters—tends to be inimical to priestly authority, to leave the mind (and society) calmer over time, and to promote civil liberty (MPL 75–79). Hume the moralist strongly favors enthusiasm over superstition, whose greater oppressiveness he associates with Roman Catholicism.

Let us now consider the polytheism-monotheism comparisons, the first of which concerns social harmony. The monotheist by raising his god to preeminence perforce lowers the others, and those other gods, along with their devotees, become full-blown pariahs. The monotheist is accordingly a great persecutor. The polytheist, on the other hand, has built-in latitudinarian principles, and even when a polytheistic culture conquers a people, the conquerors indulgently add the new faith to the existing religious structure. Of course, if the conquerors are adding a monotheistic faith, there could be problems, though mainly on the monotheistic side. "So social is polytheism, that the utmost fierceness and antipathy, which it meets with in an opposite religion, is scarcely able to disgust it, and keep it at a distance" (NHR 338). Hume reveals, albeit elliptically, the sociableness of polytheism by noting that Augustus was pleased by his grandson's refusal to sacrifice at Jerusalem, because he deemed the monotheists (merely) ignoble, not because, it is implied, he thought that they had a wrong conception of the gods. Had Augustus thought *that*, he probably would have approved a considerably more violent gesture than that of refusing to participate in the local rites. This last idea might be amplified along other Humean lines. Since groups of people are more likely to have different theoretical opinions than different feelings,[17] and since feelings can accommodate a plurality of theories better than a theory can accommodate a plurality of feelings, a feeling-based social rejection will be less common, as well as gentler, than one that is theory-based.

Hume does not deny that polytheists can be a scurvy crew at times. Their ignorance invites barbarism. Even so, he passingly observes that their cruelty is better than that which the monotheists practice. The human sacrifices of the natives of Mexico do not poison society in the way that the corresponding sacrifices of the Spanish Inquisition did, because the indigenous Mexicans chose their victims by lot,[18] whereas the inquisitors chose theirs by insidious, antiliberal design. Hume does not go into much detail on this point, but he is clearly right. An utterly random selection of a victim has an innocence about it; the selection is not indexed to the maintaining of specific beliefs, and so it could fall or not fall on anybody, like jury duty, regardless of what any of the society's members do or think. If the selection is indexed to beliefs, then incipient heterodox thinking (some of which will be helpfully innovative) must receive a powerful check, and also the fear-engendering labors of the executioners must be multiplied endlessly—finding the heretics

---

17. Hume makes this claim himself in "Of the Standard of Taste." Speaking specifically of moral feelings and theories of all kinds, he says, "The case is not the same with moral principles, as with speculative opinions of any kind. These are in continual flux and revolution. The son embraces a different system from the father. Nay, there scarcely is any man, who can boast of great constancy and uniformity in this particular" (MPL 246).

18. Incidentally, if we had to be guided by moral theories, we might do well to select them by lot, provided that we gave them strict term limits. We could be Kantians in the morning, Hobbists in the afternoon, utilitarians in the evening. We would be spared from taking any of them too seriously, and their angularities would probably cancel one another out. This would be the most natural, as well as most intelligible, method for implementing moral theories. (I owe this theory-by-lots idea to a conversation with Emily Hauptmann.)

(whose lives may be outwardly indistinguishable from those the faithful lead), making sure that they fail the relevant purity tests, and so on.

The second comparison concerns psychological fortitude. Hume here adduces the desire for emulation and achievement that polytheism promotes (which we have already noted) and the corresponding desire for ascetic self-abasement that is the legacy of monotheism. This second part calls for some comment. If a god becomes God, we might suppose that the votary merely becomes passive and inert after duly making the comparisons between himself and God. But inertness is not the consequence: the votary praises or practices various forms of self-injury, which are far from passive. "Instead of the destruction of monsters, the subduing of tyrants, the defence of our native country; whippings and fastings, cowardice and humility, abject submission and slavish obedience" succeed to the fore as the acceptable rites to perform for God (NHR 339–40). Hume does not explain why this violence occurs.

I believe that Hume is right, though we may have to have recourse to Nietzsche's essay on ascetic ideals (from *On the Geneology of Morals*) to fill out an explanation. In brief, Nietzsche's account comes to this: nobody wants to be *too* abased, even the most impotent, and so those who are abased, or who are convinced that they are, will try to demonstrate their smidgen of power (or perceived power) in self-lacerating exercises, driving themselves merrily enough deeper into the hole (thus shoring up their shaky belief in their own worthlessness, if it needs shoring, and confirming the power of the all-powerful Being, if it needs confirming).[19] Hume himself comes close, at the end of this section, to making Nietzsche's explanatory inference, and as a consequence I do not think joining Hume and Nietzsche here is to make an arbitrary pairing. Hume relates two anecdotes about persons who were bitten by animals, one that has a Greek hero, Brasidas, and the other a Catholic saint, Bellarmine. A mouse bites Brasidas, but he lets it go, saying that even a petty animal can be safe if it is willing to fight for itself. The fleas bite Bellarmine, and he lets them do so, saying that we, but not they, can expect a heavenly reward for our sufferings. A striking story, and Hume's laconic conclusion makes it an impressive Nietzschean text: "Such difference there is between a Greek hero and a Catholic saint" (NHR 340). The animals live in each case, but what we should notice is that the saint hopes for a reward

---

19. Nietzsche does not emphasize the possibility that the perception of impotence is simply false, as I have done, and although his essay is hospitable to this emphasis, I will not pursue this idea further here. Hume, however, explicitly takes a similar line in the fourth comparison, below.

merely by suffering the humiliations of infestation, by not acting, and this hope only makes sense on a Nietzsche-style explanation: Bellarmine's connivance at his own humiliation is pointless otherwise. Hume's emphases here are some evidence, then, that Hume had nearly anticipated a Nietzschean explanation.

The third comparison concerns doctrinal reasonableness. As intimated before, the monotheists have an initial advantage, so far as surface appearances go, but that advantage turns to naught on a larger view. To understand why, I should like to draw a distinction that Hume relies on, but does not make extremely plain, between the narrative and the theology of a religious practice. The narrative is the story, the plot, or the sensuous component of religious representations: Kronos's eating his children, Loki's slaying of Balder, Jesus' praying in Gethsemane. The theology, then, is the relatively unsensuous commentary on the narrative, the deeper analysis that eschews (or professes to eschew) imagery and parable in the interests of literal truth. In polytheism we have abundant narrative, but little theology. The narrative, or the narratives, as we should say, are so various and contradictory that theology does not have much of a place on which to light: it would be too comical, really, to unpack these stories, or to spend much time doing so. In monotheism we have some narrative, as always, but a profuse theology that like a vine overgrows its narrative support. The initial appearance of reasonableness attracts philosophical reinterpretation, which only converts the half-reasonableness of the original into absurdity. (Polytheism was false, but not really absurd.) Thus, the theologians fill many volumes about the Real Presence or the Trinity, and how best to understand these doctrines, which have no clear reference to ordinary bodies of evidence but about which we are assured that it is very important to have correct views. We have entered a fantasticated conceptual space, once again, similar to that which we were in while we were considering the double existence of perceptions and objects in Chapter 2.

The fourth, and final, comparison concerns the extent to which the religion penetrates either the imagination or practice. Hume does not describe the comparison in these terms, but since his discussion is diffuse, this formulation may serve to capture the various strands he brings together in it. Polytheism pleases the mind—it affords us "a true poetical religion" (NHR 349)—but its stories make no deep impression on the mind, on account of their multiplicity and noncodifiability. However, polytheism seems to sit fairly securely on practice. Cicero, who was an advanced thinker for his culture, showed no irony toward religious rituals, as when he bade his wife ("whom he highly trusted") to offer sacrifices to Apollo and Aesculapius (NHR 347). This situation mirrors, for us, the decorating of Christmas trees, a social practice in which even the village atheist can participate without qualms. Monotheism does strike deep into the intellectual reaches of the mind, and so deep that it becomes difficult for the believer to detect the absurdity in his doctrines, even though he can plainly detect them in those of other religionists. Its intellectual attractions notwithstanding, monotheism does not please the mind as a whole, and so its presence in practice is meager. The monotheistic believers are uncomfortable with this gap, and therefore "disguise to themselves their real infidelity, by the strongest asseverations and most positive bigotry" (NHR 348). They are rather like the castle builders in the *Treatise*, needing gimmicky belief enhancers to keep belief alive.

This pairing of religionists illustrates well the difference between the false consciousness that should be removed and the multiple consciousness that should be left alone. The tension between mind and practice causes the monotheist to resort to stratagems that remove, or reduce, the tension internally, but that only relocate it outdoors, so to speak: when he hurls bigoted epithets at persons of rival faiths, *he* does not feel the tension between his belief content and his life, which gives the lie to his belief, but *we* (including his addressee) feel a lively tension as an aftershock of his self-indulgent cure. (In general, it seems that do-it-yourself corrective performances, whether philosophical or popular, conscious or unconscious, usually work, if they do work, for the performer at the expense of the audience.) Since there is a straightforward harm to society because of this false consciousness, it is to be deprecated. And calling this consciousness false is fitting because of the stratagems involved, which are always intentional even if they are not conscious. With the polytheist we have simple alternation between sending a bird to Apollo and, let us suppose, thinking the thoughts of Lucretius: he is doing two things, or occupying two cognitive positions, that are incompatible only if we regard the performance of the rite as implicitly inviting us to accept the deductive closure of a theoretical system, so that sending the bird commits him to being a true believer in Apollo (whatever that might be). But no such systematicity is implied. Cicero merely forgets about his disbelief in Apollo when he sends the bird. *Not* calling this consciousness false is also accurate because there is no tension and (hence) no cover-up in Cicero. Finally, his participation in the rites of the folk religion forms an imaginative bond with the other participants, and such bonds promote, rather than undermine, social harmony. So the polytheist wins the fourth comparison on all counts.

At this point we can leave the *Natural History* and bring the present discussion to a close. The apparently orderly evolution of monotheism out of polytheism, in conjunction with the disparate effects of the two religious forms, gives us reason to believe that the route to self-correction is not straight and that straight paths should be greeted with skepticism. Theoretical indirection, however, does not threaten the possibility of normative progress, and on this latter score we do have reason to be confident. An aggressively active monotheism has waned somewhat since Hume's day (though, as recent events in the Mideast, Europe, and America remind us, we cannot expect a millennial elimination of its influence). In large measure we may thank our collective powers of self-improvement for the improvements, and thus we return to the first thesis of this chapter.

There is a close connection between giving reasons and having the hope that self-correction is possible. Because the Humean stance casts doubt on first-person-singular self-corrections, it can seem that loss of confidence is inevitable. But it is not. For if we take a view of our progress that is long enough, interpersonal and transgenerational enough, and if we do not look exclusively through the lens available to an individual person as he single-mindedly deliberates about what he can or should do to correct his steps, we shall not be in want of that moderate hope—and only moderate hope is available—which underwrites confidence.[20]

20. Throughout this chapter I have tried to reinterpret the worry about benign skeptical reflection as a worry about confidence. In this, I am once again speaking the nonrationalist language, but it is only in this language, I think, that we can satisfactorily address the important questions that Rorty raises (but does not by his own admission answer) in "Pragmatism, Relativism, and Irrationalism" (in *Consequences of Pragmatism* [Minneapolis: University of Minnesota Press, 1981]).

5

❈ ❈ ❈

Persons and Artworks

While we were still with the Sceptic, in Chapter 3, I spoke twice of a class of items that I called, without a great deal of fanfare, "objects of attention." These are modifiers of our point of view that embody points of view themselves, and they have two characteristics. The first is that their influence is intrinsically intermittent. By this I mean that they do not influence the mind constantly, but also that when they do influence it, the mind's acceptance is not entire or unreserved. The second is that their appeal is not intellectual, or primarily intellectual (if I may use "appeal" to speak indiscriminately of the satisfactions available to the mind). They satisfy our imagination and sensibility rather than our reason. These objects consequently have a strong aesthetic component, and they are, in the broadest sense of the term, aesthetic goods.[1]

A nonrationalist account of the person should give some pride of place to

---

1. My use of the word "object" is meant to be pretty colorless (as it is when philosophers speak of "intentional objects"), but the connection with the aesthetic will prompt us to deploy the much more specific sense that, for instance, informs the ethically charged concept of "objectification." Aesthetic objecthood does not, on my view, entail objectification.

these goods. In this chapter I begin—and only make a beginning with—the project of showing that these goods are not at all uncommon or unimportant (though their commonality or importance has often been unappreciated) and that the power of the nonrationalist account to explain their importance is a further recommendation of the account. The aesthetic goods I want to consider are, first of all, persons, which (because of the surprise that attends the very idea that persons have an aesthetic dimension) I discuss at considerable length. Second, I consider artworks, whose credentials as bearers of aesthetic value are more familiar to us, and so less space is needed for them—but I do wish to argue that the notion of art is less peripheral to our self-understanding as persons than it might otherwise seem if we reflect, provincially, on the various specialized activities we refer to as "the arts" or on the more shadowy entity that is still, and not without reverence, called fine art.

Nevertheless, it is one thing to seek a wider application for the notion of art, and another to insist that persons, at an important level of description, are aesthetic objects of attention. (Or so it seems: the distinctness of these claims will erode as we go along.) To call a person—or, as we might say, *the self*—an aesthetic good sounds exceedingly strange at first, and I think that the strangeness is traceable to two historical sources, both of which tend to obscure proper recognition of what should be the ordinary aesthetic dimension of the self. The first of these is the literary aestheticism[2] of the 1890s; the second is the philosophical picture of the person we have from Descartes, but whose outlines Kant sharpened. Although of the two aestheticism is the latecomer, it will be easier if we begin with it.

If it is suggested that the self has aesthetic qualities, which either admit of or are worthy of being noted and appreciated, our minds begin to wander back to the Mauve Decade, to the perfumed interiors of Pater and Wilde and Huysmans, to the connoisseurship of those who narcissistically collected exquisite sensations without drawing much of a distinction between (say) a Louis XIV escritoire and Louis XIV, the provenance of the sensations not being, for them, a matter of exceptional interest. Our minds may also wander to Nietzsche, or to certain interpretations of Nietzsche.[3] But let us stay with

---

2. This word is fairly new to the language. The *Oxford English Dictionary* records the first use in 1855, fittingly enough in a critical discussion of Tennyson's "Lotos-Eaters." The cited passage succinctly anticipates the later associations: "The *Lotos Eaters* carries Tennyson's tendency to pure aestheticism to an extreme point. It is picture and music and nothing more."

3. For instance, Alexander Nehamas's *Nietzsche: Life as Literature* (Cambridge: Harvard

the paradigm case. There is something decidedly charming—the choice of word is significant—about this aestheticism, provided it remains an affectation or pose and does not make the gritty descent into a serious lifestyle. If that happens, the charm evaporates, and the fetid air of the sickroom replaces it. When Huysmans's Des Esseintes wears a spray of Parma violets in lieu of a cravat, the regulation neckwear of the philistine, we smile at the harmless foppishness of the decision, but when he begins encrusting a tortoise with precious gems so that the animal will please the eye with its brilliant, multicolored coruscations, we start to squirm. And of course what is sauce for the tortoise is sauce for our fellow human beings, who seamlessly fit into the order of delectation providers if we succumb to the aestheticizing impulse.[4] We sense a loss, or abridgment, of humanity in this impulse.

Unfortunately, these aestheticist associations have become all but cemented to the idea that persons possess aesthetic qualities. The reason these associations are unfortunate is that the fin de siècle aesthetic is so thin that it does not even give us a passable understanding of our experience of art, much less our experience of people. We are asked to appreciate the candidates for delectation as if they had no reference to anything but the panoply of their own immediately perceivable properties (whatever those might be exactly), and it is the business of the aesthete to savor the delightful nuances of objects so conceived, which furnish the only standard of evaluation for those objects. Views of this sort were not uncommon at the turn of the century,[5] but to state the view carefully is virtually to refute it. Aestheticism discredits an extremely formalistic interpretation of the aesthetic, but not

---

University Press, 1985) can leave this impression, at least in part because of the suggestion that, according to Nietzsche, persons and literary characters may be interpreted and appraised in much the same way. There is another sort of aestheticism that also has a connection to Nietzsche, and it is implicit in the idea that if moral categories fail to make sense as applied to persons (for reasons relating to determinism), positive and negative evaluations of persons are still possible, but the evaluations have to be understood on the model of aesthetic assessment.

4. "Aestheticizing" (and its variants) are always associated with aestheticism in this chapter, never with the interpretation of the aesthetic that I prefer. It should be pointed out, however, that the aestheticist interpretation of the aesthetic is not simply a mistake: the idea that the aesthetic represents a form of value that obtains when all uses for an object are bracketed is right, but it is not the whole truth, and it does little to explain why aesthetic goods are indeed goods.

5. As in Clive Bell, *Art* (London: Chatto & Windus, 1914). Others, too, have claimed to hold the formalist type of position that Bell represents, but I think that a true formalist is as rare as a true Pyrrhonist. Still, the inducements to some kind of formalism are perpetual, and I have discussed aspects of the formalist appeal in "Is Tragedy Paradoxical?" *British Journal of Aesthetics*

more defensible interpretations, and so the connection between persons and aesthetic qualities could be advanced on other grounds.

A similar uneasiness with the aesthetics of the person is nurtured by the rationalists, but this source of uneasiness takes much longer to dispatch. Descartes supposed that there was a sharp ontological break between us and the other animals, and Kant deepened this break by matching it with an equally stark ethical dichotomy. He held that nonrational entities had a price, whereas the rational had dignity, the difference between price and dignity apparently resolving into the difference between the replaceable and the unique. If an object has a price, "something else can be put in its place as an *equivalent;* if it is exalted above all price and so admits of no equivalent, then it has a dignity."[6] One kind of price mentioned by Kant is the *Affektionspreis*, which is the value ("fancy price") we set upon objects that accord with our taste but that do not satisfy any needs—paradigmatically, for Kant, objects that exhibit what he speaks of as purposiveness without purpose, the purveyors of aesthetic pleasure. An *Affektionspreis* is a nobler thing than a mere market price (also discussed by Kant), which is the value we set upon an object that ministers to our needs, but it still falls short of dignity, which does not presuppose accordance with an appreciator's taste. Therefore, to treat a person as having properties that gratify our taste is to make that person a being for us (to speak the language of a later philosophy) and thus to diminish the value that the person possesses independently of all external appreciation.

Kant's distinction between price and dignity is problematic, however, because it seems to rely unavoidably on the notion that, in point of value, different items have a natural capacity (or incapacity) to stand in equivalence relations. There is an element of voodoo in this notion. A Brazilian rainforest is hardly a possessor of Kantian dignity, as Kant would see it, yet we do not believe that it has a "price": the flora and fauna of its ecosystem cannot be replaced, and we feel that if we did lose this ecosystem, the loss would be tragically profound. But if we were assured that we could successfully place the flora and fauna elsewhere (an assurance we do not as a matter of fact have), then we might well be able to look upon our invasions with a calmer, if not a completely calm, eye. Determinations of pricelessness and price alike

---

38 (1998): 47–62, and in "Modern Art Theories," *Journal of Aesthetics and Art Criticism* 56, no. 4 (1998): 377–89.

6. *The Moral Law: Kant's Groundwork of the Metaphysic of Morals*, trans. H. J. Paton (New York: Barnes & Noble, 1967), 96, Kant's emphasis.

depend upon the making of equivalences. If we subtract the value-positing appreciators from the act of appreciation, even in contexts where appreciations of pricelessness are made, nothing is naturally equivalent to anything else; if we put them in, everything can become equivalent.[7] This brazenly pragmatic talk is not meant to suggest that all equivalences are equally good: it would be vicious to let the loss of the rainforest be equivalent to the scratching of our little finger.[8] But I am at pains to insist that equivalences are not givens, or at least that arguing for their givenness is far more difficult than arguing for the objectivity of other kinds of value, and that if we looked beyond our habitually narrow interests, all natural objects could be regarded as bearers of priceless Kantian dignity. I rather think an extended Kantianism of this sort is what informs Heidegger's jeremiads on technology, but to extend dignity to all beings is still to set values, not to find them (and value-setting is itself technological, in Heidegger's extended sense).[9] But even if we travel down this reflectively liberalized route, which has some theoretical appeal, other problems remain that point up the idleness of this version of dignity. We do have to eat something, for example, and presumably bearers of neo-Kantian dignity are not supposed to be *edibilia*. And so we have to draw the thick and interesting ethical lines between us and nature on other grounds.

The instability of the price-dignity distinction also becomes apparent if we, insisting (against the dignity extenders) that everything has a price, rethink the entitlements to our dignity. Kant thinks that our rational will is "exalted beyond price," but the basis of this assertion is obscure. For all that Kant says, we do not have a clear sense of why our possession of rationality is such as to make us satisfy the dignitarian criteria, so to speak. It appears that we just look and see, and the judgment about pricelessness rests upon the resulting

---

7. I am supposing that a literal subtraction of one notionally separable quantity from a larger composite is possible. The point I am making here does not depend on a literal subtraction, however.

8. The allusion here is, or course, to one of Hume's most notorious passages (T 416). But there is no reason for the Humean to be shamefaced about the passage. Irrationality does not exhaust the lexicon of criticism, and the person who prefers world destroying to finger scratching can, and should be, called many *harsher* names than "irrational."

9. The self-importance that I detect in Kant's priceless will I also detect in Heidegger's conception of our relationship to nature, as presented in such essays as "The Question Concerning Technology." Heidegger lamented that we had successfully forced the truly nonhuman order into a silencing human mold, but to attribute this much power to an admittedly determined species of primates suggests that we should more profitably ease our philosophical anthropology into a more naturalistic mold instead.

intuition. This explanation is hardly satisfactory, and not merely because the intuition is contestable, but because, in this instance, we can more economically explain the occurrence of the intuition in a way that bypasses the invocation of intuition altogether. When we say that our rationality is priceless, we may be just saying that *we* cannot think of a price, that there is nothing we could imagine taking in exchange for our reason. And this seems right: we would have to use our reason even to strike the deal, and so the exchange is not one that we could be a party to, in our usual manner of conducting business. But to say that *we* cannot set the price is not to say that the price cannot be set. Another race of beings might, in that marketplace we could never enter, set prices on us, and they could do so, without any reflective discomfort, if the differences between themselves and us were sufficiently great.

To explicate the kind of difference that is needed, we might consult Hume's discussion of a related topic. According to Hume, if we lived cheek by jowl with creatures "which, though rational, were possessed of such inferior strength, both of body and mind, that they were incapable of all resistance, and could never, upon the highest provocation, make us feel the effects of their resentment," we would not lie under any obligations of justice to them, and our property relations would trump theirs (E 190). There would be an insufficient basis for genuine "society" among two species so unequal in power, and the internal social arrangements of the stronger species would outweigh those of the weaker in the imaginations of the stronger. The doctrine here is not that might makes right—which is, at any rate, too abstract to be even preliminarily helpful—but that differences of might make certain other things that we do care about, such as genuine interpersonal relationships (including those that involve resentment), virtually unobtainable. I do not see how we can reasonably expect any other consequence: if the differential abilities of two species, or two individuals, is extremely great, then considerations of reciprocity tend to fade. Smart-alecky children who advance cunning arguments for staying up past their bedtimes still get sent to bed by their parents, and the reason is that they are highly dependent beings. With different species, we do not usually stand in quasi-parental dependence relations, but other sorts of dependence are possible. (If we were roaming in a gigantic preserve set up by superior powers for their entertainment, and if they could control climatic and other life-support factors, we would be dependent on them in much the way that pets are on us.) In any event, some price or other could be attached to us in the evaluative schema of the superior power. We might not like the manner in which we are prized or contemned, but then our own distaste does not imply that we are beings who are logically incapable of being tasted, as Kant apparently supposes.

These are hard sayings. It can seem that if we allow persons to be objects of appreciation, then we have no option but to contemplate with theoretical equanimity the enslavement of beings such as ourselves in a world that differs from ours by the merely contingent addition of beings that are like us but more competent and powerful. Now the contingency of the addition—whatever that might mean—is conceivably of the greatest ethical relevance (and so we should be cautious about the "merely" in the formulation); but let us suppose, for the sake of argument, that the contingency is not ethically relevant, and then go on to ask, at a more fundamental level, what the worries are that are supposed to tie the antecedent to the consequent in the sentence above.

There are two worries at least, and they can be removed. One is that *being an object* (for whatever purpose) intrinsically invites a variety of treatments, some of them rough. Slavery is hardly an attractive example of objecthood, but we should not therefore conclude that all forms of objecthood fall within the same ethical zone. We should not suppose that any appreciation of persons must involve a policy of arbitrary usage. (It is much easier, however, to think that arbitrary usage is a threat if we are accustomed to thinking of a certain contrasting class for objects, that of rational subjects for whom, in their treatment of objects at least, *anything is permitted*—on the proviso, that is, that irrationality does not first infect the subject's options.)

The other worry is that the evil of slavery, the real evil, cannot be registered adequately unless we accept a conception of ourselves that is incompatible with our being objects: since slavery is evil, then the Kantian price-dignity distinction has to be right after all. In reply, I would argue that we can quite capably account for the evil of slavery, but that levying our criticisms at the level of objecthood provides us with too coarse a grain for the problem. (We might think again about the finger-scratching preference, and whether couching our objection in the language of irrationality does much work for us.)[10] This reply will not move someone strongly in the grip of the person-thing dualism we are considering, however, and so we need to examine the second worry further.

Let us begin by thinking legalistically about entitlements, as Kant encourages us to do. Granted, it is unnerving to think that the resentment of the enslaved is their principal entitlement to liberty. We are apt to think, "Is that

---

10. Simon Blackburn has forcefully made this point in conversation.

all? If we gelded them a bit more thoroughly or systematically than we do, would we then remove their entitlement?" Now I want to say that Hume's resentment test—if we want to call it that—does not fully capture our sense of the evil. But the evil of slavery is not just the evil of a breached *entitlement;* it is the evil we feel when the sentiments of our heart are cruelly violated, and such evils, like their opposite-number goods, are never fully captured by a legalistic test. It is thus unwise to feel that a negative answer to the "Is that all?" question must reveal a damaging omission in Hume's worldly observations about rational but weak animals. We come to expect full captures of goods and evils with rationalism, and this expectation is what makes it ethically regressive, as we shall see.

Hume says that although we would not have obligations of justice to rational but weak animals, "we should be bound by the laws of humanity to give gentle usage to these creatures" (E 190). Hume is right. There is a difference between justice and humanity, and the purview of humanity is more expansive than that of justice. Hume does not say in this passage why we should give "gentle usage," but on his behalf I would argue that humanity requires it because of the salient resemblances we perceive between us and them. (The perception of resemblance, and of which resemblances are salient, is the sphere in which we must rely on intuitions.) Not all salient resemblances need be such that they have to be registered—simply registered—by the eye, and an example would be a resemblance involving psychological operations. If we were convinced that our cats cared about their reputations, or regretted missed opportunities in their lives, we would be powerfully impressed by their psychological resemblance to us, and I believe that we would consequently become much more uncomfortable with the practice of owning cats as pets. We do not in fact sense that cats are mortifyingly missing out on life experiences, and thus pet ownership per se is not odious to most people. Certain kinds of ownership, to be sure, elicit almost universal horror. We would not happily sell a cat to someone who would wantonly torture the animal for sadistic sport; so far as sensitivity to sheer, unconceptualized pain is concerned, the resemblance between human and feline psychologies is ample enough to excite the hottest anger in us. But with human slaves we often feel that the resemblances are very close (and more so upon slight reflection), and when our fellows are reduced to the most abject impotence, our feeling of indignation never rises higher.

The most seriously felt evils are those which activate our Humean sympathy (about which I shall have more to say), and moral progress occurs when that sympathy reaches out to new provinces. That progress has never occurred otherwise. We do not think first of entitlements that flow from the possession of certain features and then look for unobvious examples of such possession; we feel lively resemblances in unexpected quarters and then, in the limit, seek to protect endangered generators of the resemblance through the appropriate legal means. The best reason that the aborting of fetuses does not seem worthy of legal proscription to many people is that although our sympathy arises naturally (as it does with a pet), it is very incomplete. Just as we put animals to sleep, after weighty reflection, so too do we perform abortions. In neither case are we happy with the decision (so strong is our sympathy), but the incompleteness of the sympathy makes the termination a feasible option, owing to the pressure of other considerations (the animal's age, the mother's youth). On the other hand, those who are most likely to feel an overmastering identification with fetuses will be those who lack (often for religiously motivated reasons) a lively sense of the want of resemblance between their own sophisticated psychological operations and the primitive ones of the fetus. Different resemblances can be appealed to by different parties, and arguments they advance can put recondite resemblances before our view, but the outcome of the moral conflicts we observe in the abortion controversy will depend, I think, on which party can get the larger culture to feel that the resemblances on which their platforms are based are the telling, imaginatively enduring ones. Whether or not the fetus possesses a particular property, or set of properties, is a nontrivial but nevertheless ancillary matter. If the sympathy is in place and to the right degree, we find, for genuine legal purposes (that is, for real-life tasks unconnected with Kant's notional legality), features that ground entitlements, but then, again, this grounding is something we institute without justifying our decision by the criteria for the entitlements.[11]

This picture of the contestants in the abortion dispute is too simple, however. There should be no presumption that either side has to win the debate conclusively for the debate to be genuine. Because fetuses are very

11. I once had a student who wrote a paper on the moral standing of the fetus, arguing that since true, full personhood is not realized until we turn eighteen (and can vote, serve in the army, etc.), human organisms from conception through age eighteen occupy the same rung, however low or high, on the ethical ladder. A singular argument, but one that should have few takers! We can presumably devise defeating conditions to protect the neonates and the seventeen-year-olds from the knife, but it is plain that the price-dignity distinction encourages us from the start to think in terms of *credentials*, and this sort of unemotional, nonresilient attention never expands our ethical horizon. Ethical progress occurs when our feelings set the rules in abeyance.

much like us, it would seem that a certain degree of ambivalence is to be expected; and ambivalence can be a moral solution as well as a moral problem. In this light, one is tempted to say that the controversiality of abortion has been exploited to bad effect. The members of our culture have, in a sense, sent a clear message about how they stand on abortion: abortion should definitely be permitted, but it should not be encouraged—and so making abortion (slightly) difficult is not morally objectionable. Making the issue turn on the personhood of the fetus, and on the entitlements that persons have, helps to create the expectation either that killing a fetus is utterly discretionary (like the clipping of a fingernail) or that killing a fetus is equivalent to killing an adult human being. Neither view seems right. But then why would we ever dream of thinking that ambivalence *had to be* problematic? It is not a practical virtue of the Kantian approach that it makes a theoretical vice of mixed feelings.[12]

At this point, we might put the difference between the Humean and the Kantian (to give names to our opposed positions regarding objecthood) in more general relief. The Kantian holds that a being has dignity if a certain property intrinsically belongs to it, and this being then possesses the property nonrelationally. It simply *has* rationality, and it ceases to occupy the logical space of objecthood as a result. On the Humean view, there is no all-or-nothing moral standing, but instead various degrees and various kinds of standing, some of which are legally reinforced and some of which are not, and moral standings are always arrived at relationally, initially through the perception of salient resemblances between sets of people.[13] Objecthood is not, on this view, alien to personhood. In the most austere terms, these are the differences between the Kantian and the Humean, and the issue is such that both sides play a strong hand. Despite the puzzles of the price-dignity distinction, which mount the more we examine them, the inarticulate belief that persons are not intelligible as mere things is powerful, and it is this belief that Kant relies on when he draws the distinction; his unapologetic insistence on the distinction, on the tenability of drawing it, gives the associated ethic an air of noble simplicity. The Humean, on the other hand, can

---

12. I do not wish to leave the impression that I consider the problems concerning abortion to be easily solved. They are not. I am merely offering a comment on the metaethical shape of the dispute.

13. Very basically, having a moral standing is having a claim *to be listened to* for a particular purpose. Moral standings are complicated, and they are affected by many different things (such as age, track records, and life experiences). The obtaining of resemblances that are deemed salient is only just the beginning of the story.

accommodate the inarticulate belief in a retail fashion (specific kinds of objectifying relationships to persons are to be deplored) while sensibly refusing to draw sharp ethical lines between us and the rest of the natural order in which we are immersed. So the opposed positions stand, but the Humean position, rightly understood, should enable us to assuage the Kantian doubts.

To begin with, since it sounds coy to insist that persons qua persons have thingly properties without adducing instances of benign objecthood, let us make an approach by considering another example where persons do not seem to be treated in the right way, and where we moreover deal with a relationship that, to many enlightened tempers, involves a peculiarly aestheticizing objectification. The example I have in mind concerns the treatment of women, in our society and in our society's visual representations, and the treatment consists in the expectation that a woman, physically or psychologically, be a broadly ornamental entity, meant to give pleasure to a (presumptively male) subject. The social treatment of women would seem to offer a most inhospitable site for a defense of the Humean position; but if the defense is successful, we shall have shown not only that the Humean can make sense of the wrongness of the "ornamental expectation," but also that aesthetic value is not tantamount to the possession of merely ornamental properties. (This second gain should be particularly impressive because, earlier, I merely allowed the case against aestheticism to rest on the case against formalist conceptions of art.)

In recent years, revisionist-minded art critics have attacked the classical genre of the nude because, as they say or insinuate, the genre objectifies the female form for the titillation of the implied spectator, who is inevitably male and located outside the picture frame. The arguments that vilify the genre can be persuasive, or at least disruptive of dogmatic slumber. John Berger, for example, has argued that in Bronzino's *Allegory of Time and Love* we see an unclothed Venus whose body is awkwardly twisted around so that while her face and eyes are turned toward Cupid on her right, her torso is frontally exposed to the spectator's gaze.[14] Once our attention is directed to this cumbersome position never occupied by a lover, it can become difficult to see what point the frontal exposure could have, other than to give the spectator a lubricious anatomy lesson. Let us simply grant, for the sake of argument, that these revisionist interpretations are, or could be, sound, and let us waive the intricate question of what our stance toward the genre should

---

14. *Ways of Seeing* (Harmondsworth, Middlesex: Penguin, 1972), 54–55.

be if the arguments are sound. Instead, I should like us to notice the intended shape of the argument. Such a depiction of Venus is a bad thing, we are meant to surmise, and the badness is of a piece with the badness of pornography; indeed, an effect of the revisionist argument is to make us entertain the possibility that the nude was pornography (or a pornography equivalent) for those cultured viewers who desired such material (but who could not accept it under a more honest label).[15] The badness of pornography, in turn, is felt to be of a piece with sexist social attitudes, and so the problem is not confined to the representational cloister, the distinction between art and life being irrelevant in this case.

I only partly accept this last reflective identification. The badness of (explicit) pornography is, minimally, the badness of art, and that, as such, is a far less serious matter, I would argue, than sexism in the workplace. The practice of art also requires the copious production of bad (or forgettable) specimens in a way that the moral practice does not. Moreover, there is a special twist to be noted (which aestheticians have often noted): in *some* sense, what is good in representation is frequently bad in reality.[16] So the art-life distinction should make some difference in principle, and claims made in one domain do not simply translate into claims in the other. But these hesitations need not really alter the shape of the revisionist argument. If a social attitude is both malign and underexplicit, then the art-life distinction has diminished relevance because the spectator often cannot draw it where the social attitude is concerned. Thus the badness will be much of a muchness, irrespective of the domain; and sexist attitudes do indeed furnish us with cases that conform to such a pattern.

Since we no longer own slaves (and are nominally nonracist), I believe that the treatment of women has become for us a paradigm case of an affectively as-yet-unwon campaign for a greater humanity. That humanity is the core issue is apparent from the talk of "objectification" that is rife when moral critics castigate sexism. It is in defense of a more humanizing stance toward women that we are most likely nowadays to hear someone say that persons are not objects. To the extent that the Humean and the Kantian can

---

15. This is very much the suggestion that Berger makes in connection with Memlinc's *Vanity*: "You painted a naked woman because you enjoyed looking at her, you put a mirror in her hand and you called the painting *Vanity*, thus morally condemning the woman whose nakedness you had depicted for your own pleasure" (ibid., 51).

16. The right way to understand this claim is a contentious matter. My own view (which I present in "Is Tragedy Paradoxical?") is that the truth of this claim generates no reflective instability.

agree that sexism is a true problem, we can straightway turn to their philosophical explanations of what makes it a problem.

In a broadly pornographic stance toward a woman, we are encouraged, the Kantian would say, to treat a woman as an object, that is to say, as so much flesh, whereas treating her as a person would minimally involve an awareness of, and respect for, her reason-using inner self. How this respect is to be manifested is never clear: we like to think that kindness ("gentle usage"?) is a component of respect, but it is not obvious to me why, on Kantian grounds, it *must* be a component. The libertines described by the Marquis de Sade regale the victims of their degradation with elaborate, and rather Kantian-sounding, justifications for their exercises, which demand the severe regimentation of naturally capricious impulses; and it could be argued that true sadism, of which there is no analogue among the lower animals, is only an option for Kantian agents, or for people who aspire to be such agents.[17] Presumably, the Kantian can somehow get over such a stile, but even if he can, there is a general difficulty that he faces. If we treat natural inclination with the suspicion that Kant encourages, then we cannot just assume that kindness (a spontaneous feeling) and respect automatically go together. The absence of an explicit account linking kindness and respect, or the taking for granted that kindness is the coin in which respect is paid, may also indicate that the Kantian conception of dignity is unconsciously parasitic on a more Humean conception of the person and, like the double-existence thesis, derives its imaginative force from the veiled host. (This parasitism also has a counterpart in the dependence, which Hegel detected, of *Moralität* on *Sittlichkeit*.)

In more general terms, the difficulty here concerns the treatment we should accord the bodies that are annexed to Kantian agents. We could call this the Other Bodies Problem, because we do not know what sorts of respect-betokening actions to perform on a body. This problem is of course a complement, in the philosophy of value, of a more famous problem that the same picture of the mind generates. We want to know how to treat a body as something other than a shell that houses the priceless, and we lack knowledge, in this framework, because we are in the dark about what would count

---

17. My thinking here was first occasioned by some remarks that Irad Kimhi made to me. Kantian readings of de Sade—which are at least (and possibly at most) suggestive readings—are the province of the very revisionist-minded, and derive from Jacques Lacan's 1963 essay "Kant avec Sade" (which appeared, in James Swenson's English translation, in *October* 51 [1989]: 55–76). See also Alenka Zupančič, "Kant with Don Juan and Sade," in *Radical Evil*, ed. Joan Copjec (London: Verso, 1996), 105–25.

as a betokening option if we pulled the plug on natural sentiment. Perhaps a serene indifference to the fact that we have bodies, insofar as such abstraction is possible, would be the least theoretically arduous option for the Kantian to pursue. The puritanism that is detectable in some understandings of nonobjectified male-female relations may be the result of following up this option. But there are attendant losses. If we think that respect is primarily an intellectual matter, then not only the rough-and-tumble of the bedroom, with its Rabelaisian earthiness and vitality, but also the polished wit of the drawing room, whose saucy double entendres are lost on all but the most spirituel, will seem adventitious and askew. We pretend that the body is not there.

The Kantian has better resources for explaining failures of respect, the instances where people interpersonally botch things up, than he has for the successes. If we focus narrowly on the failures, then the thought that persons are not objects will have greater plausibility because the failures typically reveal to us people who are being treated as though they were objects of the most arbitrarily usable kind. (It is misleading to say that their treatment suggests that they are nothing but objects, for that idiom inclines us to think that there must be a distinctive extra ingredient in a person that transforms the person from an object into a subject.) In any event, we make an unwise inference if we conclude that persons are not objects because they are not arbitrarily usable, are not the merest objects; but once the inference is made, concentrating on the failures, where we have de facto merest objects, lets us insensibly elide all distinctions within objects. Kant's error, then, lies in his refusal to attribute objecthood to persons, when he should have just acknowledged that certain objects can be degraded through arbitrary usage. What makes us degradable is of course closely related to what makes our objecthood complicated, and the nature of this complication should be our next topic.

When a prurient adolescent male looks at a picture of a woman—one not usually regarded as pornographic—and what he sees excites his sexual desire, he commonly attends to the picture so selectively as to make ridiculous the suggestion that he is even looking at the picture, particularly if it has aesthetic merit. (Let us suppose that the picture is Bonnard's erotic *Blue Nude*.) He is leaving something out of his appreciation, which we think makes for a diminished aesthetic experience. If the picture itself does not underwrite a richer experience, we think that something is lacking in the picture—pornography is commonly unerotic and uninteresting, and that is why it makes sense to distinguish pornography from erotica—rather than in the spectator. Similarly, if a man treats a woman (not a woman-picture) as pawing fodder, we also want to say that he is leaving something out of his interaction, that he is responding to what is only a part of his female colleague. For the sake of a preliminary characterization of either version of the problem, the notion of *soul-blindness*, as discussed by Stanley Cavell, may be helpful.[18] The soul-blind person sees a thing before him, but he also fails to see, or see enough of, the person that is before him.

This blindness is similar to a kind that Arthur Danto hypothesizes. He imagines a race of sensitive barbarians who, lacking the concept of art, ransack Europe in quest of merely beautiful things, which they crave.[19] If the barbarians' booty includes artworks, it is only through an accidental intersection between the set of beautiful mere-things and the set of artworks. Danto wants to propose that the barbarians would need an art-philosophical apparatus in order to avoid making accidental collocations, but this is an optional (and, in my view, undesirable) addition to the description of the barbarians' plight.[20] Like Cavell's soul-blind man, like the adolescent with the Bonnard, the barbarians strangely see everything and yet see nothing. But to what unregistered item do their incapacities attest?

Unfortunately, the ocular imagery inherent in Cavell's and Danto's stories plays us false almost at once. We are encouraged to look for something *in* the woman or *in* the painting, not visible to our earthly eye, to be sure, but accessible to our second, conceptual sight. We begin to set up the problem in Kantian terms: we expect a nonrelational ingredient that the woman and the painting, but not the mere body or the mere canvas and paint, have. These are also the Cartesian terms: if robots can be attired in hats and cloaks, then we must locate the mind in something imperceptible that hats and cloaks indifferently conceal or disclose. Because of the perplexities that arose in our earlier search for the dignity maker (or dignity canceler), I am not persuaded that this type of search will uncover anything other than an impressionistic quarry, which is unproblematic for the Humean but not so for the Kantian. But perhaps the very impreciseness of that ethereal visual field which opens to our second sight is just the pointer we need for preserving, and advancing upon, the insights of the preliminary characterization.

18. *The Claim of Reason* (Oxford: Oxford University Press, 1979), 378–80.
19. *The Transfiguration of the Commonplace* (Cambridge: Harvard University Press, 1981), 105–7.
20. The argument would take us too far afield for the present. It is enough for my purposes if we suppose (i) that artworks differ from ordinary beautiful objects on perceptual grounds, and (ii) that it is possible to imagine persons who lack the capacity to make the necessary perceptual discriminations. Danto himself rejects (i).

As noted before, in Chapter 1, ocular imagery is generally very fitting when we speak of the understanding, or of our coming into cognitive control of a thing. Yet I am struck by how comparatively inappropriate this imagery is when we speak of our feelings and of our relationships to other people, and by the auditory images that become appropriate in their stead. If I understand and accept the reason you are giving me, I may say, "I see what you mean." If I do not accept your reason, but nevertheless recognize your good faith in offering it, I am more likely to say, "I hear you, but . . ." Our hearts can vibrate to the same iron string, or we can march to the tunes of different drummers. Sweethearts say that the band is playing their song, but not that the gallery downtown is showing their painting. Political enfranchisements are sometimes described as "giving a voice" to the unrepresented: we hear the voice of the person who is in the same room with us.[21] When our feelings are engaged, strong visual images do not come unbidden to our minds, as they often do when we understand. Except perhaps at the moment of the first provocation, we do not cry "Eureka!" when we are animated by the love or hate we feel for others.

As the painting substitution suggests in the sweethearts example, it could be difficult to conceive what visual idioms would take the place of the auditory ones, and equally difficult to see how the auditory could be called upon to perform resolutely cognitive tasks. With visual items we expect to have the thing *before* us: we stand back and behold. But with the auditory we are participants, not bystanders, and our habit of saying that two or more hearts can beat in unison is a confirmation of this participatory feature of audition. Feeling requires us to expose ourselves to the other, and to the extent that we are exposed, we experience something for which our visual field furnishes an impoverished set of similes. What we see is not what we get.

Accordingly, I am inclined to think that no pictorially modeled account of the mind can ever be adequate by itself, and that we must supplement it with another that is auditory. An attraction of Hume's philosophy of mind is that this second sort of model is given its due, explicitly and implicitly. While speaking of the passions, Hume says that the mind "resembles a string-instrument, where after each stroke the vibrations still retain some sound, which gradually and sensibly decays" (T 440–41), and the pervasive associationism he observes in the mind's operations resembles the dynamism and

---

21. Lest we forget, there is the voice of conscience (or duty) as well. This language tells against the idea that the authority of conscience stems from our autonomy, for we do not really hear ourselves speaking.

rhythm of music. Hume moreover explains the resting points, the contents that the intellect can grasp, by means of the associative motions, which rest on feeling, rather than vice versa; and so it would be better to say that the supplementation, if there is one, goes in the other direction. The Humean mind tends to stay in hard-to-visualize motion, whereas its more visually manageable pauses are the exception. This is what we encounter in common life and what we should expect in a philosophy of common life.

If we return now to the notion of soul-blindness, I think we should say that although the talk of blindness is misleading, the talk of soul need not be. When we respond to another person, our own mind is animated by that person's mind, and to call this received animation "soul" is natural because of the invigorating influx we sense at the time of our response. Hume called this invigorating influx sympathy, a notion I casually introduced earlier, and it is worth noting that on one occasion he says that sympathy is "the soul or animating principle" of all our emotions (T 363). The reason he gives for this claim, in this passage, is that our pleasurable emotions dissipate and our unpleasurable intensify if they are not shared by others, and although he had made it sound, in his official account of sympathy (at T 316–20), as though sympathy were just a mechanism for simply transferring an emotion from one mind to another, it is not at all clear why the dissipation-cum-intensification mentioned at T 363 would occur if this is all that sympathy was. But the difficulty abates if we regard sympathy as being fundamentally a mechanism for making emotions participatorily available across minds, and although participation often involves a simple transfer, it just as often does not: if I am proud of you, you will probably feel more joy than pride, and if you see that I am vexed, you may be amused if you think the cause is a tempest in a teapot. Bearing in mind that sympathy can produce nontransferred emotions, we should find the occurrence of sympathy less of an unexplained explainer than it sometimes appears to be in Hume's presentation. For it would seem that our emotions require not merely *seconding*, but *expressive release*, the presence of other minds capable of an emotional response to the release; and the more generalized psychological necessity of expressive release is more easily explained than the less generalized necessity of seconding (since human animals look to their fellows with more than just the hope of having their sentiments copied and certified—which is what "seconding," in two of its senses, is).

If we let Humean sympathy provide us with our basic understanding of soul, the person upon whom soul does not register is not exactly blind, or even deaf, but, shall we say, expressively insensitive. This person would have the wells of sympathy blocked, would be incapable, or have limited capability for, participatory response. And this seems the right thing to say about the man whose treatment of his female colleagues is sexist, or about the adolescent who leers at the picture while missing the eros. Each one fails to make a response that exposes himself sufficiently to the sensibility of some other, either to that of the colleague or that of the pictured woman (or, what is also worth noting, the pictured woman's implied lover). On the basis of these observations, then, I would hazard the following view about that which distinguishes objects that are persons from those that are not: a person is an expressive being, and a being is expressive, if the person as body (that is, something sensuously accessible) is informed by a sensibility that engenders participation (on the part of other sensibilities) and whose distinctive properties are therefore more visible to others than to the person her- or himself (because they are participation-dependent). This definition has important consequences, but before we trace them, I should like to acknowledge a debt to Kant.

In his third *Critique* Kant, too, speaks of soul, and what he says is similar to what Hume says about sympathy.[22] Here, however, soul is a concept that applies to art, and Kant observes that poems, narratives, speeches, conversations, and—interestingly, in view of Kant's topic—*women*[23] can be pleasing but soulless, and that the pleasure of contemplating them is such that we can

---

22. *Critique of Judgment*, trans. James Creed Meredith (Oxford: Clarendon, 1952), 175–76 (sec. 49).

23. Kant's inclusion of women, who have dignity, with artworks, which merely have an *Affektionspreis*, points up the perhaps unexpected ease with which the Kantian approach allows us to be cavalier about dignity. Once we accustom ourselves to seeing unnaturally sharp breaks in the world, and to resisting our natural inclination, the skilled casuist can think up an intellect-pleasing story to place the break where he wants. If we think that Kant was being merely—and hence irrelevantly—hypocritical in this remark, Adolf Eichmann supplies us with a more worrisome cautionary tale in which hypocrisy is not an issue. As Hannah Arendt informs us, at his trial Eichmann "suddenly declared with great emphasis that he had lived his whole life according to Kant's moral precepts, and especially according to a Kantian conception of duty." Judge Yitzhak Raveh interrogated Eichmann further on this point, and "to the surprise of everybody, Eichmann came up with an approximately correct definition of the categorical imperative" (*Eichmann in Jerusalem* [New York: Viking, 1964], 135–36). Arendt's brief discussion is illuminating and disturbing. Did the thought that duty demands resistance to natural inclination make it easier for Eichmann to order Jews to their deaths? Did Eichmann's self-styled Kant "for the household use of the little man" (136) pander to the "little man's" exaggerated sense of his own worldly position? These are difficult questions. But what should be clear at least is that sincere acceptance of a moral theory that stresses dignity will not be prophylactic against treating people in very undignified ways.

find nothing amiss in the work (or the woman).[24] His examples do not involve the incapacity to respond, but the incapacity of the work to support response, which is just the other side of the medal, and we have, again, a situation where we are grasping for an elusive difference between two superficially similar things, the soulful and the soulless. Kant tells us that soul is "the animating principle of the mind" (apparently the perceiver's), and that it causes us to have a "representation of the imagination which produces much thought, yet without the possibility of any definite thought whatever, i.e., concept, being adequate to it." Soul is consequently not completely intelligible, according to one canon of intelligibility, but we can begin to make more sense of it, at least, if we attend to the contrast Kant draws between these "representations of the imagination," which he calls aesthetic ideas, and those that he calls rational ideas. Although his thoughts here are difficult to state, Kant wants to say that, whereas an aesthetic idea is an intuition to which no concepts are adequate, a rational idea is a concept that cannot be exhaustively specified in a set of intuitions. So if I imagine death or eternity (two of Kant's examples), I have to summon up an endless array of sensory images to approximate, at most, an exhibition of the concept, and if I perceive a work of art I would similarly need an endless array of concepts to unpack it. What would count as compliance in this second case is obscure, but I think Kant's rather dark remarks about the grasping of soul can be clarifyingly mapped onto what we can say about Humean sympathy.

Like soul, sympathy sets the mind in motion (what Kant calls a "self-maintaining" play") and does not generate a particular set of thoughts. When I expressively respond to you, my response may incline me to assent to certain propositions about you (that you are foolish, or charming, or more decent than I), but the report I am giving on you is not one that I would ever know how to finish. I instead feel something, or rather have a number of feelings that blur and meld in various ways (Hume's stringed instrument once again) and that blur and meld with the sentiments I receive from you. All of this, together with the fact that different people (and the same people at different times) will have different meldings, weakens the conviction that it would be possible for me to complete an enumeration of my thoughts about you, which

24. Although Kant, by his own lights, should be taken to the woodshed for his inclusion of women, a more generous reading, by Humean lights, is possible. His soulless woman is "pretty, affable, and refined," and this could well be the description of a merely decorative bluestocking, a woman placed on a hollow pedestal. Similarly, a soulless woman could be a woman as represented in a centerfold (a different sort of empty decorativeness).

are largely thoughts about your expressive properties. And so, there is perhaps a limit to the intelligibility of our sympathetic operations also.

So close to each other are Humean sympathy and Kantian soul that it is a pity that Kant did not see fit to apply his account of art, mutatis mutandis, to persons. Kant would have been better equipped to explain respect through soul/sympathy than through the mysterious dignity of a rational will. In his ethics, he was right to worry about the source of respect, but his rationalism clouded his vision; in his aesthetics, rationalism relaxed its hold, and he was able to lay out the materials of an alternative account. We treat a person with respect if we expressively respond to her or him, and something wins our respect if it can support an expressive response. Hume does not speak explicitly, in the *Treatise*, of the generalized sort of respect that interested Kant, but his later talk of "humanity" and "the party of humankind" (E 274–75) are sentiment-based analogues of this respect and correspond to the adaptations I have proposed from Kant's aesthetics. A backdoor rapprochement between Hume and Kant is possible after all, though we have to pair different parts of their systems in order to arrive at it.

By linking Kantian artworks and Humean persons as I have done, I have not wanted to suggest that persons are artworks, but that the two classes share a common structure up to a point. Artworks stand to persons in much the same fashion as vehicles of derived intentionality stand to vehicles of original. Just as printed words mean something because there are minds that read them, so too artworks are expressive entities because of the expressiveness of their makers and audiences. There is significant structural overlap between persons and artworks, but we need not press the claim of parity further than that. Having entered this caveat, I wish to consider what I think may be the most important element of the overlapping structure, and if my contention regarding this element is granted, we will be able at last to assign a clear sense to the notion that persons qua persons have irreducibly aesthetic properties, or that they are appreciatable objects whose potential for appreciation is special because of their peculiar interiority. We have this element if we compare the style of an artwork with the character of a person, and some observations that Danto makes can give us a place to start.

Danto develops a passage from Proust to make the claim that artworks have style and that their style is not identical to their content, even though the two may not be distinguishable to some inspections. Proust's narrator goes to the theater to see the great actress Berma act, but he sees instead the sufferings of Phèdre, Berma the actress having disappeared wholesale, for him, into Phèdre the tragic queen. According to Danto, if we were transported back to Marcel's theater, we would not witness the diaphanization of Berma, because we would see what Marcel does not, namely, the Belle Epoque flourishes that make Berma's performance "as distinguishable in style as the furniture of Nancy or the posters of Toulouse-Lautrec."[25] We would truly see Berma act because we would see the *art* in her performance, not just the performance itself; the "art" is merely another word for Berma's style, or that which is lost on Marcel.

There are a few prickly questions this little story raises, some of which I should blithely like to pass over without expending too many words. If Marcel is not alive to Berma's style, then by Danto's criteria he is like the barbarian who lacks the art concept; and this is a far-fetched supposition, since, if anybody has the art concept, it is surely a demure aesthete like Marcel. Danto's presentation also makes it sound as though art is invisible to the generation that produces it, and that is surely an overstatement. And finally, and most significantly, it seems that the features Marcel is alleged not to see are those which are genuinely ornamental: the signature of Berma's acting that is akin to the signature of Nancy furniture is something we can straightforwardly enough isolate from what centrally concerns us—the realization of Phèdre or the excellent crafting of a chair.

Such a signature is what is sometimes pejoratively called style, but what I (following Kant here) would pejoratively call mannerism instead. Our ongoing interest in art is not really an interest in the cultural history of mannerism (though art often serves that historical motivation well). But it is possible to redescribe Marcel's blindness as a failure to see how Berma herself contributes an important ingredient to the realization of Phèdre; and this Berma-ish ingredient, which is of greater aesthetic interest, can also be called style—deep style, if we want to distinguish it from style understood as mannerism. To bring out Marcel's blindness more precisely, we can then mark a distinction between (i) perceiving Berma-as-lost-in-Phèdre and (ii) perceiving Berma-as-Phèdre. In (ii), but not in (i), we can separately identify the performance and the role. Clearly, the performance and the role *are* different things, and so if we cannot disentangle them, the explanation must lie in the phenomenological position that we occupy. We can suppose that someone like Marcel could have the experience of (i), but I think that, more realistically, the experience of (i) picks out the phenomenological position of Berma herself. When she plays Phèdre, she cannot separate the style she imparts to the role from the role itself. (This is of course not the same as

---

25. Danto, *Transfiguration of the Commonplace*, 163.

saying that when she performs, she forgets her own extratheatrical identity.) At least some of Berma's spectators can, and they have the experience of (ii).

Berma's deep style, invisible to her, is ineliminable from our appreciation of the acted work. Why? Danto does not leave us with much of an answer to this, because he explicates his core insight about style in what I think is a wrongheaded way, one that cannot make sense of deep style. He unconvincingly assimilates stylistic properties to referentially opaque representational properties, so that Berma's contribution to the performance of her role becomes continuous with a person's contribution to the holding of the (false) belief that the Morning Star is not the Evening Star. My intention here is not primarily to criticize Danto, but we should note that if the assimilation goes through, then it seems that when the "art" of a work becomes explicit enough for us to see it, the "art" also becomes aesthetically negligible, to the extent that it is understood to be a reliquary for discarded representational commitments.[26] Danto's insight fares better, therefore, if we take it out of Danto's hands and say that Berma's style matters because we take a lively interest in witnessing how a sensibility can inform Racine's words and move us far more than the words themselves can, or move us, thanks to Berma's talents as an actress, in a fresh, unaccustomed way. The person of Berma invigorates the role and is thus something other than a tacked-on affectation or performative tic.

In the case of nonacting persons we may with propriety speak of style as well, and it is important for the same reasons. But since "style," as applied to persons, calls to mind the fripperies of old-time aestheticism, it is desirable to replace or supplement it with a less lurid term, and I propose "character," which I construe in a very wide sense. I do not mean just what we sometimes call a person's "moral character," which is virtually a synonym for integrity (or the lack of it). I include what we think of as temperament or personality, and the whole sentiment-based texture of the mind that is communicable via Humean sympathy. If it were not so archaic, "complexion" in the sense of "habit of mind as revealed in the body" would probably be the best word choice for what I am after, but talk of character will do.

I would also comprehend successful exercises of wit under character, because wit is so dependent on the speaker's context and the speaker's sensibility for its success. Hume says that "no one has ever been able to tell

---

26. Danto's death-of-art views are consonant with this downbeat conclusion, which in any event seems plainly false for other reasons: one should not mistake the end of a certain historical or philosophical conception of art for the end of art as such.

what *wit* is, and to shew why such a system of thought must be receiv'd under that denomination, and such another rejected" (T 297, Hume's emphasis), and he assures us that "the most profound metaphysics, indeed, might be employed in explaining" its different varieties (E 262). Both claims are correct because we are dealing with something akin to Kant's imperfectly explicable aesthetic ideas. And once we recognize that wittiness is a character trait, in this extended sense, we open a space for all sorts of siblings: wryness, humor, pathos, quirkiness, moodiness, effervescence, and so on. If we think about the people we know, and try to articulate what it is that makes them the persons that they are, I suspect that we shall almost immediately begin retailing notions such as these.[27] We will usually be confident about which ascriptions are the right ones to make, but at the same time we will often be at a loss to explain what grounds the ascriptions. For what particularly guides our determination here is truly a something-I-know-not-what, inasmuch as we are incompletely known to ourselves.

With respect to our character, or style, we are pretty much in the position that Berma is in when she plays Phèdre. From the inside, we are not able to separate our thoughts and actions from our character: all that lies open to our gaze are the thoughts we entertain and the actions we perform, and our character as such does not pass before us as something about which we can deliberate. But the people who know us, gladly or not, have the outside view, and they are able to make the distinction. I am not saying that we are debarred from knowing our characters, but only that such knowledge has to be routed through other minds, either literally (others tell us what we are like) or by veridical imaginings (we project ourselves into the position of the others, and try to divine what they would say). Because our imaginations tend to be weak and unreliable, the first approach is much the best. But in either case, there is a second-person privilege for character identifications, and what our fellows identify is for their consumption, as it were, not ours. They want to spend time with us, or avoid us, for reasons that are first-person invisible and that pertain to ourselves insofar as we possess objective qualities.

This conception of the self, according to which character, or style, is an

---

27. Danto writes, "It is the qualities of character and personality which make us so interesting to one another as individuals, which arouse in us those feelings of love and hatred, fascination and revulsion, and which escape classification in terms of the regimented distinctions that have defined the mind-body problem" (*Transfiguration of the Commonplace*, 160). In my view, this is the most penetrating sentence in Danto's book, though Danto himself does not pursue his own suggestion. This discussion of the aesthetics of the person may be regarded as an attempt to furnish the beginnings of a follow-up.

essential aspect of the self, represents a *démarche* in the direction of a truly non-Cartesian understanding of who we are. For on this conception our minds have an *outside*, and this is not the same as the outside of our bodies, since what others appreciate in us is mental (though not unembodied). Similarly, when we appreciate a painting, we are responding neither to unconceptualized color configurations nor to states of mind that lie behind the painting and that so to speak stand in a transcendent relation to the canvas and paint. (These are the options that both Danto and the formalist give us: what needs to be resisted is the thought that these are the only options.) That this externalized mind is a real alternative to the Cartesian picture can be shown more clearly still if we consider, briefly, another picture of the mind, more widely known, that is not as different as it first promises to be.

It is sometimes thought that the postulation of a wide operational scope for unconscious mental activity occasioned the decisive defeat for rationalism. When we learn that the ego is not the master of his own house, that represssed infantile wishes can exert extensive—but undetected—influence over conscious beliefs and actions, we naturally begin to imagine contrasts between the superficiality of Descartes and the profundity of Freud. This surmise is much too quick. Unconscious mental activity, generally speaking, can be handled without strain within a rationalistic framework, as Leibniz's *petites perceptions* were, and even the distinctively Freudian unconscious admits of a rationalistic interpretation. For the manifest, conscious self is a screen for the unconscious, and it is possible for the conscious self to peel back the screen, by performing the right steps, and thereby lay bare the contents of the unconscious. There is a very strong rationalist resonance in this procedure, and Descartes, with his customary acuteness, actually anticipates the Freudian mental architecture, and even the Freudian strategy: the evil genius whom the meditator fears could very well be the meditator himself, and he comes close to making the possibility of this massive self-deception explicit in *Meditation Two*, when he acknowledges that he is capable of producing his fantasies, which he cannot yet dismiss as mad. And his groping toward the light can then be regarded as a self-analysis, similar to Freud's initiating psychoanalytic deed, that is meant to undo the threat of this possibility and thereby heal the wayward imagination that feels a threat. In both Descartes and Freud the right sort of inward turn will reveal the mind to itself, and the difference between them largely concerns the number of turns that the inward screw must take. On the view that the mind has an outside, however, there is no place within us where we can even look for the desired self-knowledge, and acknowledging this limitation on the reaches of self-reflexivity involves us in a more dramatic (but, as we are coming to expect, a more self-effacing) critique of the Cartesian picture.

This picture of the mind is more incomplete than simply false (inward turns are frequently revelatory, though in ways that are more ordinary than those that psychoanalysis primes us to anticipate), but the readiness with which we take it to be complete yields a falsity of its own. However, I present Descartes and Freud as unlikely confederates mainly to bring out more pointedly the objectivity of the self. And here we are poised to take notice of the innocuousness of the objectivity. So long as we are gripped by the image of a mind that owns, or reclaims, parts of itself, we shall countenance a split between the owning subject (or master subject) and an ownable object (or object analogue). Ownership, in a literal sense, institutes such a split, and it is worthwhile for us to see how.

If we are able to make an owner-type appropriation of something, we have a powerful tendency to regard that which we appropriate as being not quite a bare object as a result. Locke's well-known view that we make property by mixing our labor with bare objects is an example of this imaginative principle, and we naturally treat owned objects with a form of consideration that we do not show to unowned. For an amusing example of this consideration, recall the scene in *Dr. Strangelove* when Colonel Bat Guano, ordered by his superior to break into a vending machine, demurs (in a slightly hurt tone of voice): "But that's private property!" Even though nobody thinks that vending machines are not objects, their being owned softens our sense of what can be done to them, and they ride on their owners' coattails. But only if the owner has done the softening does the object ride at all.

It is easy, but not innocent, to transfer the ownership model from literal instances of the ownership relation to the relationship between the mind and its contents. (This move is not dissimilar to the Kantian emplacement of entitlements—a legal device—on the ground floor of the moral life, prior to the institution of the laws with which we are best acquainted.) If we wink at the transfer, then we have already made it very difficult to accommodate the benign objecthood of the self. We will feel that if what our minds appropriate is an unruly part of the mind itself, the appropriation softens the objecthood. The slogan "Where id was, there shall ego be" illustrates this idea: the id is a hard psychological lump until the ego recognizes it and thereby confers some of its own clarity (or fancied clarity) on the id. Mixing our subjectivity would thus seem similar to mixing our labor. But if our minds are not of a sort that will enable one part to mix in this fashion with another, save poetically, then there is no basis for the ownership model. By contrast, the aspects of character I have insisted on are unlike the id in that they are generally undangerous to the person whose aspects they are, nor are they candidates for control.

Our characters, even if they do not furnish us with candidates for control, can make us unhappy, and so make us desire control; and I do not mean to deny this obvious thought: that an unhappy character poses serious problems for a person. But there is not much that we, through introspection or analysis, can do about the source of unhappiness, and to recognize our objecthood duly is to recognize that some people have characters that are wired for misery and others for settled contentment, and that most of us lie somewhere in between. And, as the Sceptic reminds us, this thought "must . . . be obvious to the most careless reasoner, that all dispositions of mind are not alike favourable to happiness, and that one passion or humour may be extremely desirable, while another is equally disagreeable." Unhappiness would never exist if a person could "elude all attacks, by the continual alterations of his shape and form" (MPL 168). Knowing our place in the world is, in part, knowing that we have a place.

The objective self is the externalized complement of the internalized world we saw in Chapter 2 but did not label as such. An embodied mind is not multipresent; most of the world must be tucked away from view, but we are able to think about the world, and not just world fragments, because we imaginatively construct it without our being aware that we are doing the constructing (until we do philosophy, perhaps). This imaginative construct we could call an "internalized world" because we do not simply find its content in our experiential field: this world is derived from our mental operations in conjunction with what we do find. So too I want to say that an embodied mind is not wholly present to itself; although much of the self is present, an important part of us must be tucked away. Yet we are able to think about ourselves, and not just self fragments, because we obtain the content of our nonfragmentary self through our experience with others (and, again, without being aware of how we do it until philosophy brings us to book). In both cases, we arrive at our conceptions through the mediation of the seemingly extrinsic, or (as I would prefer to say) through a necessary indirection.

To strengthen further the sense that selves have innocuously appreciatable objective features, we might notice a remarkable connection between the two sources of that discomfort which the aestheticizing of persons produces. We have devoted much attention to the Kantian ethical source, but the other source, our discomfort with old-time aestheticism, also has some connection to Kant. The theoretical position that licenses the aesthetes' poses is a radicalization of the Kantian aesthetic, which enjoins us to contemplate an object without interest.[28] Bell and other formalists pushed Kant's Aesthetic Imperative, so to speak, beyond anything Kant envisaged, inasmuch as "interest" for them was understood so severely as to encompass the conceptual classification of percepts, but the element of continuity between their views and Kant's is, all the same, what makes aestheticism seem, depending on our sympathies, either gloriously self-transcendent or inhuman. Kant holds that when we look at objects aesthetically, we disengage them from our purposes, and looking at a person this way *is* problematic. But as I said earlier, looking at a nonperson this way is problematic, too, since the purposes to be disengaged do not concern merely narrow self-interests (which are sensibly deprecated) but those which we consult when we explain what something is or what it means to us. The virtue of a knife, to use a shopworn example, is to cut, and if a knife is abstracted from its métier we really do not know what to make of it apart from whatever we make of its nonknifish properties or parts. A statue of a knife would not be used for cutting, to be sure, but we should still carry its use in our eye as we look at the statue. Cutting *that* out will put us on the fast track to hard-line formalism, and so the Kantian formula has to be rewritten if it is to avoid having the radicalized aesthetic as its logically purified and rightful heir. And a defensible rewrite will surely not retain a promiscuous proscription on interests, as the original does.

In sum, I hold that only false aesthetic and ethical views would lead us to be uneasy about the appreciation of persons. If we think that appreciating a person entails holding him or her ornamentally at arm's length, we have a false aesthetic. If we think that treating a person decently is to attend selectively, as much as possible, to his or her rational will and its concerns, we have a false ethic. (Selective attention, upheld by principle or incapacity, can take the high road as well as the low.) If we stay in the temperate zone, avoiding both the chilly aesthetics and the tropical morality that rationalism promotes, we shall also find that people are much richer, ethically and aesthetically, than we would otherwise find them. I want to say more about this.

---

28. Kant narrowly defines disinterestedness (in sec. 2 of the third *Critique*) as indifference to the existence of the contemplated object. We typically have much more in mind than this; and as Kant's discussion proceeds, so does Kant. In my remarks about the Kantian aesthetic, I align interest, more liberally, with the having of purposes.

First of all, let us return to the genre of the nude, as understood by Berger, and to the social attitude (which he thinks the genre expresses) that can be stated as the expectation that women are to be on display, rather than to act. Now I am impressed that Berger does not back off from the aesthetics of the person entirely, even though he may not officially realize it. He praisingly speaks of paintings—they are few in number, he thinks—that show wholly or partly unclothed people without the spectatorial idealizations that for him are endemic to the classical nude, and these, he says, depict the (merely) naked body. These paintings, which include Rembrandt's *Danäe* and Rubens's *Helen Fourment in a Fur Coat*, receive praise because they show persons who are reassuringly banal and ordinary: the women are relatively unposed, a little awkward and hesitant, and not preternaturally voluptuous. In the disclosure of their ordinariness "lies the warm and friendly—as opposed to cold and impersonal—anonymity of nakedness."[29] Since anonymity does not sound particularly warm and friendly (we think of Kafka), we press on expectantly to see what keeps this anonymity from being cold and impersonal, and it seems that the interposition of the artist (who is the woman's lover) between us and the image is the supplier of the warmth. Of course, all paintings require causal interpositions on the part of an artist, but here the interposed item is the artist's own real-world stance toward the beloved, which stance the spectator is then led into and which consequently makes him (or her) feel more like an eavesdropping guest than a voyeur.

This gloss on the genre of the "warmly naked," if we can speak of such a genre, gives us what we need to make sexual objecthood innocuous: intimacy. Persons in intimate relationships are routine appreciators of their partners' aesthetic properties, and these, to repeat, are not just bodily properties, but the bodily as expressive of the partner's sensibility. The aesthetic appeal of the sexual properties diffuses itself onto other aesthetically accessible properties, as Hume was aware (T 395), and these are also the properties upon which friendships are built. More important, diffusions onto the offspring of sexual unions also occur, and the love of parents for their children has a direct aesthetic reference that we have great difficulty comprehending on nonaesthetic grounds. But let us restrict our attention for now to the friendship component of the relationship between two partners. Ideally, amorousness should be reinforced by friendship, which is free of "those feverish fits of heat and cold" (MPL 189) that make amorousness unstable (but that also make it an "agreeable torment") and whose scope extends well beyond that of love.

---

29. Berger, *Ways of Seeing*, 59.

Friendship, as a phenomenon independent of sexual love, provides us, then, with the second category of personal aesthetic appreciation we should consider.

In a sense, our friends are more gratuitous than our lovers and families (particularly if we suppose that friendship is unessential to the relationship between ourselves and our lovers and family members). Our friends do not really help us accomplish anything, nor do they satisfy primitively specifiable urges, and typically enough, no "offspring" is produced except that of words and shared actions, which are heard or seen but by a few and which perish unrecorded. These facts alone would suggest a strong analogy between friends and artworks.[30] We need only to think of Plato's bottom-line question about art—what cities has Homer helped you to govern lately?—to see that a similar query is natural for friendship. Yet we associate readily with each other, despite not being able to justify the association in extremely precise terms. Certain temperaments are felt to be so similar to our own that we delight in the affinity (the power of resemblance again), and we repair to them for the refreshment that expressively luxuriating in their company affords both us and them. We do not want, or expect, too much harmony between us and them, however, because we also desire to be taken out of ourselves, to hear strings of words we would never utter in soliloquy, to undertake plans of action we would never pursue alone. For this reason, friendships not uncommonly develop between fairly different sorts of persons, and odd couplings thrive owing to their very oddness, provided there is an underlying affinity the oddness conceals. Whether the friend is closer to or further from us in felt affinity, the attraction is only explicable if we situate it in the space of the aesthetic—or the erotic. (If we reject the aestheticizing conception of the aesthetic, we are left with the possibility that, on solely cognitive grounds, the aesthetic and the erotic may not be distinct from each other. In both kinds of attraction we are drawn by something whose drawing power is less than fully explicable to us. I am not saying that the two are the same, however, since we can obviously distinguish them on noncognitive grounds.)

Needless to say, the space of the aesthetic includes negative as well as positive attractions: our enemies as well as our lovers and friends, and hatreds

---

30. Indeed, in "Of the Standard of Taste" Hume had written, "We choose our favourite author as we do our friend, from a conformity of humour and disposition" (MPL 244). More recently, Wayne Booth has explored a similar idea in *The Company We Keep* (Berkeley and Los Angeles: University of California Press, 1988).

can engender contexts of intimacy that eerily resemble those of love. Claims made about the negative instances parallel those about the positive, though sometimes the parallels are inversions, as with intractable hatreds that arise between people who resemble each other closely. Disagreeably aware of their resemblance, they take pains to emphasize to themselves and to others the minute differences that separate them, thus heightening the color that the differences have and making them more noticeable. This phenomenon has been aptly called the narcissism of minor difference, and it is the opposite number to odd-couple friendships, for here we have people who are oddly kept apart. Because we usually do not spend, or desire to spend, much time around our enemies, except in our imagination (that ever-serviceable battlefield), we need not concern ourselves with them further. Although there is an aesthetics of the enemy waiting to be written, our actual consortings with those whom we prize provide us with more straightforward material for study.

If we suppose that the appreciation of the person is best confined to a coterie of intimates, we should attempt to explain this confinement. If we do not explain it, the stipulation will seem ad hoc and merely face-saving for the Humean, whereas, if we come clean, I am confident that the explanation will only add new force to the nonrationalist account. There are three reasons for thinking the confinement desirable.

First, there is a definite element of risk in allowing ourselves to be an object for another. We let others see us in such a way that we give them the wherewithal for mockery and manipulation. We let them have everything they need to have in order to make us appear ridiculous—nothing can be more comical than a human being—and the power to make ridiculous is one form of the power to control. But manipulation of a more familiar kind is also a possibility. Those who know our aesthetic properties also know how to play their own tunes upon us: if someone is acquainted with the recesses of our character, seeing what we do not see, that person will in principle know how to box us in psychologically and score self-serving victories at our expense. And this manipulation may be bidirectional. Soured love relationships furnish many examples of internecine exploitation.

Any sensible person should recognize the dangers of intimacy. But such a person should also recognize that many splendors of civilized life are closely allied to these dangers; and we should therefore take a little care not to be too precipitate in parading naked (in all senses) before others, and we should therefore avoid concluding that nakedness as such is the problem. William James said that it was not to the saint, but to the repenting sinner, that the full meaning of life was revealed, and we might recast that statement, in line with our purposes, as follows: it is not the mere subject, but the subject who becomes an object, who will feel the richest sentiments, and have the most sterling values, of which we are capable. Objecthood has a cost, we might say, but that cost is scarcely prohibitive. Hume perceptively observed that "almost all animals use in play the same member, and nearly the same action as in fighting; a lion, a tyger, a cat their paws; an ox his horns; a dog his teeth; a horse his heels" (T 398). Curiously, the great naturalist does not say what we fight and play with, but it seems clear that language is our "member" and that we use language in all sorts of object-presupposing and object-identifying ways when we play and fight with each other. Declawing the cat and deobjectifying the person are efficacious, industrial-strength expedients for dealing with the problems that fighting raises, but they are hardly genial remedies.

The second reason for restricting the appreciating audience is that our objecthood is banal, to use Berger's word. We are much more anonymous than we fancy, and even though the particular circumstances of our life can erase this anonymity, the fact of our objecthood contributes considerably, as such, to the state of affairs that makes us yearn for erasure. This is just a return to the point about the Kafka and Rembrandt versions of anonymity. The first version is our natural lot; the second is the lot we attain with our intimates; and we exemplify each. The first is unpleasant because we think we are more interesting than we are. It is a harmless and sociable fantasy to suppose that we are fascinating to our fellows, provided that it does not motivate too many of our actions (in particular, any attempt to prove that the fascination is more than a fantasy), but we feel pain when reality impinges on the illusion that conceals the whim. (Parties and other social gatherings are sometimes disquieting for this reason. The truth begins to break through, as we smell the moldy cheese of which we are all made.) Naturally, then, we seek to closet ourselves with a few trusty intimates who are in on the game, as it were, and whose candor and affection help to reverse the emotional charge that our original anonymity carries.

This last remark lets me add a needed codicil to my earlier statements about our associative bent. The clustering of like temperaments is only a partial explanation of love and friendship. Temporal and spatial contiguities also account for their occurrences. This fact may seem hardly worthy of any notice (but of course! we do not strike up friendships with thirteenth-century Tibetans), but its triviality abates if we remember that spatiotemporal contiguity can be the cause of, and on that basis supply reasons for, our being interested in another, just as much as a temperamental affinity. There are people whom we care about originally as a result of finding ourselves with them at a particular place and time. Our being marooned with them, if we wish to call it that, not only forces us to look for resemblances we would otherwise have ignored but also forges the relevant resemblances through creating a shared history in that place and time. This cockeyed causation occurs outside of narrowly personal relationships, as Hume (with his feeling for the oblique) sensed: "A stranger, when he arrives first at any town, may be entirely indifferent about knowing the history and adventures of the inhabitants; but as he becomes farther acquainted with them, and has liv'd any considerable time among them, he acquires the same curiosity as the natives" (T 453–54). Our interest in towns and countries is generally fainter than our interest in particular people, and if a strong bond involving the fainter variety of attachment is propinquity-producible, so to say, then we have every reason to believe that the livelier variety is also, since bonds between people are easier to sustain than bonds between a person and a locality.

The codicil should be included because it draws my earlier statements closer to the actual workings of society. We do not simply gravitate toward those of like mind; our circumstances in part produce the likeness—that is, make it possible for the likeness to be a Humean natural relation—to which we gravitate. Boswell once opined to Johnson that he thought that Aristophanes was wrong in thinking that each person had a missing half somewhere, the restoration of whom would ensure felicity, because (Boswell said) fifty persons could fill the bill as well as one. To this, Johnson replied: "Nay, fifty thousand."[31] Johnson had the more accurate number, but he was wrong if he supposed that a person would meld with each of the fifty thousand in the same way (or would not undergo differential character modifications). We become different persons, in the sense of acquiring different shapings of our character, because of our associations: a truth that needs to be taken seriously, since the rationalist self-conception subtly disposes us to think that, irrespective of the way our life histories go from here, we are the same person across the alternative possibilities. But that is not so: we become who we are

---

31. Hume made use of the missing-halves myth in his essay "Of Love and Marriage"—in order to assist the two sexes in accepting the "amicable sentiment" that they should brook "no pretensions to authority on either side" (MPL 560). The use (and Hume's expansion) of the myth take up the bulk of the essay, which Hume eventually withdrew from the collected *Essays*. The picture of human love that the myth fosters is just a bit too precious for a Humean, is it not?

through a particular life history, and who we are is not who another might have been. The context-dependence, and moderate plasticity, of our characters, to which these observations call attention, takes us to a third reason for restricted appreciation.

A person's character can become so refined, through suitable historical associations, that the people who are able to appreciate it appropriately are perforce a small number. This is an idea Hume explores in his brief beautiful essay "Of the Delicacy of Taste and Passion," which is most un-Kantian in the aesthetically aware stance toward people that its author unobtrusively assumes and recommends. The idea I wish to retrieve from this essay comes from the second half but requires the background of the first.

Hume begins by claiming that we have two ways of registering "beauty and deformity of every kind" (MPL 4). The first is what Hume calls delicacy of passion, which we might call reaction delicacy, for a person who has it reacts to all affective stimuli that reach him; such a person undergoes the whole gamut of emotions that the world's goods and evils arouse. The second is delicacy of taste, which we might call detection delicacy, for a person who has it is not prey to the volatile behavioral manifestations that afflict the delicate reactor, but he imaginatively detects all the emotional nuances of the experiences that his hot-blooded brother, in the hurry of his spirits, cannot detect. (The delicate detector is the person who, in grosser physical tastings, is able to discriminate the leather from the iron tastes in a hogshead of wine.)[32] The reactor and detector are each finely attuned to the same experiences, but the one is overwhelmed by his experiences, while the other has a knowing detachment from them. Taste is more reflective, in a good sense, than passion: exercising taste does not flood the mind, as passion can, with affects that saturate it to such a degree that our attention is wholly absorbed by a single object. Hume holds that these two delicacies are incompatible, and that the delicacy of taste is far superior to that of passion.

One wonders whether delicacy of taste is the unequivocal good that Hume takes it to be, and whether a false delicacy (corresponding to the false refinement Hume criticizes some authors for) could be more than just inaccuracy in one's fine detections.[33] Be that as it may, Hume bases the superiority of the one delicacy over the other on (i) its conduciveness to that "agreeable melancholy, which of all dispositions of the mind, is the best

---

32. As in the *Don Quixote* episode regarding the two wine-tasting kinsmen, which Hume positions prominently in "Of the Standard of Taste" (MPL 234–35).

33. My "False Delicacy" examines these issues.

suited to love and friendship," and (ii) its conduciveness to the satisfaction of that disposition (MPL 7). Delicacy of taste makes us desire personal contact and at the same time helps to realize a peculiarly intimate variety of it.

Hume presents meager argumentation for (i) and (ii), but that is not a serious problem since (i) and (ii) gain plausibility more from each other than from what Hume says about each separately. The increasingly delicate detector will be an increasingly rare, and in a sense endangered, bird: his judgments will tend not to square with those of others whose taste is less delicate, with mutual incomprehension as a common result, and a sadness on the more delicate side that is not shared by the less (since he, the delicate detector, does not feel that there should be incomprehension, whereas the other, with callow *de gustibus* folk aesthetics, expects little else). An example: cinéastes will sometimes call a particular film unendurable, while others who go to a film once a year, watching the same piece, will be enraptured. In both cases the emotion is authentic (that is, not faked through external perturbing influences); the first taste is superior to the second, and yet the first cannot be made fully apparent to the second, because the occasional filmgoer is not a film lover, and the habituated heart has reasons that the unhabituated knows not of. The film example may make us suspicious of the genuineness of the phenomenon, since the practice of the arts generally has well acquainted us with connoisseurs who annoyingly profess to see more than others see. But the phenomenon arises for many other practices, and in some of these—the assessment of athletic performance, for example—the worry about snobbery, which is the (not wholly illegitimate) source of our suspicion in the art cases, seldom or never takes hold. We should resist, then, any merely general suspicions about the superiority of putative refined perceptions. The altering of our perception through habituation is one of the chief reasons why disputes of taste are so intractable and why they are not, for all that, pseudo-problems. Like our conviction concerning the continuing world, a conviction that unites us, our convictions concerning taste, which divide us, raise some of the most remarkable questions that our embodied nature generates.

In life as in art, the person who pauses over events and does not simply pass through them will have his delicacy heightened and be somewhat unfitted for the company of those whose taste is less delicate. That is, he will be less satisfied with such company. Notwithstanding this fastidiousness, he will be better suited for friendship because whenever he detects concordances of character (itself requiring delicacy), the resulting friendship will have a higher value and may be more enduring.³⁴ That the friendship has greater value could be fairly obvious, but in view of what Hume says, its greater endurance is not, although the staying power seems to be related to reflective stability. Interestingly, Hume regards delicacy of taste as something we grow into (detectors are made, not born), and friendships that begin on an indelicate plane acquire reflective stability through the refinements of the persons involved. "The gaiety and frolic of a bottle companion improves with him into a solid friendship: And the ardours of a youthful appetite become an elegant passion" (MPL 8). Persons who have "well digested their knowledge of both books and men" will be content to taste but few of either, and the detector's response to the world will be confirmed by the response of the detector's lover or friend: the "solid friendship" or "elegant passion" could not long subsist if one of the parties did not, by looking beyond the relationship, have a more enlarged, cosmopolitan view of things. We truly gain our own soul by gaining another's, and the other's is ours only if we both lose, through reflective tasting, a bit of that active world where the less reflective prosecute their designs.

And so, the more delicate our taste, the narrower our circle of intimates, or, better yet, the more rewardingly intimate our circle becomes. For intimacy is not merely protracted exposure to another person, but an exposure that makes people mutually visible and collectively invisible. Families illustrate well this dual property. An outsider to the family circle is often puzzled by an apparently insignificant remark that one family member makes to another and that strikes the recipient as deliciously droll or sends him into a towering rage. These are the earmarks of intimacy. The family members understand each other well (and all too well), but their mutual understanding is lost on their visitor. And if this occasion for co-occurrent concealment and revelation arises naturally in the most primary human associations, we must expect such occasions to become more numerous when the associations grow more secondary and refined. The intimacy is more invisible to the outsider the further up the refinement scale we go. And with this imperfect comprehen-

---

34. There is a difference between "being highly valued" and "having a high value" that becomes apparent here. I am not intending to suggest that friendships between less delicate detectors cannot be as heartfelt (and so, in a sense, as highly valued) as friendships between those who are more. But insofar as we think that value is somehow correlated with irreplaceability (and we do think this, some of the time, and Kant's view of our dignity is one expression of the thought), we have grounds for thinking that friendships between the more delicate have a higher value. (However, the notion of objective value, implicit in the last sentence, is in tension with some strands in the Sceptic's thinking, and so, clearly, more needs to be said.)

sion across the exclusionary boundary of intimacy we have returned to the kind of antinomy that the contretemps in our film example presented.

Familial intimacy is thrust upon us, but the other forms arise through a dialectic inherent in the aesthetic dimension of the self. Furthermore, I think it is difficult to explain what intimacy is, or why it is important, unless we acknowledge the aesthetic dimension. Nor do we need to worry that the refinement of taste (and thus the aesthetic enrichment of the character) will refine a person out of all company, and so replace intimacy with privacy. Good wine needs no bush: an aesthetically pleasing person, like an ultimately successful avant-garde artwork, creates the conditions for his appreciation if those conditions are not already in place. The appreciators may be few, a happy few, but that should not be an in-principle problem, as we have seen, because the desire for appreciative confinement sprouts in tandem with the power to retain appreciation satisfyingly. These observations, incidentally, enable us to detect the fustian in Nietzsche's pronouncements about the free spirit, and it will not be a rank digression to explain one superiority of the Humean version of the free spirit.

There is a rather straight line, conceptually (but of course not historically) speaking, between Hume's person of delicate taste and Nietzsche's free spirit. Their resemblance is obscured, I suspect, by a tendency to interpret the free spirit as a basically Kantian agent whose freedom is no longer constrained by reason. (This tendency is arguably assisted by some connivance from Nietzsche himself.) Yet the resemblances are there. Hume's person is retiring, not fully an actor in the world; so too is the free spirit. The detector has digested books and men; the free spirit has been "at home, or at least has been a guest, in many countries of the spirit."[35] The detector is hard to please and hard to appreciate; the free spirit has "fore- and back-souls into whose ultimate intentions nobody can look so easily, with fore- and backgrounds which no foot is likely to explore to the end."[36] Both figures ground their most personally weighty judgments in their taste. Their chief difference is also striking. Hume never says that the detector should *try* to cultivate esoteric withdrawal, whereas Nietzsche regularly uses the language of intention, at just this point, in characterizing the activity of a free spirit.[37] The mawkish

---

35. Adapted from *Beyond Good and Evil*, trans. Walter Kaufmann (New York: Vintage, 1966), sec. 44.
36. Ibid.
37. Though not exclusively. In section 40 of *Beyond Good and Evil* he says that "around every profound spirit a mask is continually growing," and this does not sound intentionalistic.

hermeticism that puts us off in Nietzsche derives largely from his attribution of self-concealing intentions to his ideal character. Hume's detector does nothing at all to create himself, but a self is created nonetheless, and the detector's freedom of spirit is the subtler because he does not make any ado about it. This comparison shows us that the Humean characterization of the free spirit is more sweetly reasonable, but also more consistent with the rest of Nietzsche's picture, which makes us suspicious of conscious intentions, than Nietzsche's own characterization.

Now that we have examined the various reasons that either effortlessly or with modest effort restrict the appreciation of persons, this introduction to the aesthetics of the person is nearly complete. One variation on the intimate relationship calls for additional comment, however, and the variation is unusual both in that it need not be the cause or effect of spatiotemporal contiguity and in that it can play an overtly ethical role in a person's deliberations. I have in mind role modelings from afar.

Persons routinely make vivid impressions on others when they romantically capture their imaginations and inspire them with a familiar kind of hero enthusiasm that is not vicious. This plainly involves an aesthetic appreciation. When an inner-city youth is captivated by a basketball hero and affects the overall style of his imaginary mentor—his on-court deportment, his verve, his professed (if not expressed) values—he is more truly treating his idol as an aesthetic object than Wilde ever did when he affected psychical distance. This sort of attachment from afar is extremely pervasive. Political candidates may carry the image of Lincoln or Kennedy in their eye; intellectuals, a favorite writer or thinker (one might think of Harold Bloom's anxiety of influence as well as Hume's more pleasant anxiety of emulation); teachers, someone who had a deep pedagogical impact on them; artisans, the families who made them feel the dignity of their trade or the master workman who communicated their sense of exacting standards; younger generations, members of the older generations (the Shropshire lad thinks, as his train leaves the station, of "the men who made a man of me"). Even though there is actual acquaintance in many of these cases, the acquaintance seldom involves much, if any, intimacy: we often do not know our teachers very well, for example. But the lack of mundane intimacy is compensated by a strong imaginative intimacy, as it is with the authors we favor, and so our relationship to the other in these cases is continuous with our relationships with friends and lovers.

Role modeling has negative instances also, and these typically arise when we pull back distastefully from a course of action, or go through with it under duress. Dietrich von Choltitz, the general whom Hitler commanded to raze the French capital, refused to carry out the order, because he did not want to be known to posterity as the Man Who Burned Paris. During the Cuban missile crisis, Robert Kennedy advised his brother not to invade Cuba by surprise, because such an invasion would disagreeably resemble the Pearl Harbor attack. Many homeless persons will delay asking passersby for money for as long as possible because they know what figures they cut in the eyes of those whom they importune. These examples disclose sympathy-imbued mental operations that are only slightly more elaborate than those in Hume's own text.[38]

Clearly, in both positive and negative versions of role modeling there is an ingredient of what Rousseau called *amour propre*, or living in others. Rousseau painted *amour propre* in the darkest colors imaginable, and many have found the painting persuasive. And to the extent that Rousseau put his finger on genuine evils, we must regard them as the bad outcomes of risky exposures to other people (exposures whose better outcomes justify the risks). But not all of Rousseau's effect comes from his documentation of genuine kinds of intrasocial enslavement. Some of it results from his pandering to that readily bribed part of our nature which recoils indignantly at the suggestion that we exist for others in a way that we do not for ourselves. It is not for nothing that Nietzsche once called Rousseau the "moral tarantula" that bit Kant:[39] the blanket hostility to *amour propre* and the blanket aversion to the appreciation of persons are at bottom the same feeling. We are unlovely zealots if we think there is something amiss with the examples we have canvased. To a more delicate taste, Rousseau's painting would have been improved by a thinner impasto.

Let us now take up the second aesthetic good I wanted to examine: artworks. Unlike persons, artworks raise no excited cries of disbelief if we say that they are purveyors of aesthetic satisfactions, for these satisfactions are—until recently perhaps—what we have always expected of them. Consequently, we do not have to labor for this claim and fill another chapter. But there is another question, which artworks pose and which persons did not, and it is worth a brief examination. I said at the outset that the nonrationalist

---

38. Not all generals, statesmen, and homeless persons care about their role models, of course. But this is not to say that caring about them is dependent on what is merely a contingent fact, our having had a good upbringing. For the goodness of our upbringing is not itself contingent in any important sense.

39. *Daybreak*, preface, sec. 3.

account should give artworks reflectively more prestige than the rationalist account does. Yet that prestige may amount to little, because artworks occupy such a small niche in our lives. True, some of us take an interest in the arts, with varying degrees of seriousness, but most people do not. Adapting what Hume says about philosophy, we could even go so far as to say that over those who do take the interest, the empire of art has very limited authority; we leave the gallery, and the aesthete is lost in the man (or woman). Marginality is the new issue. Is there a problem that it raises for the nonrationalist account?

First, we might just accept the marginality, and through this acceptance dismiss any problems. Philosophy occupies a small niche in the world (that is, few people pursue it), and although that smallness is reflectively endorsed in the Humean conception I have set forth, its importance is not the same thing as its smallness. We could make similar provisions for art.

This answer will not serve for long, however. If the nonrationalist psychology is right, then people are creatures guided by a partnership between stolid habit, on the one hand, and rather racier emotions and imaginings, on the other. That being so, it would be empirically surprising if we were not widespread appreciators of a form of art, since art, as Plato maintained, appeals so strikingly to the emotions and imagination. Not much, of course, appeals to our sense of habit, and that is why habit is stolid. This appeal distinguishes art from philosophy, which does not really give the emotions and imagination much, or as much, to grab. This is true, preeminently, of the Sceptic's own philosophy, which uncolorfully advises us not to reconceive the emotion- and imagination-conformable objects of everyday experience too drastically. The color, the sentiment, is present in the Sceptic's view, but an uncommon delicacy of taste is needed to discern it.

Second, we might say that persons, as described in these pages, are the artworks of prereflective life, and therefore we are wrong to look in the prereflective order for a certain class of artifacts that correspond to the contents of our museums, our symphony halls, or libraries. This idea is not unattractive, but here I think we run into a matter-of-fact hurdle: artworks are not simply isomorphic deposits of persons, even though the features in which they resemble persons are arresting. Persons and their fellow appreciators still have their lives to lead—artworks have no life and are not subject to the moral assessments that living agents are—and there are things we expect of artworks that we do not expect of persons (such as a level of excellence that only exceptional works of art attain).

Nevertheless, the proposal to look for something besides arty-looking artifacts is promising, and we should follow this lead. To begin with, we could shift our focus from fine art to those forms of art which even now we do not hesitate to call "low": pop music, pulp romances, television sitcoms, comic strips, and the like. These items certainly play a larger role in everyday life than do their more elitist cousins, and perhaps they give us our passkey. But I am not convinced that we can let the investigation rest with them, because the lower art forms do not reveal much about the source of the aesthetic pleasures they provide if we critically examine the works in these forms themselves.[40] We do not understand why we thrill with pleasure while listening, as Roquentin did, to the most hackneyed song lyrics, wearily sung, if we look no further than the conclusions that an inference from the aesthetic qualities of the tune (or the lyrics) to the listener give us. Andrew Sarris once ascribed to Charlie Chaplin a frayed lace valentine heart, and it seems that this should be a good description of the heart of Everyman if we were to explain the low-art phenomenon from the inside out. Perhaps so: but let us first try approaching from the outside in, to see why we are so ready to exult, like Roquentin, in the merest nothing from Tin Pan Alley.

In the spirit of John Dewey, who wanted to integrate aesthetic satisfactions into everyday life, we would do well to look for ur-versions of art outside the gallery, and their values should be recognizably artistic and not merely aesthetic in a more generalized sense. Although the aesthetics of art and the aesthetics of nature (and, more broadly, the nonartifactual) have nontrivial similarities, and are intricately related to each other, there is a difference between them that we should be careful to observe. "Art" is cognate with "artifact" and "artifice," and the conceptual connection is of more than etymological interest. The artistic is concerned with conscious design, with pretense and simulacrum, and with the exceptional, unaccustomed moments—the epiphanies—that purposeful pretense can deliver; and we bear all this in mind whenever we survey or interpret a work of art. "What an insipid comedy should we make of the chit-chat of the tea-table, copied faithfully and at full length? Nothing can please persons of taste, but nature drawn with all her graces and ornaments, *la belle nature*" (MPL 191–92). Beautiful nature: not just any old slice of life, but a slice that is so carefully selected that the principle of selection yields us simultaneously a slice of art. Of course, the test for the exceptional is its naturalness, after a fashion. A work should not dazzle

---

40. This is controversial, because there is an inclination among some people today to regard any attempt to differentiate high and low art on *aesthetic* grounds as hopelessly suspect. I do not think that this suspicion can be borne out, but I cannot pursue this topic here.

the mind with merely ingenious conceits, nor should it violently assault our emotional dispositions. We should be able to take to it naturally, to appreciate it, in that respect, as if it were a piece of nature. And so, Hume's praise (at MPL 191) of Addison's definition of literary artistry—writing whose sentiments are natural without being obvious—is well awarded, for this brief formulation calls attention to both the artificial component and the test for artful success. (And indeed, the formulation qualifies as an enlightening example of artistry in its own right by its own standard.) These reflections reveal to us a bit of the intricacy of the art-nature relation I just mentioned, but the greater complexity of art, which presupposes nature while contrasting with it, prevents art from being simply reducible to natural beauty. If we prescind from its linguistic meaning, the "chit-chat of the tea-table" can be appreciated for the relative euphoniousness of the sounds we hear—and it is possible that, so far as the sounds themselves are concerned, the "chit-chat" will be more beautiful than the ode the poet sings. Yet this beauty is not the beauty of art.

If we look for the protoartistic in our experience, I think we will find it in two areas. The first I call saturnalia events; the second, memorializations. Although these terms sound as if they might refer to things forbiddingly remote from ordinary consciousness, that appearance is erroneous because we do not usually have any need to group together the items I am grouping, and so we do not have a ready-to-hand label for them.

In the course of a typical year we celebrate a variety of holidays, generally with our families or with others whose relationship to us is affectively important: Christmas, Passover, Thanksgiving, the Fourth of July, birthdays. Frequently, to be sure, we are miserable at these times, which can be awash in bathos and hokum. But let us not be crabs, and we should, at any rate, be more impressed by the necessary element of fantasy in the celebration of these days rather than the dreary letdowns that regularly occur (but that are also not universal). It is enough that these celebrations influence our taste, and not our will, as Hume said while considering (T 586) our refusal to pay a shilling for the rebuilding of a house whose deformity, we know, gives pain to its owner (which, for the moralist, involves another sort of letdown itself). These days of the year are special events; imaginatively we feel special, and our souls catch a generous flame, if only for a moment, from those who share the event with us. At midnight, to be sure, our coaches turn back into pumpkins, but that hardly funds an objection. The extraordinary would fatigue, as well as lose its point, logically speaking, if it became ordinary. These times I call saturnalia events, not because licentiousness is their accompaniment, but because on these occasions we feel that the quotidian rules of our existence do not apply. We live, in a trice, a little beyond our means, as they are specified in our various moral economies. We get a chance to rib the straitlaced fellow with the diplomatic immunity of the king's fool, and *he* gets a similar shot at us. We meet with people we may seldom see, and even if the last six months bring us the same news, the same jokes and rantings, that we have heard for the last six years, the repetition can be reassuring.

Humble stuff, you say, and so it is, but lest we be too sniffy, we should recall that the celebrations that sanction and make possible these moods and forms of behavior are the highlights of the year for a great many persons, and are ardently anticipated in their imagination and revisited in their memory. And I do not think that this importance could simply be a function of a deeper alienation that imposes a psychological demand for saturnalias because quotidian existence is so grindingly unrewarding. Alienation can exacerbate the need for saturnalias (and concomitantly cause us to exaggerate their standing in the calendar), but I do not think that alienation can create the need. In the most desirable social arrangements that are in our power to produce, we would still have a need for the holiday because the nonholiday world is monotonous. Habit, upon which we base our mental lives and without which they lose coherence, is ultimately boring, and it naturally generates a desire for the contra-habitual, a desire that can itself be satisfied within the habitual framework (our holidays occur as periodic punctuations of the year). The best life conceivable must have a strong component of habit in it, for it would not otherwise be a life at all, and hence the need for Mardi Gras would seemingly spring eternal in the human breast.

Saturnalia events are not confined to the public calendar: we have our private grids as well.[41] If we ask one person to open her photograph album, and another to give a chronology of his life, we shall see and hear a parade of punctuations: the first bicycle, the first automobile, sixteenth birthdays, prom nights, baseball championships, graduations, marriages, job promotions, career changes, purchasing a house, taking a vacation in Hawaii, getting one's name on the door of the firm, having a prestigious one-man art show, receiving a prize for newspaper reporting, being fêted on retirement from the

---

41. "A gloomy, hair-brained enthusiast, after his death, may have a place in the calendar; but will scarcely ever be admitted, when alive, into intimacy and society, except by those who are as delirious and dismal as himself" (E 270). We will not fully understand the attractions of "hair-brained" enthusiasm unless we fully acknowledge the meanings of the ordinary calendar.

bank. The list is endless, and by including the sappiest Americana along with more sophisticated specialities, I have tried to show something of the range that the list possesses as well as the formal commonalities of the items on the list.[42] Once we throw the private in with the public, the set of moments by which people identify and define themselves will appear large and various, and characterizing the set in protoartistic terms will not betray an elitist bias.

It should be noted that not all special events are saturnalias exactly, though many of these behave in a surprisingly similar way. Many of the most colorful and extraordinary times of our lives are occasioned by circumstances that run the gamut from mildly unpleasant to ghastly, and they are consequently circumstances that we would never choose to put ourselves in. Catastrophes are good examples. People who weather hurricanes, survive plane crashes, witness riots, or who extricate themselves from snafus while traveling abroad are often extremely quick to tell us about the scrapes they got through and, indirectly, how they rose to the occasion and proved their mettle. The precariousness of the reality confers a luster on the anecdotal representation, and we see the glow in the face of the raconteur. None of these people would ever propose calling up a hurricane or a plane crash so that they could enrich their characters and glean more material for boffo stories, but the unsummoned events allow them to live lives a little out of the common grain nonetheless, and they are tacitly thankful for the opportunity. We must put a great deal of stress on the fact that these events are unchosen. Their imaginative hue would change utterly if we knew that someone had chosen them. The world is indeed a vale of soul-making, but we are disturbed if we suspect that the world has been arranged with a view to realizing soul-making intentions. (We are disturbed whether the chooser is located outside the world or, like a hypothetical seeker of plane crashes, within it.) That a certain indisputable kind of flourishing on our part has morally unchoosable presuppositions is another of the curiosities of the mental-cum-moral life of animals such as ourselves.

Let us turn now to what I have called memorializations. We love to leave monuments to ourselves and to each other, or to the self that we imagine that we and others have. Houses are perhaps the most common examples. We take pride in stamping our plot of turf with some mark or other that lets the world know that we passed through it, and the patient labor that people put into

---

42. We might transfer and update Hume's test for psychological explanations: if a theory of value cannot explain why the first bicycle or the prom night is important, it is probably a defective theory.

feathering their nests, and that knows no surcease, attests to this pride. Hume said that a man who shows us a house "takes particular care" to point out, among other things, "the little room lost in the stairs, anti-chambers, and passages" (T 363), and the pleasure of the exhibition cannot be traced to the mere utility of the "lost" rooms, important though that is, but also to the owner's proud decision to have those rooms put in the house (or to buy a house that had such rooms). Like the chambered nautilus, we forever build our domiciliary shells.

Much more than our houses can be included under this metaphor. From houses we can turn to the memorializations of work. We want our work to be good, and for its goodness to stand as a record of ourselves. (The mark of the workman need not be different from the work, as Descartes correctly observed.) The work we do can have very intangible effects—glad memories in another person's mind for having made our acquaintance—but those effects are monuments, after a notional fashion, still. It is difficult, I think, to conceive an adequate reason for the powerful bond that the majority of persons have, or want to have, with their work unless we connect their work to themselves as more enduring and less self-contained expressions of the persons that they are. And this is memorialization. Penury, or the threat of it, drives many of us to accept the particular jobs we have, but even if we removed these factors, we would still find in ourselves an itch to make marks that others recognize and applaud. Nobody enjoys eating the bread of idleness, and I think that our discomfort is largely due to a vague (or not so vague) awareness that unless we are employed, our foothold in existence becomes more tenuous: we insensibly drift into that inner world where none will follow us, where we cease to be of interest to others (and, finally, to ourselves). We have an opportunity here to be reminded that "ourself, independent of the perception of every other object is in reality nothing" (T 340), and just as our perceptions give us our surveyable characters, our actions give us surveyable monuments of, and to, those characters.

My pairing of saturnalia events and memorializations as the ur-versions of art owes much of its inspiration to the Dionysian-Apollinian duality in Nietzsche's *Birth of Tragedy*, a work whose suggestiveness makes it more widely ranging in its import than it is sometimes thought to be. The nonimagistic Dionysian arts of music and dance intoxicate their practitioners, making them participants in episodic performances. During the Dionysian revel "the slave is a free man; now all the rigid, hostile barriers that necessity, caprice, or 'impudent convention' have fixed between man and man are broken. Now, with the gospel of universal harmony, each one feels himself not only united, reconciled, and fused with his neighbor, but as one with him." The imagistic Apollinian arts of painting and sculpture generate art*works*, nonepisodic material deposits that we calmly contemplate rather than performances we whirlingly immerse ourselves in. As intoxication is the physiological correlate for the Dionysian forms, dreams are the correlate for the Apollinian, and if we are moved by what we contemplate, we say, "It is a dream! I will dream on!"[43] The imagination is moved to linger, where the passions were prompted to continue their participation, and the two classes of forms complement—and, as Nietzsche later says, perfect—each other.

This contrast is very much mirrored (or echoed?) in my account. Nietzsche's portentous, oracular style of utterance, coupled with the ostensibly narrow concerns of his book, have hindered us from duly appreciating the contrast. Hume, who is akin to Nietzsche in his nonrationalism, allows us to see that these concepts have an unexpected and application that enhances their plausibility. The "cautious observation of human life" (T xix) shows us little rooms in the stairs, not mystery rites from the dark abysm of time, but these barely noticed phenomena display the relevant concepts, and if Nietzsche is right about the centrality of the Dionysian and Apollinian impulses, right that they arise "without the mediation of the human artist,"[44] then we should be able to find them, in some form or other, in those circumstances of ordinary human culture which were not too lowly for Hume to investigate.[45]

Incidentally, as I close this survey of the aesthetically valuable elements in our experience, I am now in a position to note that persons and protoartworks sometimes present themselves inseparably to our minds. Hume was fond of a story concerning Alexander the Great, of which the Prince of Condé was also fond and whom Hume quoted. When his soldiers refused to follow him to India, Alexander told them, "Go! Go tell your countrymen, that you left Alexander completing the conquest of the world" (E 252, T 599). Here we have a charismatic man who fires the imagination, but who also promises an exceptional experience to those who remain with him, and so a person and

---

43. *Birth of Tragedy*, sec. 1.
44. Ibid., sec. 2.
45. There is moreover, for Hume, a deeper reason to investigate the lowly. In a remarkable passage in "Of Refinement in the Arts," he writes, "The same age, which produces great philosophers and politicians, renowned generals and poets, usually abounds with skilful weavers, and ship-carpenters. We cannot reasonably expect, that a piece of woollen cloth will be wrought to perfection in a nation, which is ignorant of astronomy, or where ethics is neglected" (MPL 270–71).

an ur-version of art aesthetically coalesce. Interesting events (or achievements) follow in the wake of the more interesting people, and prizing the two apart can be difficult. And because joint inducements are stronger than single ones, we have every reason to be alarmed, as Hume was, by the Alexander figures, whose greatness unfolds itself in such socially destructive ways. Greatness has socially constructive, as well as socially invisible, instantiations, and the Humean critic should point both kinds out to us, redirecting our sentiments from injurious objects to those which withstand a severer scrutiny.

Finally, we should be struck by the centrality, in general, of the aesthetic goods. If we understand persons aright, not confining our understanding of the aesthetic to the framework of the various etiolated aestheticisms, and if we understand art aright, not confining it to the museum and the school, we shall conclude that aesthetic goods are among the very greatest goods. In fact, we shall be rather inclined to agree with G. E. Moore, who, at the conclusion of his influential treatise on the foundations of ethics, wrote: "By far the most valuable things, which we know or can imagine, are certain states of consciousness, which may be roughly described as the pleasures of human intercourse and the enjoyment of beautiful objects."[46] Moore put forward this claim because he thought personal and artistic pleasures were the only ones we valued for their own sake, intransitively, and indeed, if my argument is cogent, Moore's thought is correct. Hume gave indications that he would have agreed as well. When he described a paradise, at the beginning of his discussion of that justice we need to practice in our conditions of moderate scarcity, he said that for a person who lived there, "music, poetry, and contemplation form his sole business: conversation, mirth, and friendship his sole amusement" (E 183). The textual evidence is somewhat exiguous, but Hume is depicting a fantasy, a kind of dream, and in the *Treatise* he had recommended that we "recollect our dreams in a morning, and examine them with the same rigour, that we wou'd our most serious and deliberate actions" (T 219). These pages, in fine, are a new and Humean kind of philosophical testimonial to what we think of as "the Bloomsbury values," but a Bloomsbury liberalized beyond its original boundaries, and therein, I hope, lies the novelty of the testimonial.

---

46. *Principia Ethica* (Cambridge: Cambridge University Press, 1922), 188.

Retrospect

In these pages I have attempted to clarify a certain conception of the embodied person. Although the mental transitions I have charted here are perhaps natural to make, they are often, and even typically, unclear; and to make them clearer, as well as to close our irregular circle, I will now look backward to see where we have been. A retrospect is arguably a more fitting view than a prospect for a skeptical philosopher to occupy, but apart from observing an aesthetic propriety, we may learn a few new things by treading over our old footsteps. It is through repetition that resemblances become salient to the mind's eye, and in a skeptical system (if I may be allowed to co-opt, for a rhetorical purpose, a word fraught with rationalist associations) looking at the same patch of terrain in various lights and from various angles may be indispensable for securing conviction in both the author and the reader.

To begin this retrospect, I should like to return to the target of my criticism, rationalism. We might, unfortunately at the risk of some grandiloquence, refer to this target as the "Enlightenment self-understanding," a way of thinking about ourselves that is difficult to state precisely in nonmetaphorical terms, but that we can roughly characterize as follows: A person consists of two broad classes of components that stand in a distinctive relation to each other. In the first class belong those psychological faculties that are essentially dependent on our embodiment, and being embodied should be understood liberally to include not only our physiological hardware but also the various dispositions we have in virtue of having bodies (such as a tendency to be fatigued, or to prefer the more contiguous good to the more remote). These faculties are the senses, which in the natural course of events yield relatively unreflective beliefs, and the emotions, which similarly yield relatively unreflective values. By calling such beliefs and values unreflective

I primarily mean that not much thinking goes into their manufacture, but I also want to incorporate another idea, and this takes us directly to the second type of component and to the distinctive relation. Some of the beliefs we acquire through the natural avenues are false, some of the values bad, and calling them unreflective serves to remind us that we do not generally and consciously select the contents of our mixed bags. That our bags are mixed is hardly cause for amazement, but the rationalist turn begins if we suppose that we have a faculty that corrects our beliefs and values, makes them truer, on the basis of merely intellectualistic criteria.

The role of reason, the corrector, is to accredit beliefs and values to the extent that they possess a Cartesian-style "clarity," which I have parsed as a certain kind of rule-expressibility. This clarity is not the ordinary sort we prize when we are trading in Locke's marketplace (or even for the most part in Mill's marketplace, that of ideas). It is the clarity that only a more fastidious customer requires, an inquirer whose copious reflections have inculcated in him a desire to be immunized in advance against error or hollowness. There is no purchase for such an extravagant form of clarity outside of reflection, for attaining this clarity serves no purpose, satisfies no interest, that is specifiable independently of the reflection that normatively nurtures it. The demand for this clarity arises naturally, however, because our minds detect no mistake in the articulation of the demand, and therefore seeing the demand as questionable, as a problem and not simply as a given, involves our stepping outside rationalism. I have tried to explain the rationalist target in Chapter 1, as well as to exemplify, in my own discursive procedure, the nonrationalist competitor, and this dual display of the target and the critical perspective on the target was my first (and far from negligible) task. Subsequent chapters offered what I hope were collateral illuminations of the two perspectives.

My second task, after explaining rationalism, was to show what exactly goes wrong with it if the wrongness is not primarily of an intellectual sort. We might have thought that, in view of the artificially exalted standards that rationalism encourages, the chief objection to rationalism would be that its standards are too difficult or impossible to satisfy. This is not the main line I have pressed, however. The most trenchant criticism of any position always calls into question the desirability of satisfying the standards the position presupposes, and I have attempted a most searching criticism of rationalism. The central problem with rationalism is false heroism. We obtain through rationalism a self-conception according to which we are able, potentially, by means of various belief- and value-purification exercises, to invest our beliefs and values with a magnificent global order or tidiness. The independent intellect is capable of performing the exercises and surveying the order. A strong note of heroism is discernible in both the procedures and the results envisaged in the application of the procedures: we have to have a titanically self-reflexive single-mindedness of intention in order to carry out the purifying exercises and to abide in the purified state. By couching the criticism of rationalism in these terms I am speaking the language of the nonrationalist, obviously, but we then must go on to ask what makes rationalistic heroism suspect, that is, what makes it unworthy of reflective endorsement. As for the falsity of the heroism, it is possible to offer considerations that the rationalist should accept as cogent, if not decisive. In brief, the heroism is false because it deprives us of a desirable (and desirably moderate) confidence in our powers or, alternatively, it engenders a misplaced confidence in them. (The problematic character of the military virtues affords a useful comparison with the virtues of reflection, according to rationalism.) I make out the case for false heroism in respect of rationalism in Chapters 2 and 3, using materials found in Hume, that archetypal nonrationalist whom I iconically invoked in Chapter 1 but upon whom I actively depended for my conceptual moves here.

In Chapters 2 and 3, I have hopes that I have made a contribution to Hume interpretation by showing how different (and not, as by Hume's exegetes, usually related) parts of the Humean corpus reflect each other. Nevertheless, I have mainly wished to situate a seminal figure from the past within the frame of a present concern, to make him a partner in a conversation. Since Hume is both an inspiration for me as I trace some of the implications of nonrationalism and thematically the cynosure of this project, he turns out to be—in an unlikely but nevertheless acceptable (and Humean) sense—a hero. This fact is of some importance. I seek embodiments for those stances which I reflectively approve, and in doing this I hope to evince fidelity to nonrationalist principles.

The criticisms of rationalism in these two chapters parallel each other to an extent, but they are directed at different engagements of the human mind. Chapter 2 dealt with our framework of beliefs, and showed that rationalist reflection (i) causes us epistemically to disavow a non-rule-governed movement of the mind along resembling perceptions, and (ii) results in a skeptical condition I have called malign, the malignity lying in the mind's incapacity, or diminished capacity, for reflective commitment to its beliefs. Malign skepticism is largely a notional difficulty, since belief is too hardy a perennial to be extirpated by reasoning, however circumspect initially; and yet a tincture of this skepticism is present whenever relativism gains a foothold in the imagination (as it sometimes does). In any event, the rationalist viewpoint, as uncorrected by sentiment, leaves us in an underattached mental position that can be described as disembodied. The disavowal in (i) is concomitant with the skepticism of (ii), and their dialectical connection allows us to make sense of the idea that rationalist heroics are false. I should also remind us that the skepticism I have laid incriminatingly at the door of rationalism is not the same as the skepticism I have been at pains to laud, and the differences between the two, as well as the resemblances that justify my using "skepticism" for both, can be concisely restated along these lines: The malign skeptic reaches his skepticism through a reliance on overly intellectualized arguments, and his commitments to belief are indiscriminately attenuated. The benign skeptic reaches his through sentiment and habit, and his commitments are selectively attenuated, beliefs with narrowly intellectual recommendations arousing the greatest suspicion.

Chapter 3 dealt with the evaluations that flow from the fabric of our sentiments, and sought to show that if rationalist reflection were efficacious in managing our occasionally troublesome passions, it could do so only by strengthening or weakening the ethically bad dispositions along with the good. (The conditions for efficaciousness are the conditions for another form of disembodiment.) This mismanagement of our passions would occur because the corrections the rationalist wants to make are anchored in the adoption of a point of view that is too abstract, too weakly related to our particular circumstances. Moreover, if the adoption were to be beneficent, we should have to regard the vouchsafed point of view as being simply an object of attention (in much the same way that an artwork is), and not as a binding requirement of rationality. These points of view are to be found as ingredients in various ethical theories, namely, those which purport to tell us, in accordance with a favored general principle, what it is that we should do; and although I did not pursue the matter in any detail, the paradigms of such theories are the familiar Kantian and utilitarian options. An interesting feature of my treatment of rationalism is that these ethical theories occupy, in the space of value, a site similar to that which malignly skeptical campaigns occupy in the space of belief: the ethical theorist and the malign skeptic are both motivated by a distrust of common feeling; they each look for merely intellectual solutions to problems that usually arise nonintellectually; and when the contents of their deliverances are elaborated, those contents seem, to nonadepts, more or less chimerical. Furthermore, I do not want to say that ethical theories (on my restricted conception) are good accounts of value that unfortunately have not been perfected in principle or followed in practice, but I do want to say instead that they are bad accounts that extratheoretic circumstances have luckily prevented from producing untoward effects on either reflection or practice.

My third task was then to show where an acceptance of benign skepticism, that which is in harmony with the most naturalized conception of ourselves, leaves or leads us, particularly with regard to our "moral sentiments" (as eighteenth-century thinkers would say). An ocean of philosophy opens before us here, and the final chapters only begin to take us into the water. I believe that it is difficult for us to accept a nonrationalist interpretation of ourselves, but I am also persuaded that if we do accept such an interpretation of ourselves, the selves we accordingly survey will have less surface dash, perhaps, than the less mature selves we saw in the rationalist mirror, but they will definitely have more interesting recesses, more to reward the delicate perceiver. One of these rewards concerns the notion of reward itself. It sometimes seems that a rejection of rationalism would lead us to resignation, quietism, or merely a bemused (and slightly resentful) abandonment of reflection. I do not think that this saturnine state of mind is at all warranted; and there is no reason to think that the Humean should *abandon* the Enlightenment self-understanding (if that were possible). Human beings maintain, strengthen, and revise their beliefs and values in a piecemeal way over time, and with a varying tempo, and without much of a theoretical apparatus to guide or license their moves. The self-consciously Humean reflector can at least assist this progress by expressly seconding those operations of the mind and those practices of the culture which promote a defensible confidence and by expressly contemning the operations and practices that do not. The job of a Humean critic is probably more cautionary than constructive, but given our whimsical condition, this is job enough. Just as we cannot expect an intellectually straight path out of our deliberative puzzles, so too we cannot reasonably hope that we shall avoid making wayward turns, within reflection or without. In Chapter 4 I sought to show how benign skepticism naturally accommodates both the large-grain sense of social progress and the small-grain sense of psychological difficulty and misgiving, and to show then how things are both better and worse than they appear under the rationalist picture of our situation. To buttress these two senses, I explicated Hume's genealogical account of monotheism, treating monotheistic religion as the primitive rehearsal of rationalistic philosophy. Polytheism is ethically superior to intellectually more creditable monotheism, but both are problematic, and yet it is only the slow process of cultural refinement that reveals to us how they are problematic, and why, from a very late perspective indeed, polytheism unexpectedly wins the palm.

Polytheism emerges, by the same token, as the rehearsal of nonrationalism, and this identification made it possible for us to explore another kind of consequence of benign skepticism. We may feel an elevated vertigo if we accept the skeptical critique of rationalism. We may entertain that ever-uncanny thought that nothing guides us as we sift through our puzzles. In reality, however, we are seldom left dangling. If theory fails us, other things can fill the deliberative breach; and if we are Humeans, we should expect the breach to be filled. Now the gods of polytheism were artworks in the form of persons, and indirectly they guided action and informed sensibility. These gods never existed, as we know, and so their influence on the mind was predicated on ignorance. But artworks, and persons qua artworks, can perform offices similar to those which these illusory entities performed, and they can do so without our remaining mired in ignorance. Their indirect but nontrivial influence was the subject of Chapter 5. In this chapter I sought to show that persons possess an aesthetic dimension (which rationalism conceals from us), and how persons are understandable as aesthetic goods and how in this capacity they do some of the work done by illusory ethical theories. I also wanted to show in this chapter that the aesthetic goods we typically find in art are not restricted to artworks and their audiences, as we sometimes think, but are much more widespread, and are thus more important than they at first appear.

And so we end. In the Conclusion of the second *Enquiry* Hume wrote that virtue, on his representation of it, no longer wore the "dismal dress" with which the religionists and philosophers had often attired it: "nothing appears but gentleness, humanity, beneficence, affability, nay, even at proper intervals, play, frolic, and gaiety" (E 279). Hume's desired association of virtue with levity and good cheer is part of an effort to make ethical seriousness a more discreet and delicate notion than it has generally been. I have painted the reflective self with the colors Hume used for virtue, hoping to abet a similar design. And to speak aphoristically in conclusion, the reflective self should smile, I think, when it sees its image, and this smile is the token of its true seriousness.

Index

abortion, 137–38, 138 n. 12
abstraction, 48, 70
absurdity, 52, 125–26
  reduction to, 4, 23–24, 40, 75
achievement, collective, 108 n. 6, 111
Adam, 105
Addison, Joseph, 169
adulation, 120–21
aesthetic and erotic, relations between, 157
aesthetic and moral, relations between, 84, 86, 113, 113 n. 9, 140. *See also* art and life
aesthetic experience, 85, 142. *See also* appreciation
aesthetic goods, 129–30, 131 n. 4, 173–74, 180
aesthetic ideas (Kant), 147, 151
aestheticism, 130, 130 n. 3, 131, 131 n. 4, 139, 150, 154, 174
aesthetic perfection, 120
aesthetics, 55, 148, 155
  of enemy, 158
aesthetic satisfaction, 166, 168. *See also under* pleasure
aesthetic success, 67
Affektionspreis, 132, 146 n. 23
afterlife, 37
Alexander the Great, 9, 173–74
alienation, 27, 170
Allegory of Time and Love (Bronzino), 139
ambition, 75, 81, 89
ambivalence, 138
amour propre, 166
amusement, 58, 91, 174
animals, 94–95, 107–10, 118, 136, 141, 159, 171
  difference between human and other, 95, 132, 136

Antipater, 78
anonymity, 156, 159
Apollinian-Dionysian duality, 172–73
Apollo, 126
aporia, 25
appearance, momentary, 97, 98 n. 2
appearance/reality gap, 28–31, 41
appreciation (aesthetic), 131, 135, 142, 152, 154, 157–58, 161, 164–66
arbitrary usage, 135, 142
Arendt, Hannah, 146 n. 23
arguments, 47, 74, 77, 134
  abstruse/byzantine, 5, 23, 66, 69
  and point of view, 63
  antidemonstration (Hume), 16–18
  artificial, 63–64, 80–81
  malignly skeptical, 24
  misfortune of, 7
  perceptual-variation, 39, 41, 43–44, 44 n. 12
  refined, 105
  Sceptic's identification of microscopes with, 68
  scope and power of, 5
  therapeutic, 21, 61
Aristophanes, 86, 160
  missing-halves myth, 160, 160 n. 31
art, concept of, 130, 143, 146, 149
art, death of, 150 n. 26
art, low, 168, 168 n. 40
art and life, relations between, 140, 171
art and nature, relations between, 168–69
artifice (of politicians), 116
art-religion, 119
arts, civilizing, 103
artworks, 80, 84, 130, 143, 146 n. 23, 147–48, 157, 166–67, 180

asceticism, 124
associationism, 144
associations
  constantly conjunctive, 16, 105
  of ideas, 37
  of persons, 159–61, 163
astronomy, 75, 89
attention, 155. *See also* inattention, objects of attention
autonomy, 144 n. 21

backsliding, 49
bafflement, 24
Baier, Annette, 22 n. 2, 24 n. 4, 39 n. 10
Beattie, James, 20 n. 8, 55
beauty, 97, 143, 161, 168–69, 174
belief
  inability to sustain, 21, 50
  in continued existence, 16, 25–27, 31, 33, 35, 38
  in distinct existence, 25
  in external world, 24–25
  influences on, 96, 100
  in mind-independent object, 49
  precipitate, in the arts, 51
Bell, Clive, 131 n. 5, 155
Bellarmine, 124–25
Berger, John, 139, 140 n. 15, 156
Berkeley, 3–4, 4 n. 3, 7, 29, 48
Berkeleyans, 47–48
Berma, 148–51
Bible, 86
Blackburn, Simon, 44 n. 13, 135 n. 10
Blackmur, R. P., 88
blindness, 109, 149
  soul-blindness, 143, 145
Bloom, Harold, 165
Bloomsbury, 174
Blue Nude (Bonnard), 142
Bonnard, Pierre, 142–43
Booth, Wayne, 157 n. 30
boredom, 5, 58, 170
Borges, Jorge Luis, 5, 68
Boswell, James, 160
Brasidas, 124
Bronzino, 139
Brueghel, 87–88
Buñuel, Luis, 65
Buridan's ass, 54

Caelia, 84, 113
calendar, 170, 170 n. 41
Callicles, 103
carelessness, 3, 53, 61, 73, 84
causation, 96
cause and effect, 37. *See also* inference, causal
Cavell, Stanley, 143
Chaplin, Charlie, 168
character (of a person), 148, 150–51, 154, 161–62, 172
character, ideal, 88
children, 134, 156
choice, 110
  of body, 65
  reasoned, and random selection, 54
Christianity, 116
Cicero, 77–78, 81, 125–26
clarity, 4, 14–15, 153, 176
clarity and distinctness, 13
Cleanthes, 79 n. 9
cogito, 9
coherence (normative), 96
coherence, perceptual, 31, 34–36, 44 n. 11
colors. *See* qualities, secondary
comedy, 168
comic, the, 5, 7, 62, 91, 158
commonsense understanding of world, 4 n. 3, 28–29
complexion, 150
concrete universality, 82–83
Condé, Prince of, 173
confidence, 25, 27, 42, 51, 93, 107–8, 111–12, 127, 127 n. 20, 177
conservatism, 19–20, 94, 98, 100–101, 103, 107, 111
consistency, logical, 4
constancy, perceptual, 34–36, 41, 44 n. 11
  distinguished from coherence, 36
contiguity, 37, 160
contingency, 60, 75
contradiction, 10, 24 n. 4, 32–34, 97, 110, 125
conversation, 7, 84, 174, 177
correction, collective, 94, 98, 127. *See also* achievement, collective; self-correction
criticism, 81, 87–88, 98, 104, 114, 174. *See also* self-criticism
  revisionist art, 139–40
cruelty, 106, 136
Cupid, 139
curiosity, 58, 119 n. 14

custom, 15, 33
Cynics, 79

Danäe (Rembrandt), 156
Danto, Arthur, 143, 142 n. 20, 148–50, 150 n. 26, 151 n. 27, 152
deafness, 77, 145
death, 77, 147
deduction, 17 n. 7, 21
deductivism, 10
delicacy, 79, 102, 161–63, 163 n. 34, 167, 179.
  See also taste
  reaction and detection distinguished, 161
Demea, 79 n. 9, 117 n. 13
demonstration, limits of, 16–18, 89
Dennett, Daniel, 11–12 n. 5
deobjectifying persons, 159
Derrida, Jacques, 6
Descartes, 8–9, 19, 28, 30–31, 59, 97, 99, 103, 130, 132, 172
  Meditations: Two, 152; Three, 12, 122; Four, 13; Six, 14
  similarity to Freud, 152–53
Des Esseintes, 131
detector, delicate. See delicacy, free spirit
determinism, 46, 130 n. 3
deus sive natura, 9
Dewey, John, 168
diaphanous phenomena, 15, 149
dignity, 59, 108–10, 132–33, 138, 141, 143, 146 n. 23, 148
Diogenes, 80
Dionysian-Apollinian duality. See Apollinian-Dionysian duality
disembodiment, 21, 74, 82, 115, 178
Disembodiment Argument, 21, 27, 47, 56
  sobriquet explained, 27
disinterestedness, 155 n. 28
diversity of life, 23, 85
Divine Comedy, 85
Dr. Strangelove, 153
Don Quixote (character), 10
Don Quixote (novel), 68, 161 n. 32
double existence, doctrine of, 25, 27, 40–41, 43–44, 44 n. 11, 46 n. 15, 47–48, 125, 141
  offspring of causal and resemblance inference, 41
  relation to perceptual-variation argument, 44
duck-rabbit, 64

education, 99, 116 n. 12
  Bildungsroman, 26
ego, 152–53
Eichmann, Adolf, 146 n. 23
Eliot, T. S., 13
embarrassment, 24, 42
embodiment, 10, 38, 69, 74, 77, 82
emotions. See passions, sentiments
emulation, 53, 80, 84, 110, 119, 165
encouragement, 100
endorsement, 26, 50–51, 78, 96, 112, 177
Enlightenment self-understanding, 175, 179
enthusiasm, 122, 170 n. 41
entitlements, 135–37, 153
Epictetus, 63
Epicurean, the, 74–75, 78, 84, 91, 112
equivalence, 132–33
ethics, 11, 17, 74, 79–80, 82–84, 88, 148, 173 n. 45, 174, 178
erotic, the, 142, 146, 157
error, 4, 4 n. 4, 118, 122, 176
evils, 77–81, 136
  proper method for dealing with, 79
exile, 75
existence
  continued and distinct distinguished, 25
experiments, 25, 39
explanation, causal, 27, 39, 113
expressiveness, 148
expressive release and response, 145–48
external assistance, 9
externality, 54
eyes, microscopical (Locke), 64, 74

false consciousness, 90–91, 126
families, 157, 163, 163 n. 34, 164
Family Values, 106
fanaticism, 55 n. 20
fancy. See imagination
fancy price. See Affektionspreis
fantasy, 49
fear, 120
fetus, 137, 137 n. 11, 138
fictions, 41–43, 77
fideism, 116 n. 11
Fogelin, Robert, 24
followable rule, 15–16, 52
Fontenelle, 75–76, 81
forgetfulness, 80
formalism, 131, 131 n. 5, 139, 152, 155

fortitude, psychological, 124–25
free spirit, 164–65
friendship, 88–89, 156–58, 162–63, 163 n. 34, 174
Freud, 76, 152–53
"Funes the Memorious" (Borges), 68, 74

Gainsborough, Thomas, 55
galleylike motion. *See* imagination; inference, resemblance
gaps, mental, 34
Guano, Colonel Bat, 153
Geist, 10
generality, 70–71, 97
general points of view, 97–100
genius, 16
glory, military. *See* military glory and virtues
God, 99, 109–110, 117 n. 13, 120, 124
　belief in 9
　idea of, 12
　of philosophers, 49, 115
gods, 115, 118–20, 124
God's-eye view, 72–73
goods and evils, 77, 81. *See also* evils
good sense. *See* sense, good
government, 19

habit, 2 n. 1, 15, 17, 83, 103, 150, 167, 170
habit-compatibility, 83
habituation, 162
Hampshire, Stuart, 89 n. 14
harmony, social, 122–23
hatred, 52, 95, 151 n. 27, 157–58
Hauptmann, Emily, 123 n. 18
Hegel, 10, 26, 50, 71, 141
Heidegger, 106, 133, 133 n. 9
Helen Fourment in a Fur Coat (Rubens), 156
Heraclitus, 108
heroism, 9, 55–56, 74, 84, 93, 110, 114, 176–78
Hobbists, 109, 123 n. 18
holidays, 169
Homer, 157
horror, Lockean, 65
houses, 171–72
humanity, 131, 136, 140, 148
Hume
　accepts modern philosophy, 44
　allied with Gainsborough, 55
　as naturalist, 159
　as nonrationalist, 6, 173
　as practical moralist, 37, 87, 114, 122
　association of virtue with good cheer, 180
　awareness of evil, 79 n. 9
　Berkeleyan moves of, 48
　both naturalist and skeptic, 57
　content of worldview, 25–26
　describes paradise, 174
　favors polytheism, 122
　footnote in "The Sceptic," 84–85
　gap-mindedness, 33
　"good" and "bad," 3
　increasing pessimism, 116 n. 12
　ironic tone, 7
　not a positivist, 53
　on obligations to rational but weak creatures, 134, 136
　on preferring the scratching of one's finger, 133, 135
　on skeptical argument, 4
　philosophical responses to, 1, 3, 7
　reconciliationist psychology, 46, 46 n. 15
　return to philosophy, 57
　worldly vs. unworldly, 23
Humeanism, 175–80
　not irrationalist, 94
　worries about, 20 n. 8
Huysmans, J.-K., 130–31

id, 34, 152–53
ideal critic, 113
ideal-observer theory, 82
identity, nonhuman, 91
identity, personal, 42, 66
ignorance, 118–19, 180
illusion
　of censor, 50
　optical, 29–30, 33, 81, 97
　radical, 29, 90
imagery, auditory, 144
imagery, ocular, 15, 143–44
imagination, 5, 95, 120–21, 129, 134, 147, 151–52, 170, 173, 178
　and generality, 71
　and inference, 17
　contrariety in operations of, 46
　effects on or within, 13, 33, 65, 82, 85, 91, 97–99, 118, 125, 158
　finds something/nothing to grasp, 19, 48–49

glides (galleylike motion), 25, 34–36, 41–43, 44 n. 11, 103
  modeled on physical relationships, 72
  possible moves for, 52–53
  revivified by sense perception, 38
  seemingly trivial properties of, 56, 58
  trivial qualities of, 51
  two operations of, 43
imaginings, 167
immaterialism, 48
impasse, 27, 54, 56–57
imperatives, 13–15, 100, 146 n. 23, 155
impressions and ideas, 37
impudence, 108
inattention, 53–54
inclination, natural, 58–59, 111
indirection, 33, 110, 127
inertia, 35 n. 9, 42
inference, causal
  and first *Enquiry*, 18
  cements universe, 37
  claim to secure all beliefs, 37–38
  contrasted with demonstration, 17
  horizontal and vertical, 40, 121
  not entrusted to reasoning, 18
  not undermined by Hume, 18
  of animals, 118
  presupposes belief in continued existence, 27, 31
inference, moral, 17
inference, probabilistic, 36
inference, resemblance (resemblance-based) unavailable, 49
  belief in continued existence rests on, 27, 36–37
  happens to mind, 55
  denial/disavowal of, 40–41, 45, 56
  double-existence thesis weakens credentials of, 43
  name for galleylike motion, 35, 54
  nontrivial work of, 38
  not respectable, 41
inferences, need for, 68
innate ideas, 10
intellect
  and whole person, 66–67, 126
  great light in, 14
  unreliability of, 2, 4, 94, 177
  whether will should follow, 14
intellectual awareness, 67

intellectuals, 106–7
intention, 164, 164 n. 37
intentionality, 148
interest and interestedness, 97, 99, 133, 155
intermittent influence, 100, 129
intimacy, 84, 89, 110, 156, 158–59, 162–63, 165
intuition (Kantian), 147
intuitions, 99, 134
irony, 44, 49, 107, 125
irrationalism, 6, 8, 20, 93–94, 98, 100–101, 103, 111
irrationality
  charge of, 59, 66, 104, 133 n. 9, 135
irreplaceability, 163 n. 34
is/ought, 16

James, Henry, 23
James, William, 158
Jesus, 115, 125
John in the tie shop (Sellars), 45
Johnson, Samuel, 4, 76, 160
judgment, evaluative, 97–98, 100
Judt, Tony, 106 n. 5
justice, 134, 136

Kafka, 156, 159
Kant, 82, 91, 142, 146 n. 23, 147 n. 24, 148, 151, 155, 155 n. 28, 166
  contrasted with Hume, 16, 34. *See also under* persons
  Critique of Judgment, 146–47
  on human distinctiveness, 130, 132–33, 133 n. 9, 135, 137–38
Kantian aesthetic, 155, 155 n. 28
Kantian agent, 141, 164
Kantianism, 100, 133, 178
Kantians, 123 n. 18
Kennedy, Robert, 166
Kimhi, Irad, 141 n. 17
kindness, 141

Lacan, Jacques, 141 n. 17
latitudinarianism, 122
laughter, 5, 44, 59, 62, 81, 87
legality. *See* entitlements
Leibniz, 8–9, 152
life, improvement of, 61
Locke, 29, 44–45, 64–68, 153, 176
Lockeans, 40

186　　　　　　　　　　　　　Index

Louis XIV, 130
love, 13, 63, 89, 95, 144, 151 n. 27, 156–59,
　　160 n. 31, 162–63, 165
　representations of, 139, 146, 156
lowly, the, 173 n. 45
Lucian, 79
luck, 54, 69–70
Lucretius, 126

Machiavellians, 109
Mackie, J. L., 89 n. 15
macroscope, 72–73
madness, 52
mannerism, 149
Marcel (Proust's narrator), 149
marginality, 102, 167
marvelous, the, 118–19
matter
　denial of, 4–5
　meanings of, 4 n. 3
media, artificial, 63
Memlinc, 140 n. 15
memorialization, 169, 171–72
memory, 65, 170, 172
Meno, 12
Meno psychology, 34
metafiction, 42–43, 110
metajudgment, 90
metaperspective, 73
metaphilosophy, 101
metareason, 8
microscope, 63–64, 68, 72–73
Middlemarch, 85
military glory and virtues, 114, 177
Mill, J. S., 71, 176
mind
　and bodily constitution, 32
　as a whole, 129. *See also under* intellect
　as having an outside, 152
　as reclaiming itself, 153
　bearing its own survey, 24 n. 4
　defining property of embodied, 33
　difficulties with rationalist version of, 11
　human and other animal, 95–96
　movement (motion) of, 26, 61, 70 n. 7, 118,
　　145, 177
miracles, 37, 118
monads, 9
Monet, 87
monotheism, 93, 115–16, 120–27, 179

Mont-Saint-Michel, 86
Moore, G. E., 4, 174
moral conflicts, 137
morality, 155
moral sense. *See* sense, moral
moral standing, 138 n. 13
moral tarantula, 166
moral valet, 110
Morning Star/Evening Star, 150
Mrs. Siddons (Gainsborough), 55
Mrs. Siddons as the Tragic Muse (Reynolds), 55
multipresence, 32, 35, 38, 154
music, 1, 144–45, 174
mysticism, 55

naked, the, 156, 158
narcissism, 158
narrative, 125
nationalisms, 102–3
naturalism, 95, 107, 110, 133, 179
　and evolution, 11 n. 5
　and modern philosophy, 46
　and skepticism, 57
　defined, 11, 11 n. 5
　normative aspects of, 79
　types of, 11 n. 5
naturalness, malign, 74
nature, 18, 27, 57, 74, 83, 112, 133, 168–69
　human, 108–11
Nehamas, Alexander, 130 n. 3
neorationalism, 16
necessity, 94–95
Nietzsche, 80 n. 10, 100, 109, 130, 130 n. 3,
　　164–66, 172–73
　Birth of Tragedy, 119–20, 172–73
　On the Genealogy of Morals, 124
　similarities to Hume, 6, 26, 46, 70, 83, 124,
　　124 n. 19, 125, 173
nonrationalism, 8, 55, 177
　and benign skepticism, 55
nonsense, 53. *See also* absurdity
normativity, 94–95, 97–98, 101, 113, 176
　and inability, 50 n. 17
　and repetition, 83
　naturalistic explanation of, 96
　relationship to the descriptive, 13
Norton, David Fate, 20 n. 8
noumenal/phenomenal distinction, 41
nude (genre), 139, 156

Index

object, 135, 153
  use explained, 129 n. 1
objecthood, 135, 138–39, 142, 153–54, 156, 159
objectification, 129, 139–40, 142
objectivity, 153
objects of attention, 63, 84, 96, 129–30
objects, value-invested, 78
ocean, 37
omnipresence. See multipresence
opacity, deliberative, 54, 73. See also luck
opacity, referential, 150
Other Bodies Problem, 141
overinterpretation, 121
overvaluing, 91
ownership, 153–54

pain, 136
Paracelsus, 86
parricide, 89
participation, 144–46
Pascal, 34, 80
passions
  and external objects, difference between, 31
  control of, 63, 69–70, 85, 178
  flattery of, 55, 82
Pater, Walter, 130
patriotism, 89
Pears, David, 24, 28
Penelhum, Terence, 116 n. 11
perception, 64–66, 98 n. 2
perception and object, 25–28, 47
  categorial neutrality vs. categorial mixture, 28
  confounded by vulgar, 28–29
persecution, 122
personhood, 137 n. 11, 138
personification, 117
personification of faculties. See protopersons
persons
  aesthetic dimensions of, 130–32, 148, 151 n. 27, 154, 156, 180
  and artworks, 148, 167
  and objects/objective, 135, 139–40, 142, 151, 154
  as embodied, 30, 175
  as expressive, 146
  components of, 175
  Humean vs. Kantian conceptions of, 138–48

non-Humean philosophical picture of, 130
  transgenerational combinations, 19
perspective, 22, 57–58, 68, 75, 83, 85, 176, 180
  artificial, 68–69, 73
  benignly skeptical, 22
  characterized, 68
  horizontal and vertical, 73
  (intra)mental, 70–71
  reference to embodiment, 69
pessimism, 114, 116 n. 12
petites perceptions, 152
Phantom of Liberty (Buñuel), 65
Phèdre. See Berma
Philo, 79 n. 9, 117 n. 13
philosophers, 49–51, 86, 180
philosophy
  academic, 102
  as medicine of mind, 69
  elimination of, 63
  exposes frailty, 105, 154
  modern, 25, 39, 39 n. 10, 44
  naturalized, 20 n. 8, 101, 112, 167
  oddity of, 103–4
  similarity to religion, 51, 115
  true, 108
Philosophy Elimination Theorem, 63
pig and koala (Rorty), 66
place, knowing our, 154
Plato, 8, 10, 12, 24, 86, 157, 167
Platonist, the, 74–78, 80–87, 112
pleasure, 5, 78, 90–91, 139
  aesthetic, 132, 168
  Epicurean, man of, 91
  origin of Hume's philosophy, 58
Plutarch, 75, 81
poetry and poets, 1, 42, 125, 174
point of view, 22, 51, 63, 83, 85, 94, 113, 129
  correction of monotheistic, 121
points of view, general. See general points of view
polygamy, 87–88
polytheism, 115–27, 179–80
pornography, 140–42
porphyry, 44–45
porter and letter, 31–32, 34
power, inequality of, 134
practice, 63, 82, 88, 91, 102, 104, 111, 125–26, 179
pragmatism, 117
prereflective order, 104

Price, H. H., 35 n. 9
price, 132–33
price-dignity distinction, 132–33, 135, 137 n. 11, 138
pricelessness, 132–33
pride, 95, 110–11
probabilities, 77
progress, 99, 127, 136, 137 n. 11
projection, 117–19, 121
proof, 62 n. 1, 69
propensity, 2 n 1. *See also under* reason
property, 76, 153
Proteus, 91
protoartistic, the, 173–74
protopersons, 2, 46
Proust, 148
puritanism, 142
purposiveness without purpose, 132

qualia, 46
qualities, primary, 4 n. 3, 47
qualities, secondary, 44–45, 47, 64
quietism, 179

Ramsay, Allan, 55 n. 20
random selection, 54, 123
rationalism, 7–9, 155
　aesthetic contrast with nonrationalism, 55
　and self-sufficiency, 9
　break with, 83
　commitment defined, 9
　conceals irrationality, 93, 114
　impediment to believing, 11
　in historical context, 8–10
　its theories reclassified as artworks, 85, 104
　noncredibility of, 12
　reformulated as normative, 14
　reformulation elaborated, 15
　worry about living rationalists, 10
　wrongness of standards, 89, 176
rational ideas (Kant), 147
rationality, 133–34, 138, 178
Raveh, Yitzhak, 146 n. 23
realism, naive, 47
realism, scientific, 4 n. 3
reason
　as mixing itself with propensity, 2, 57, 112
　as slave of passion, 1–3
　choice between false and none, 24
　contrasted with rationalist version of, 8

correction of, 22
Humean conception of, 3, 6, 24
Hume's arguments concerning, 16–20
in exchange for reason, 134
naturalized, 17, 114
of animals, 95
power and scope of, 3, 8, 22
role of, 176
reasonableness, 2–3, 6–7, 93–94, 101, 125
reasoning, refined, 20, 53
reasoning, uncertainty of, 18–20
reciprocity, 134
recollection, 10
recognition, 115, 120. *See also* self-recognition
refinement, 105, 161, 173 n. 45, 180
reflection, 95–96, 101–14, 121, 136, 176
　and Lockean horror, 65
　and practice, 88
　conditions necessary for, 102–3
　Humean conception of, 94–95, 179
　philosophical, 26, 85
　refined, 63, 69–70, 70 n. 7, 73, 75, 101
reflexion, 97–98
　cool, 114
Reid, Thomas, 20 n. 8
relationships, interpersonal, 134, 143, 156, 160, 165
relativism, 177
religion, 51, 114–16
　penetration of, 125–27
Rembrandt, 156, 159
repetition, 83
resemblance
　and perceptual constancy, 36
　between human and other animals, 11, 66, 136
　between monotheism/polytheism and rationalism/nonrationalism, 115
　between perceptions/ideas, 25, 37, 177
　importance of, 37, 66–67, 137, 138, 138 n. 13
　projection of, 118
resemblance inference. *See* inference, resemblance
resentment, 134–36
respect, 141–42, 148
Reveries of a Solitary Walker, 56
Reynolds, Sir Joshua, 55
rightness, detection of, 67
role modeling, 165–66

Index   189

Roman Catholicism, 38, 122
Roquentin, 168
Rorty, Richard, 6, 66, 103–4, 127 n. 20
Rousseau, 56, 166
Rubens, 156
rule, 137 n. 11, 176. *See also* followable rule
  ambiguous between ruling and recipe, 15
  as containing instances, 15
  recalcitrance to formulability in, 16
  to fix property relations, 19
  universality as involving, 82–83
rule-avoidances, 16

Sade, Marquis de, 141, 141 n. 17
Sarris, Andrew, 168
St. Bartholomew's Day massacre, 38
Sartre, 106
saturnalia events, 169–72
Sceptic, the, 61–91, 94, 97, 104, 111, 112–13, 154, 163 n. 34, 167
  on control of passions, 63, 69
  on effects of philosophy, 108
  on great vacancies of life, 33–34
  on reasoning, 19
  on religion, 49
  on secondary qualities, 44
  on values, 44
Schopenhauer, 55
science
  logic of, 13
  not naturalized, 46
  refined reflections tested, 53
scientism, 11 n. 5
second-person privilege, 151
self, 42, 69, 154, 172, 180
self-consciousness, 94
self-correction, 93, 110, 126–27
self-criticism, 98
self-esteem and self-worth, 93, 119. *See also* dignity, pride
self-knowledge, 151–53
self-recognition, 56, 66, 73
self-reflexivity, 24, 24 n. 4, 27, 177
Sellars, Wilfrid, 45
Seneca, 63
sense, good, 58, 94–95
sense, moral, 62, 113
sense, normative, 95–96, 99
sense, religious, 116

senses, 175
  distrust of, 10, 30
  faith in, 51
sensibility, 6, 23, 34, 49, 113, 122, 129, 146, 150, 156
sentiments, 142, 179
  changes in, 23
  concerning life and happiness, 74–75
  correction of, 16, 22 n. 1, 98, 98 n. 2
  influencers on, 84
  natural but obvious, 169
  seconding of, 100, 145
seriousness, 3–6, 8, 62, 90, 116, 180
sex, 76, 142, 156–57
sexism, 140–41
Shaftesbury, 62
Significant Form, 86
Skepticism (Hegel), 26 n. 6
skepticism
  affective, 89
  benign, 55, 93–94, 101, 107, 111, 114, 116 n. 11, 178–80
  benign and malign distinguished, 22
  malign, 39, 53, 57, 112, 177–78
  strategy of benign, 22, 27
  true, 57, 60
slave metaphor. *See* reason as slave of passion
slavery, 135
  social enslavement , 88, 166
smiles, 91, 180
Socrates, 12, 13, 98
solidity, 48, 48 n. 16
solipsism, 58
soul, 145–48
soul-blindness. *See* blindness
soullessness, 146–47, 147 n. 24
Spanish Inquisition, 123
Spinoza, 8–9, 13, 73
Sterne, 62, 79 n. 9
Stoic, the, 74–75, 77–87, 112
Stoicism (Hegel), 26 n. 6
Stoics (ancient), 79
Strawson, Galen, 50 n. 17
Strawson, P. F., 11 n. 4
Stroud, Barry, 24
style, 148–51
subject, 139, 153
subjectivity, 153
supernaturalism, 11, 111
superstition, 116 n. 12, 118, 122

sympathy, 118, 136–37, 145–48, 150
Swift, 79 n. 9

taste, 113, 135, 157 n. 30, 161–63, 167–69
  disputes of, 162
temperate zone of culture, 109
Tennyson, Alfred, 130 n. 2
tests, 136
theism, genuine (Hume), 117
theology and theologians, 115, 125
theory and theoretical opinions, 87, 123, 123 n. 17, 171 n. 42, 178, 180
theory/practice distinction, 14
Toulouse-Lautrec, 149
tragedy, 62
transparency. See clarity
"true world" (Nietzsche), 26

ugliness, 80 n. 10
unchoosable presuppositions, 171
unconscious, the, 152
underinterpretation, 119
unhappiness, 154
Unhappy Consciousness (Hegel), 26
uniformity, principle of, 17
universalizability, 83
Utilitarianism (Mill), 71
utilitarians and utilitarianism, 123 n. 18, 178

value, 90–91, 163, 163 n. 34, 171 n. 42, 174–76
Venus, 139–40

view, point of. *See* point of view
view from nowhere, 73
virtual movement, 70 n. 7
virtue, 13, 79, 88, 99, 114, 180
vision, darkening of, 78–79
voice, 98, 100, 144, 144 n. 21
von Choltitz, Dietrich, 166
vulgar, 91
  belief in continued existence, 27, 41
  metaphysics of, 26
  view, Humean conception of, 29

walking, 30–31
warring-subsytems picture of mind, 2–3
whimsical condition of mankind, 59, 179
Wilde, Oscar, 130, 165
will, 14, 55, 133, 133 n. 9, 148, 169
  preceded by intellect, 14
Williams, Bernard, 54, 103, 111
Wilson, Edmund, 23
Wind, Edgar, 55, 55 n. 20
wit, 62 n. 1, 150–51
Wittgenstein, 55
women, 139–42, 146–47, 147 n. 24, 156
work, 172
world
  as object of belief, 26
  continuously existing, 15, 162
  internalized, 154

Zeus, 115
Zupančič, Alenka, 141 n. 17

www.ingramcontent.com/pod-product-compliance
Lightning Source LLC
Chambersburg PA
CBHW031551300426
44111CB00006BA/272